Collins

Real Lives
Real Listening
Advanced B2–C1

Sheila Thorn

Collins

HarperCollins Publishers
77–85 Fulham Palace Road
Hammersmith
London W6 8JB

First edition 2013

Reprint 10 9 8 7 6 5 4 3 2 1 0

© HarperCollins Publishers Ltd 2013

ISBN 978-0-00-752233-0

Collins® is a registered trademark of HarperCollins Publishers Limited

www.collinselt.com

A catalogue record of this book is available from the British Library.

Printed in China by South China Printing Co. Ltd

HarperCollins does not warrant that www.collinselt.com or any other website mentioned in this title will be provided uninterrupted, that any website will be error free, that defects will be corrected, or that the website or the server that makes it available are free of viruses or bugs. For full terms and conditions please refer to the site terms provided on the website.

Photos of Jill in Units 7 and 13 © Sheila Thorn. All other images are from Shutterstock.

Free teacher's notes and answer keys available online at:
www.collinselt.com

Contents

My Family

Judy lives in Sevenoaks, a beautiful town in Kent, south-east of London. She is the mother of four children. She also works full-time as a teacher in a private girls' school. During nearly the entire interview one of Judy's sons, Rupert, is playing the piano in another room, which makes this unit more challenging.

This is an English as a Lingua Franca unit (ELF). Marilena is a Romanian woman in her early 30s. Seven years ago she decided to leave Romania and come to London. She now works in the operating theatres of a busy hospital in east London together with her colleague and line manager, Jill, who also appears in the interview. Marilena understands spoken English very well and communicates effectively, although she does make a number of phonological and grammatical errors. Jill speaks clearly, but quickly, and she has retained her North Welsh accent.

Randy is a trained actor, musician and composer from Montana in the USA who is currently living in London. He has a strong American accent, despite having lived in the UK since 1999. This interview was recorded in a large Victorian pub during one afternoon in early summer and there is a lot of background noise (music, people talking and calling out, etc.). It is a good example, though, of real life listening.

Supplementary Units

Eileen was born in Watford in north-west London, but she now lives in Walthamstow in east London with her husband and two children. She has a strong east London accent.

Hannah (aged 20) and Luke (aged 18) are the daughter and son of Judy in Unit 1. As with a lot of young people they speak very quickly.

A Typical Day

Supplementary Units

A Place I Know Well

Supplementary Units

Teacher's notes and answer keys available online at: **www.collinselt.com**

About the author

The author, Sheila Thorn, is an experienced teacher and materials writer with a particular interest in authentic listening. She is the founder of The Listening Business: www.thelisteningbusiness.com

Acknowledgements

Books, articles, lectures and workshops by the following people have been invaluable in helping me to develop the approach to authentic listening I have used in the *Real Lives, Real Listening* series: Gillian Brown, Ron Carter, Richard Cauldwell, John Field, Jennifer Jenkins, Tony Lynch, Mike McCarthy, Shelagh Rixon, Michael Rost, Paul Seligson, Adrian Underhill, Mary Underwood, Penny Ur and J.J. Wilson.

My grateful thanks to the following people and institutions for commenting on and piloting these materials:

Maria Sforza and Heather Wansbrough-Jones at *South Thames College, London*, Carol Butters, Sarah Dearne, Michelle Parrington and Justin Sales at *Stevenson College, Edinburgh*, Jonathan Fitch at *The Oxford English Centre*, Hazel Black and Chris Jannetta at *English for Everyone, Aberdeen*, Sasha Goldsmith at *Rands English Language Tuition*, Elizabeth Stitt at the *University of St Andrews*, Sophie Freeman, Jen McNair Wilson, John Marquis, Harriet Williams and Jo Whittick at *English in Chester*, Dariana Cristea, Beverley Gray and Keith Harris at *Loughborough College*, Catherine Marshall and Michelle Scolari at *Bellerbys College, London*, Kath Hargreaves, Julia Hudson and Eric Smith at *Embassy CES, Oxford*, Andy Wright at *Queen Mary, University of London*, Zoe Smith at *OISE Bristol*, Elizabeth Bray and Mike Powell at *Coventry College*, Joe Ferrari at *Dundee College* and Julia Isidro at *Kings Oxford*.

I am also extremely grateful to all the people who kindly allowed me to interview them for these books, particularly those for whom English is not their first language.

This book is dedicated to my father and to Jill for their constant love, support and encouragement, and to my late, and greatly missed, mentor Jean Coles.

Introduction

Aims

The main aim of the *Real Lives, Real Listening* series is to provide busy teachers with ready-made listening materials which will effectively *train*, rather than just test, their students in listening. A parallel aim is to boost students' confidence in their listening skills by exposing them to authentic texts. A further aim is to introduce students to the grammatical structures and idiomatic expressions which are typically used in informal spoken English.

The series reflects the latest academic theories on the process of decoding listening input and the importance of authentic listening practice in language acquisition. The series also reflects our new awareness of the huge differences between spoken and written English highlighted by recent research on spoken English corpora.

Authenticity

Unlike the listening texts typically found in coursebooks, each text in *Real Lives, Real Listening* is 100% unscripted. This means that students are exposed to the features of spoken English which they encounter outside the classroom and generally find so daunting. These features include assimilation, elision, linking, weak forms, hesitations, false starts, redundancy and colloquial expressions.

The *Real Lives, Real Listening* series is carefully designed to include both native and near-fluent non-native English speakers, reflecting the fact that most of the English which is spoken these days is between non-native speakers of English.

Content

The series is at three levels: Elementary (A2), Intermediate (B1–B2) and Advanced (B2–C1), with 15 units for each level.

The books are divided into three sections: *My Family, A Typical Day* and *A Place I Know Well.* There are five units in each section. The first three contain a wide variety of focused exercises which the teacher can select from, depending on the needs of their students. These units are graded in terms of difficulty, from easier to more challenging. The final two units in each section are for revision purposes. Here the speakers recycle, naturally, the lexis and grammatical structures found in the previous three units. Every unit contains verbatim transcripts of the listening texts and useful glossaries.

Extensive piloting of these materials has shown that students at all levels experience a huge sense of achievement when they find they can actually understand a native or competent non-native speaker talking at a natural speed. The *Real Lives, Real Listening* series provides them with that opportunity.

Sheila M. Thorn

My Family

UNIT **1** Judy

Judy lives in Sevenoaks, a beautiful town in Kent, south-east of London. She is the mother of four children. She also works full-time as a teacher in a private girls' school. During nearly the entire interview one of Judy's sons, Rupert, is playing the piano in another room, which makes this unit more challenging.

A Discussion

Discuss these questions in pairs or small groups and share your answers with the class:

1. Judy is the mother of four children. She also works full-time as a teacher. What do you expect her to talk about during this interview?

2. What are the advantages and disadvantages of a) growing up in a large family and b) being an only child?

B Normalisation 1: Anticipating the next word

This exercise is designed to help you get used to Judy's voice.

Listen to Track 2. There is a word missing from the end of each excerpt. Try to guess the missing word and write it down. Then listen to Track 3 to check your answers. How well did you guess?

1. _____
2. _____
3. _____
4. _____
5. _____
6. _____

C Normalisation 2: Questions

Judy talks about her family. Listen and answer the questions.

1. What do we find out about the interviewer from the very start of this interview?
2. What does Judy's daughter Hannah do?
3. Why is Hannah living at home at the moment?
4. How many boys and girls does Judy have?

A True/False

Judy talks about the dynamics between the children and her. Answer true or false. Be prepared to give reasons for your answers.

1. _____ Judy and her husband would have liked more children.
2. _____ The children often fight amongst themselves.
3. _____ Judy's husband has to leave for work very early in the morning.
4. _____ Sometimes Judy can't be bothered to stop the children arguing.
5. _____ The interview takes place in the summer.
6. _____ The interviewer asks Judy if it's hard to make the children revise for their exams.

B Gap-Fill (Transformations)

Judy talks about how stressful it is during the lead-up to the children's exams.

This is a difficult exercise because you need to identify and then change the words Judy uses to make them fit the gaps. You may need to listen to the excerpt several times to complete the task.

1. Judy says she has more _____ _____ with her own children than with the children she _____.
2. Judy has been feeling very _____ during the run-up to the children's exams.
3. In two weeks' time the children will have _____ their exams.
4. Judy plans on _____ the end of the exams with a bottle of wine.

C Questions

Judy talks about the summer holidays and her daughter Hannah. Listen and answer the questions.

1. Why do Judy and her children particularly like the summer holidays?
2. What does Judy enjoy doing in her free time?
3. What has Hannah been doing exactly since she left school?
4. Why is Hannah probably feeling a bit anxious at the moment?
5. Where will Hannah work for a year if she does well in her first- and second-year exams?
6. Would Judy prefer Hannah to do a three-year or a four-year degree course?

D Cloze

Judy talks about how Hannah copes with living at home during the summer holidays, after being independent at university.

Before you listen, try to predict which words, or which types of words (nouns, adjectives, prepositions, parts of verbs, etc.) will fill the gaps. Listen and check your answers.

Again this is a very challenging exercise, with 23 gaps in just 33 seconds, so you will probably need to listen to the excerpt several times to complete the task.

I: Interviewer   J: Judy

I: How, how _____ you _____ the dynamics with Hannah _____ away, being quite _____-up, and then coming back home _____ and _____ in to family _____?

J: I think she finds it _____ _____ and she says we _____ her like a _____...

I: Mmm.

J: ...but being in _____ of when you _____ and what you do _____ university, that _____ really_____ when you're fitting in with family and _____...

I: Mmm, hmm.

J: ...um, so I think she finds that a bit_____.

I: Mmm.

J: And I find it tough when we all have to _____ _____ in the morning and she _____. *(laughs)*

I: No, that would _____ a bit of resentment I _____ imagine.

J: Yeah.

E Questions

Judy talks about getting the children to help around the home. Listen and answer the questions.

1. What has changed a lot since Judy was a child?
2. What are you no longer allowed to do as a parent in England?
3. What are children encouraged to do at school?
4. What does Judy have to offer her children to ensure they help in the house?
5. What is the weekly allowance which children receive from their parents called?
6. What will Rupert do housework in exchange for?
7. Which computer game is Toby a big fan of?

8. How tall is Toby in feet and inches?*
9. Who does Luke like to spend his free time with?
10. Does Hannah have to be bribed to help around the house?

An inch is 2.54 cms. There are 12 inches in a foot. A foot is 30.48 cms, so Toby is one metre, 88 centimetres tall.

F True/False

Judy talks about how Hannah and the boys get on. Answer true or false. Be prepared to give reasons for your answers.

1. _____ Judy says the arguments the boys have with Hannah are different from the ones they have with each other.
2. _____ Judy expects the boys to be less protective of Hannah as they get older.
3. _____ The boys have already protected their sister on several occasions.
4. _____ Judy says Hannah finds the boys quite childish at the moment.
5. _____ Judy teaches at a primary school.

G Gap-Fill

Judy talks about the rest of her family. As with Exercise D, try to predict your answers before you listen.

1. Until about 10 years ago Judy regularly used to meet up with her brother and sister at _____ and during the _____.
2. Now Judy's sister lives a day's _____ away in Yorkshire.
3. Judy and her sister often talk on the _____.
4. Judy says when she talks to her sister it's the _____ as _____, but she does _____ her.
5. Judy's brother now works in the USA, but Judy sees him more _____ than her sister.
6. Her brother regularly comes to London on _____ and _____ in to see Judy and her family.
7. Judy says her brother makes a big _____ because he lives so far from his _____ and family.
8. Judy sees her parents several _____ a year.
9. She says her parents are always _____ to have any _____ of her and her children at _____ _____.
10. One reason Judy likes staying with her parents is that her mother does all the _____ and brings her _____ in bed in the morning, as does the interviewer's _____.

A Hedging and qualifying statements

It is very common in British English to qualify statements rather than to make direct statements. This is probably one of the reasons British people have a reputation for being reserved.

1. quite

    Judy and the interviewer use the word *quite* throughout her interview:

    > The interviewer says that it must be *quite hard work* to be the mother of four children. Judy replies *Yes, it's quite busy...*

    > Later Judy says of her children *quite often somebody's arguing with somebody.*

    > She says *It's quite tiring being the peacemaker.*

    > She says *my husband comes back quite late at night.*

    > When talking about her daughter's exams, Judy says *it matters quite a lot.*

    > She says Hannah *finds it quite hard* to fit back in to family life during the holidays.

2. a bit

    Another way of making statements less direct is to use *a bit*, as in these examples from the interview:

    > Judy says Hannah finds it *a bit tough* to be home again after being away at university.

    > The interviewer says that Hannah staying in bed when everyone else has to get up *must cause a bit of resentment.*

    > When talking about Hannah being the only girl with three brothers the interviewer says *That must be a bit tough.*

    > The interviewer says she feels *a bit guilty* that her father still brings her tea in bed in the morning.

    > Now write a series of statements about yourself and then qualify them using **quite** and **a bit**.

B Colloquial language

There are a number of colloquial expressions during the interview:

1. to be into something – to enjoy something very much

    When talking about Toby, Judy says: *Roomscape, it's a computer game he loves.*
    The interviewer replies: *OK. He's into that...*

2. to treat someone like something – to deal with someone in a certain way

    When talking about her daughter Hannah, Judy says: *she says we treat her like a child.*

3. to pop in – to visit someone for a short time

    Judy says that when her brother comes to London on business he *pops in* to see her and her family.

4. to cope with – to deal with

    The interviewer says it must be difficult teaching children all day *and then you've got yours to cope with as well.*

5. a bit tough – rather difficult

    When talking about Hannah having to fit in to family life when she's home for the holidays Judy says: *I think she finds that a bit tough.*

Now make a series of statements about yourself using these examples of colloquial English.

C The gerund

There are numerous examples of the gerund in the interview where the verb changes to the –ing form, for example after certain verbs and prepositions.

Interviewer: *And do you find yourself **playing** the peacemaker?*

Judy: *they've got exams **coming** up*

Interviewer: *Is that difficult – **making** them do their revision?*

Interviewer: *So how long till you're clear of all that – when you finish **teaching** and the children finish their exams?*

Interviewer:	*How are you going to celebrate, if you like, **finishing** their stressful period?*
Judy:	*Well, the summer holidays are really nice, not **having** to get up.*
Judy:	*the boys hate **getting** up*
Judy:	*And I like **going** for lots of walks as well.*
Interviewer:	*How have you found the dynamics with Hannah **being** away, **being** quite grown-up, and then **coming** home again and **fitting** in to family life?*
Judy:	*...but **being** in charge of what you eat and what you do at university, that doesn't really work when you're fitting in with family and mealtimes...*
Judy:	*And there are so many reasons you can't go weekends and holidays – there's **studying** to be done and exams and sport commitments...*
Judy:	*mum insists on **cooking** and **bringing** me tea in the morning*

Now make a series of statements using the gerund.

D Listener response

We use the following phrases, words and sounds to indicate to a speaker that we are following what they are saying, both in face-to-face conversations and on the telephone:

a) I see.
b) Right.
c) OK.
d) Mmm, hmm.

Look at the following extracts from the interview:

a) I see.

Judy:	*Sometimes they get on well, but quite often somebody's arguing with somebody.*
Interviewer:	*I see.*

b) Right.

Judy: *Um, he's out in the evenings quite a bit because he works at The Telegraph.*

Interviewer: *Right.*

c) OK.

Interviewer: *So how long till you're clear of all that – when you finish teaching and the children finish their exams?*

Judy: *Another two weeks.*

Interviewer: *OK.*

d) Mmm, hmm.

Judy: *Rupert wants CDs, so Rupert does things to get a new, a new CD.*

Interviewer: *Mmm, hmm.*

Now practise using these listener responses in conversations with other members of the class.

E Second conditional

When talking about being the mother of four children and planning a large family, Judy says:

> *And the theory was that if we had an even number they'd* [i.e. they would] *play together nicely.*

This is a classic use of what we call the second conditional. Here the subtext is that this was a good plan in theory, but not in practice.

Here is another example of the second conditional based on a true story:

> My friend's mother bought a male puppy and a female puppy from the same litter and was amazed a couple of years later when she found the female was pregnant. She said: 'I thought if I *got* two puppies from the same litter they *wouldn't* mate because they were brother and sister.'

Now try to make up your own second conditional sentences.

A Dictation

 to

At times in her interview Judy speaks very quickly and consequently some words are not pronounced clearly.

Work with a partner. First listen to the excerpts from Judy's interview and write down how many words there are in each item. Then listen and write down the words you hear. After that check your answers with another pair.

1. (___ words) _____
2. (___ words) _____
3. (___ words) _____
4. (___ words) _____
5. (___ words) _____
6. (___ words) _____
7. (___ words) _____

B Fluency practice 1 – elision and the glottal stop

When speaking quickly in English, a process called 'elision' often occurs, most frequently with words ending in –d and –t. This results in these sounds not being pronounced when the next word begins with a consonant. For example, a speaker will say *las' night* instead of *last night*, *jus' got here* instead of *just got here*, or *trie' to* instead of *tried to*.

Another feature of informal spoken English is the *glottal stop*. This happens when the speaker tightens his or her throat and very briefly stops the air from getting through. This results in the /t/ sound at the end of words such as *got* or *lot*, or the /t/ sound in words such as *bottle* or *kettle* not being fully pronounced. This can make it difficult for you to recognise words containing this feature.

This gap-fill exercise focuses on words which you probably know already, but whose pronunciation has changed because of elision or Judy and the interviewer's use of the glottal stop.

Try to fill in the gaps before you listen to the excerpts, then listen and check your answers.

1. That _____ be quite hard work, I would imagine.
2. Yes, it's _____ busy...
3. She's home at the _____ for the holidays...
4. _____ the theory was that if we had an even number _____ play together nicely, two at a time.

5. Well, the summer holidays are really nice, _____ having to get up.
6. my _____ comes _____ quite late at night...
7. she's _____ done her first year studying biology
8. _____ is _____ going well?
9. so the first lot _____ fine
10. And if that _____ work then she _____ does a three-year degree.
11. So _____ _____ crucial.
12. I _____ make him do anything.
13. She _____ to be good.
14. That _____ be a _____ tough.
15. And they're _____ protective?
16. so far the opportunities _____ been there
17. My brother _____ to America...

Now listen and repeat each phrase or sentence after the speaker, imitating the speaker's pronunciation.

C Recognising a word from hearing the first syllable

This exercise is designed to encourage you to think ahead when you're listening.

Listen to Track 25. Try to guess the missing word just from hearing the first syllable and write it down. Then listen to Track 26 to check your answers. How well did you guess?

1. _____
2. _____
3. _____
4. _____
5. _____
6. _____

D Fluency practice 2 – weak forms

The words between the stressed content words are known as grammatical (or function) words. These are the words which bind the speaker's content words together and they are a major contributing factor to the rhythm of English speech. These grammatical/function words tend to be unstressed, which makes them difficult to distinguish. Listen to these excerpts and fill in the missing grammatical/function words.

NB Because this is a listening training exercise don't try to predict the answers before you listen!

1. She's home _____ the moment _____ the holidays...
2. _____ the three boys _____ still _____ school _____ still living _____ home all the time
3. I can tell _____ the tone _____ your voice that hasn't actually worked.
4. this time _____ year
5. particularly with the exams _____ really count
6. I like going _____ lots of walks as well.
7. Hannah's _____ away at university – _____ _____ _____ first year _____ university I think.
8. _____ is _____ going well?
9. And she's waiting _____ the results _____ this lot?
10. So she'll be _____ university _____ two years...
11. but as he's now rather larger _____ me _____ six foot, two...
12. And Hannah? What _____ you do with Hannah?
13. I probably see him more often _____ my sister.
14. he's a long way away _____ all his friends _____ family
15. _____ it's quite a nice break _____ me _____ well...

Can you hear what has happened to the missing words in the stream of speech?

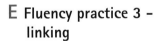

Now listen and repeat the sentences and phrases after the speaker, imitating the speaker's pronunciation.

E **Fluency practice 3 – linking**

Linking occurs when the end of one word runs_into the start_of the next word. It is very common in informal spoken English, but less so in more formal English, such as speeches or lectures.
The most common linking occurs between the letter –s at the end of a word when the next word begins with a vowel, as in these examples from the interview.

Hannah's_at university. She's_ home at the moment for the holidays.
Well, the summer holidays_are really nice..
I like going for lots_of walks_as well.

However, linking also occurs with other sounds, for example when one word ends in the same letter as at the start of the next word, as in this example from the interview:

you're a mother of_four

Linking also occurs when the consonant, or consonant cluster, at the end of one word runs into the vowel at the start of the next word:

I would_imagine...
I just let them get_on with_it...
you're not_allowed to smack your children

Linking also occurs when the final letter –s merges with the start of the next word, as in this example:

It's_quite tiring being the peacemaker.

Mark where you expect linking to occur in these excerpts from the interview. Then listen and check your answers.

1. and they're all teenagers now
2. it's not so hands on with nappies and things
3. Are they all living at home?
4. two at a time
5. You don't have two that get on better than another two...
6. Um, he's out in the evenings quite a bit because he works at The Telegraph.
7. He's into that, yeah.
8. that kind of thing
9. to an extent
10. I think she finds them quite immature.
11. We could all meet up at Christmas and holidays.
12. When I talk to her it's like, you know – it's the same as ever.
13. I probably see him more often than my sister because he comes to London on business and pops in.
14. And he makes a big effort because he knows he's a long way away from all his friends and family...
15. mum insists on cooking

Now repeat numbers 1, 3, 4, 7, 8, 9, 10, 11, 12 and 15 after the speaker, imitating the speaker's pronunciation.

F Sentence stress

It is important that you are able to recognise stressed words in a stream of speech because these are the words that carry the speaker's meaning. Each speaker stresses the words he, or she, feels are necessary to get his, or her, message across. Listen to these excerpts from Judy's interview and mark where the stressed words occur.

NB Unlike scripted listening passages, this exercise is not suitable as a predictive activity because the stressed words are personal to Judy and the interviewer and therefore cannot be predicted by looking at the written script in isolation.

1. Did you plan to have a big family?
2. he's out in the evenings quite a bit
3. I've found it enormously stressful...
4. this is her first year at university, I think
5. she left school two years ago
6. And it matters quite a lot...
7. And if that doesn't work then she just does a three-year degree.
8. And I find it tough when we all have to get up in the morning and she doesn't.
9. you're not allowed to smack your children
10. I think discipline is harder now at school and at home.
11. They probably need incentives.
12. I can't make him do anything.
13. Now my sister it's a day's drive, really.
14. And I think your brother's in America now?
15. I probably see him more often than my sister...

G People talking over each other

In real life, as opposed to coursebooks, it is very common for two or more people to talk over each other at the same time. Fill in the missing words in these excerpts from the interview where the participants are talking at the same time.

Please note this is a very difficult task that many native speakers would find tricky!

    I: Interviewer   **J:** Judy

Excerpt 1

I: *OK. So you're... Yes, you've just got to hold on...*
J: *The _____ _____ _____ _____.*
I: *(laughs)*

Excerpt 2

J: *Er, to get a placement you have to get a 2:1 these days and there aren't enough placements _____ _____ ...*
I: *What do you mean by 'placement'?*

Excerpt 3

J: *Er, and they're always very keen to have any combination of us...*
I: *Mmm.*
J: *...at short notice, and...*
I: *Oh, that's_____, _____ _____?*
J: *...yes...*

Excerpt 4

I: *...and I feel a little bit guilty that he's bringing me tea in bed but um...*
J: *Yes.*
I: *...they like to do it, _____ _____?*
J: *Yes, yes, _____ _____ _____.*
I: *We'll always be their _____.*
J: *Yes.*

A Gap-Fill

Fill in the blanks in these new sentences with words you heard during Judy's interview. The words are listed in the box to help you.

charge	crucial	equivalent	get on	hands-on	involved
keen on	nappies	notice	pocket money	pops in	range
results	revision	right	to cope	treat	

1. I don't think it's _____ that Aaron gets twice as much _____ _____ as me just 'cos he's a bit older.
2. My new manager is really _____-_____ – she wants to be involved in everything.
3. One of the things I hated doing when the kids were small was washing their _____.
4. There's a huge age _____ in our class – from 18 to 72.
5. It's funny, but my mum and dad _____ _____ much better now they're divorced.
6. I'm finding it a bit difficult _____ _____ at work at the moment as we're so short-staffed.
7. I can't come out tonight – I've my exams next week and I need to do some _____.
8. She's a great nurse, but she does tend to get too emotionally _____ with the patients.
9. I need to make a doctor's appointment to get the _____ of those tests I had last month.
10. It's really _____ that I get to work on time tomorrow because we've got someone from head office coming in.
11. How can I _____ you like an adult when you do such childish things?
12. Who's in _____ of the photocopier?
13. What's the _____ to $200 in euros?
14. My friend normally _____ _____ on a Friday on her way home from work.
15. I like salads, but I'm not very _____ _____ celery.
16. Sorry it's short _____, but would you be available to babysit on Friday?

B Transformations

Change the word in each bracket that appeared in the interview to form a word that fits the gap, if necessary.

Here's an example to help you:

*Example: I can make you a sandwich if you're (hunger) **hungry**.*

1. Sheffield used to be a very (industry) _industrial_ city, but it's changed a lot since I was a student there.
2. I can't imagine her ever (smack) _____ her children.
3. My favourite science fiction author is Terry Pratchett – he's got a brilliant (imagine) _imagination_
4. We're trying to find new ways of (incentives) _incentive_ our staff and I was wondering if you've got any experience in this field.
5. I never drive in central London because I get too (stressful) _stressed_.
6. I think my older brother (resentment) _resent_ it when I was born so we've never got on.
7. Paris is really expensive at the moment in (compared) _comparison_ with London.
8. The dog died, despite the vet's best (effort) _efforthers_
9. We (combinations) _combine_ our summer holiday this year with doing family history research, which killed two birds with one stone.
10. We're leaving at six, and I don't want any (arguing) _argument_ from you three kids, you hear?
11. She's quite (hope) _hopeful_ she'll pass this time.
12. It's a bit noisy out in the garden because our neighbours are having some kind of (celebrate) _celebration_
13. Is Dan your (biology) _biological_ father?
14. You need to be very (discipline) _disciplined_ to be self-employed.
15. In some countries (bribery) _bribe_ the police is quite normal.
16. I once met someone who was (relationship) _related_ to William Wordsworth.
17. Remember Jane's a (commitments) _committed_ Catholic, so she never eats meat on Fridays. We'll have to have fish instead.
18. I've put my name down for a (cooking) _cookery_ course at my local college.

C Prepositions and adverbs

Insert the correct preposition or adverb into the gaps in these sentences based on the interview.

1. Do you watch much television when you're _____ home?
2. You have to be careful _____ Mike – he'll do anything _____ a laugh.
3. I can tell _____ your face you're annoyed _____ something.
4. I don't want to argue _____ you, so let's just leave it.
5. My brother works _____ Muscle In - that new gym in the High Street.
6. I'm hoping _____ a white Christmas again this year.
7. This project seemed never-ending when we started it, but at least now the end is _____ sight.
8. It's a lovely day. Shall we go _____ a walk?
9. They've offered me a new job, but it's _____ accounts and it sounds really boring.
10. Anyone who drinks and drives should lose their licence permanently _____ my opinion.
11. Could you possibly look _____ my tropical fish while we're away?
12. I didn't have time to see Clare, but we had a nice long chat _____ the phone.
13. It's been at least five years since we met, but he looked just the same _____ ever.
14. Let's meet up next time I came to Cardiff _____ business.
15. Why don't you come _____ and sit with us?
16. It's impossible to get a table at Poon's there _____ such short notice. Why don't we get a takeaway instead?
17. My father always insists _____ driving which makes my mother really cross.
18. Would you like breakfast _____ bed tomorrow morning?

I: So, um, Judy, you're a mother of four.

J: That's right.

I: That, that must be quite hard work, I would imagine.

J: Yes, it's quite busy...

I: Yes.

J: ...and they're all teenagers now so **(1) it's not so hands-on with nappies and things**, but equally difficult.

I: Mmm.

J: And they go to bed much later.

I: Mmm. Are they, are they all living at home?

J: Hannah's at university. She's home at the moment for the holidays...

I: Mmm.

J: ...and the three boys are still at school and still living at home all the time.

I: OK. Um, what, what's the age range?

J: Hannah is 20 and Toby is 14.

I: OK. Did, did you plan to have a big family?

J: Yes.

I: Yeah.

J: And the theory was that if we had an even number they'd play together nicely, two at a time.

I: Mmm. And I can tell from the tone of your voice that hasn't actually worked.

J: No, they fight in various combinations.

I: Really. You don't have two that **(2) get on** better than another two or...

J: Um, it changes. You know, sometimes they get on well, but...

I: Right.

J: ...quite often somebody's...

I: Mmm.

J: ...arguing with somebody.

I: I see. And do you find yourself playing the peacemaker, or is that more your husband?

J: Um, he's out in the evenings quite a bit...

I: Mmm.

J: ...'cos he works at **(3) The Telegraph**.

I: Right.

J: Um, so... **(4) And sometimes I just let them get on with it.**

I: Mmm, hmm.

J: It's quite tiring being the peacemaker.

I: Well, you're a teacher so you're... you're working with children all day and then you come home and you've got yours **(5) to cope with** as well.

J: Yes, yes, um... If you've had a bad day at school then...

I: Mmm.

J: ...sometimes you hope for them to be very good in the evenings.

I: Right. Um, I guess this time of year – it's June now, so they've got exams coming up, is that, is that difficult – making them do their revision?

J: Yes, and your own children you're so much more emotionally involved than the children you teach.

I: Mmm, hmm.

J: Um, so yes, I've found it enormously stressful, particularly with the exams that really count.

I: Yes. So how long till you're, you're clear of all that – when you finish teaching and the children finish their exams?

J: Another two weeks.

I: OK. So you're... Yes, **(6) you've just got to hold on**...

J: The end is in sight.

I: *(laughs)* Right. How are you going to um, celebrate, if you like – finishing this stressful period?

J: Um... bottle of wine? *(laughs)*

I: Mmm, hmm. Right.

J: Well, the summer holidays are really nice, not having to get up. Um... the hours get later and later because my husband comes back quite late at night and the boys hate getting up and don't have a reason they have to, so **(7) lie-ins are very nice**.

I: Yeah.

J: **(8) It's a treat**. And I like going for lots of walks as well.

I: Right. Do the children come with you?

J: Not often these days.

I: No. OK.

J: Sometimes get one or two to come with us.

I: Mmm, hmm. Um, Hannah's been away at university – this is her first year at university, I think.

J: Yes.

I: But she had **(9) a gap-year** as well.

J: Yes, she left school two years ago. She had a gap-year and she's just done her first year studying biology.

I: OK. And is that going well?

J: She hasn't got her exam results yet...

I: Right.

J: ...but so far it's going well. She's had... Um, they have two sets of exams per year so the first lot went fine.

I: OK. And she's waiting for the results from this lot?

J: Yes.

I: Yeah. OK.

J: And it matters quite a lot because er, to get **(10) a placement** you have to get a **(11) 2:1**...

I: Mmm.

J: ...these days... and there aren't enough placements for everyone.

I: What do you mean by 'placement'?

J: So she has a year in industry.

I: Mmm, hmm.

J: So she'll be at university for two years, then a year out in industry if she gets a placement, then back for her final year.

I: And if that doesn't work then she just does a three-year degree.

J: Yeah, three years straight, so you're transferred from the four-year course to a three-year course...

I: I see.

J: ...if you don't get a placement.

I: Right. So that's quite **(12) crucial**.

J: Yes.

I: How, how have you found **(13) the dynamics** with Hannah being away, being quite grown-up, and then coming back home again and fitting into family life?

J: I think she finds it quite hard and **(14) she says we treat her like a child**...

I: Mmm.

J: ...but **(15) being in charge of** when you eat and what you do at university, that doesn't really work when you're fitting in with family and mealtimes...

I: Mmm, hmm.

J: ...um, so I think she finds that **(16) a bit tough**.

I: Mmm.

J: And I find it tough when we all have to get up in the morning and she doesn't. *(laughs)*

I: No, that would cause a bit of er, **(17) resentment** I would imagine.

J: Yeah.

I: Um, but you grew up, you had two younger...

J: Yes.

I: ...siblings, didn't you – a brother and a sister.

J: Yes, I'm the oldest.

I: Can you see parallels with your family then and now?

J: I think a big difference is that um, discipline has changed. I think um... Well, you're not allowed **(18) to smack** your children...

I: Mmm, hmm.

J: ...and they're encouraged to um, argue their case at school and um, I think discipline is harder now at school and at home.

I: Mmm, yeah. So if you ask your children, for example, to do the washing up...

J: They probably need **(19) incentives.**

I: Mmm, hmm. Yes.

J: So um, **(20) bribery** is fine, in my opinion.

I: What, what do you mean by bribery? Not money?

J: Um, **(21) pocket money**. Um... Rupert wants CDs, so Rupert does things to get a new, a new CD.

I: Mmm, hmm.

J: Um, Toby – access to Roomscape, but as he's now rather larger than me at **(22) six foot, two**, um, I can't make him do anything.

I: Mmm. When you say Roomscape, that's like a...

J: Roomscape, it's a computer game he loves.

I: OK. **(23) He's into that**, yeah.

J: Yes.

I: What about Luke?

J: Um, Luke likes to be allowed to go out when he wants to go out with his friends. Um...

I: Mmm. So you offer him later times to come home – is, is that the incentive?

J: That, that kind of thing.

I: Yeah, and Hannah? What can you do with Hannah?

J: Um, Hannah's actually... She's, she's keen to please. She's...

I: OK.

J: She, she wants to be good.

I: Mmm. All right. How... What's the relationship like with Hannah and having three boys? That must be a bit tough.

J: Um, I think they don't argue with her in the same way...

I: Mmm.

J: ...so that's good.

I: Yep.

J: Um, I think they do look after her to a, **(24) to an extent** and I think that will be more in years to come.

I: Mmm.

J: I think she'll feel very well looked after by having three brothers, um...

I: And they're quite protective?

J: Yes, yes. I mean so far the opportunities haven't been there because they're still...

I: Mmm.

J: ...well, Toby's only 14.

I: Mmm.

J: Um... I think she finds them quite **(25) immature.**

I: Yes, well she, she would, yeah. And I've met her and she's..

J: Not only they, they are younger than her, but I think emotionally they're...

I: Mmm.

J: ...you know, girls they grow up quicker than boys, probably.

I: Yes. Do, do you find that with your school that... with the schoolchildren as well?

J: Um, we're... I only... It's a single sex...

I: Mmm.

J: ...so only girls, so yes, if I think about the equivalent year group um, the 14-year-old girls compared to Toby, yes...

I: Mmm.

J: ...they seem more grown-up.

I: OK. Um, your brother and sister – do you see them much?

J: Um, not too much, no. Um, a few... No, 10 years ago we were all close together.

I: Mmm.

J: Um, we could all meet up at Christmas and holidays.

Now my sister **(26) it's a day's drive**, really.

I: Mmm.

J: And er...

I: Where, where is she?

J: She's in **(27) Yorkshire**.

I: Right.

J: And there are so many reasons you can't go. Weekends and holidays – there's studying to be done and exams and sport commitments. Um, so talk on the phone...

I: Mmm.

J: ...and see her sometimes and...

I: Do, do you miss her?

J: Yes, yes. When I talk to her it's like, you know – it's the same as ever. But....

I: Yeah. Oh, that's good.

J: Yes.

I: And I think your brother's in America now?

J: Yes, my brother moved to America so um, I probably see him more often than my sister because he comes to London on business **(28) and pops in**.

I: Oh, I see. Right.

J: And he makes a big effort because he knows he's a long way away from all his friends and family, so he brings the family over in the summer.

I: Do you see your mum and dad much?

J: Um, try to see them several times a year.

I: Mmm. Right.

J: Er, and they're always very keen to have any combination of us...

I: Mmm.

J: ...at short notice, and...

I: Oh, that's brilliant, isn't it?

J: Yes. So yes, we... and we're made very welcome. And it's quite **(29) a nice break** for me as well because mum insists on cooking and...

I: Oh, that's good.

J: ...bringing me tea in the mornings. *(laughs)*

I: That's, that's lovely. My dad does the same. He, he's 90 now and I feel a little bit guilty that he's bringing me tea in bed but um...

J: Yes.

I: ...they like to do it, don't they?

J: Yes, yes, mum loves it.

I: We'll always be their children.

J: Yes.

7. Words and Phrases

1 **it's not so hands-on with nappies and things** – there isn't so much physical work involved as when we used to have to change the children's nappies when they were small (nappies - a nappy is a square or rectangular piece of thick paper or cloth fastened around a baby's bottom)

2 **(to) get on** – to have a good relationship with someone, e.g. Do you get on with your boyfriend's mum and dad?

3 **The Telegraph** – a famous broadsheet newspaper, traditionally right of centre politically

4 **And sometimes I just let them get on with it**. – And sometimes I just leave them to it. i.e. I don't try to stop them.

5 **to cope with** – to deal with; to manage something difficult

6 **you've just got to hold on** – you just have to manage, or cope, for a while longer

7 **lie-ins are very nice** – If you have a lie-in you stay in bed in the morning longer than normal. For example a lot of people have a lie-in on a Sunday morning because they don't have to go to work.

8 **It's a treat**. – It's a special, enjoyable thing.

9 **a gap-year** – A lot of young people take a year off, or have a gap-year, between school and university, either to travel and see the world or to get some work experience and earn money.

10 **a placement** – A university degree course generally lasts three years in the UK. However, sometimes students do a placement in their third year, i.e. they work for a year in a field related to their degree, and they then return to university for a fourth and final year of study.

11 **a 2:1** – If you take an honours degree the highest grade you can get is a First. A 2:1 (pronounced 'two-one'), or Upper Second is the second best grade you can get. There is also a 2:2, i.e. a Lower Second and a Third Class honours degree.

12 **crucial** – important; essential; necessary

13 **the dynamics** – the relationships between all the different members of the family - the three boys, their sister and their parents

14 **she says we treat her like a child** – she says we behave towards her, or deal with her, as if she's still a child

15 **being in charge of** – being in control of

16 **a bit tough** – *(in this case)* a bit difficult

17 **resentment** – *(in this case)* the feeling you get when someone else is able to do something that you can't

18 **to smack** –to hit with the palm of your hand

19 **incentives** – an incentive is something which encourages someone else to do something. For example parents telling their children they'll pay for driving lessons if their children do well in their exams.

20 **bribery** – If you bribe someone you offer them money or presents or something they want to try to make them do something for you.

21 **pocket money** – the (generally weekly) allowance some parents give their children

22 **six foot, two** – six feet and two inches or six foot and two inches (An inch is 2.54 cms. There are 12 inches in a foot. A foot is 30.48 cms, so Toby is one metre, 88 centimetres tall.)

23 **He's into that…** – He enjoys that very much. e.g. My brother's really into skiing.

24 **to an extent** – to some degree; a certain amount

25 **immature** – childish, i.e. young for their age

26 **it's a day's drive** – it takes a day to drive there by car

27 **Yorkshire** – an area of north-east England comprising three counties: North Yorkshire, West Yorkshire and East Yorkshire

28 **and pops in** – and calls in to visit for a short time

29 **a nice break** – a nice short or mini-holiday

UNIT 2 Marilena

1.Pre-Listening Comprehension

This is an English as a Lingua Franca unit (ELF). Professor Jennifer Jenkins and other English language experts point out that around four-fifths of the English spoken in the world today is between non-native English speakers. This unit gives you practice in understanding a non-native English speaker.

Marilena is a Romanian woman in her early 30s. Seven years ago she decided to leave Romania and come to London. She was a qualified operating theatre nurse in Romania and she now works in the operating theatres of a busy hospital in east London.

Marilena's colleague and line manager, an operating theatre sister called Jill, also appears in the interview. Jill is from North Wales, but she also moved to London in her early 30s.

Marilena understands spoken English very well and communicates effectively, although she does make a number of phonological and grammatical errors. Jill speaks clearly, but quickly, and she has retained her North Welsh accent.

A Discussion

Discuss these questions in pairs or small groups and share your answers with the class:

1. What are the possible reasons for Marilena's decision to leave Romania and come to England?
2. How much do you know about Romania – its geography, its recent history, its language, etc.?
3. Have you ever been to Romania? If yes, what was it like? If no, would you like to go? Why/Why not?

B Normalisation – Freestyle listening comprehension

Marilena talks about her immediate family.

1. What do you learn about Marilena's family from this first section?

2. What do you learn about Marilena's character?

3. Can you identify at least two of the four grammar areas Marilena has problems with?

A True/False

Marilena talks about her sister in England and her nephews and nieces.

Listen and decide if each statement is True (T) or False (F). Remember to give reasons for your answers.

1. _____ One of Marilena's sisters lives with her.
2. _____ The two sisters get on really well.
3. _____ Marilena's sister came to England because Marilena asked her to.
4. _____ Marilena's sister trained as an electrical engineer.
5. _____ All Marilena's grandparents are dead.

B Questions

Marilena talks some more about her family in Romania and the UK.

1. How many nephews and nieces has Marilena got?
2. Who shares the house with Marilena?

C Questions

Jill talks about her family in North Wales.

1. Jill and Marilena have worked in the same operating theatre nearly every day for the past two years, but Marilena knows very little about Jill's family. What are the possible reasons for this?
2. How long is it since Jill's sister moved back to the town in North Wales where she and Jill were born?
3. Who is Teddy?
4. What does Jill's sister work as?
5. What does the expression 'she's off' mean in this context?
6. Jill talks about her aunts and uncles. What does the expression 'they're getting on a bit' mean?
7. How does Jill feel about not seeing her aunts and uncles more often?

D Gap-Fill and Transformations

Marilena talks some more about her parents and her brother and sister in Romania.

Make changes to the actual words Marilena uses (where necessary) so that they fit the gaps. Try to predict your answers before you listen.

1. For the first few years after coming to England, whenever Marilena talked about her parents she _____.
2. Now when she _____ her parents, she feels her _____ is in the UK.
3. Marilena feels there is less _____ in the UK between rich and poor people.
4. She qualifies this by saying that perhaps there is discrimination in the UK, but when people discriminate in the UK they do it '_____.'
5. Marilena hasn't noticed a big _____ difference in the UK.
6. She says rich people in Romania tend to feel very _____ of themselves.
7. Marilena doesn't like people who are rich but who haven't worked _____.
8. Marilena's sister in Romania also works as a _____ and her brother is a _____.

E Cloze

Marilena talks about why she left Romania. Try to predict your answers before you listen.

I: Interviewer   M: Marilena

I: What, what's the reason you came here? Why, why...
M: *(laughs)* I don't think, I don't think we have enough _____!
I: OK.
M: I was married in Romania and er, I wasn't happy in my _____.
I: Mmm.
M: And I tried to _____ _____ from my husband. I, we couldn't divorce because he wa... he didn't agree to _____.
I: I see.
M: And I make a plan, a _____ plan to run away from him.
I: Wow!
M: *(laughs)*
I: To, to England?
J: It's all quite exciting, _____.

M: *(laughs)*

I: Wow!

M: Yes, yes. And I came to England.

I: And it _____?

M: It worked, yeah.

I: He didn't come after you?

M: Er, he _____. In that time we need visa.

I: Oh, I see.

M: When... Because I left in 2005 and we.... By 2007 we need visa, and it was lots of procedures to... And he couldn't find me anyway. And during two years he find somebody else.

I: Oh, OK. So it was quite _____ for you to divorce?

M: No... Ah, yes, because I was away.

F Questions

Marilena talks about her new husband.

47

1. Who introduced Marilena to her future husband?
2. Who wanted to get married most – Marilena or her husband-to-be?
3. Why did Jill miss 'the do', i.e. the social event organised by Jill's colleagues to celebrate Marilena's wedding?

G Gap–Fill and Transformations

Marilena talks some more about her new husband.
Make changes to the actual words Marilena uses (where necessary) so that they fit the gaps. Try to predict the answers before you listen.

48

1. Marilena's new husband hadn't been _____ before.
2. It seems he's very _____.
3. Marilena says he follows the _____ in the Bible.
4. He believes that if you do something _____ to somebody, then something even _____ will happen to you.
5. The interviewer says Marilena's husband is probably very _____.

H Questions

Marilena talks some more about her husband.

49

1. What did Marilena's husband qualify as in Romania?
2. How much is the average monthly salary for a nurse in Romania at this time?
3. Which industry does Marilena's husband work in now?
4. How many hours does he spend at work?

5. Who thinks these are long hours – Marilena or the interviewer?
6. Which two words (one negative and one positive) mean the opposite of fat?
7. Who thinks Marilena's husband is good-looking?
8. What does a person have to have to be truly attractive, according to Marilena?

I Gap–Fill and Transformations

Marilena talks about her sister in England and we find out more about Marilena.

Ask your students to make changes to the actual words Marilena, Jill and the interviewer use (where necessary) so that they fit the gaps. Ask your students to try to predict their answers before they listen.

1. A synonym for the verb 'to fight' is 'to _____'.
2. If no one wants to _____ dinner then they order a _____.
3. Marilena says her sister likes to _____ people.
4. Someone who enjoys telling people what to do is called '_____'.
5. Jill says Marilena is 'quite _____-_____ at work' because she doesn't get stressed even if something goes horribly _____.
6. Marilena says people who get stressed easily tend to _____ younger.

J True/False

Marilena talks about her sister's life in Romania. Listen and decide if each statement is True (T) or False (F). Remember to give reasons for your answers.

1. _____ Marilena's sister only has £100 of her own money to live on for a month after she's paid her mortgage.
2. _____ Marilena says food is much less expensive in Romania than in London.
3. _____ Marilena's sister and brother-in-law's joint income per month is £400.
4. _____ When Marilena goes back to Romania on holiday she gives her sister £1,000.
5. _____ Marilena is planning to return to Romania once she has saved enough money.

K Cloze

Marilena talks some more about her sister's life in Romania. Try to predict your answers before you listen.

I: Interviewer   M: Marilena

I: Poor... I feel _____ for your sister now.
M: But they... Don't feel sorry for them! They are _____! *(laughs)*
I: OK.
J: They don't know any _____, do they? It's just...
M: Yes.
I: No, that's right. Do they live in a nice _____ of Romania?
M: Bucharest, which is...
I: OK.
M: ..._____, which is...
I: Yeah. I've seen a...
J: Big city.
M: Big city.
I: ...documentary. It was... I think Ceausescu, he _____ down a lot of the big _____, didn't he? And he made a big palace...
M: Yeah.
I: ...and a... _____.
M: Yes, yeah.
I: And a lot of the old houses, they _____.
M: Yeah, yeah, yeah.
I: And they built all these very modern, _____ houses.
M: Yeah, that... high _____ and...
I: Yeah. Do they live in something like that?
M: Yeah.
I: Oh, _____.

L Gap-Fill and Transformations

Marilena talks about her grandparents. Try to predict the answers before you listen.

1. Marilena's grandparents used to live in the _____.
2. They didn't have a proper _____, but they had a small _____.
3. They used to _____ all the food they needed.
4. We call this type of farming '_____ farming'.

A Communication and grammatical accuracy: Part 1

It is interesting to note that although Marilena makes a number of grammatical errors, none of these have any impact on communication – Jill and the interviewer understand exactly what she means. In fact it is only the phonological differences that cause problems with communication.

In this first section imagine that Marilena has asked them to help her with her English.

Here is a list of the main grammar areas Marilena has problems with:

A   Comparatives and superlatives
B   Second conditional
C   Confusing the simple past and the present perfect simple
D   Definite and indefinite articles
E   It was/There were
F   Negatives
G   The passive
H   Plurals
I   Possessive and personal pronouns
J   Prepositions
K   The present simple
L   3rd person final –s
M   The simple past
N   Word order

First identify the problem area(s) in these excerpts from the interview using the codes above. Then try to make each excerpt more accurate.

Example

When talking about her parents, Marilena says:

> *if it wasn't them, I wasn't here*

Grammatical problem area(s): **B and J**

More accurate version:

if it weren't/wasn't for them, I wouldn't be here

1. When talking about coming to England, Marilena says:

   No, I came in my own.

   Grammatical problem area(s): _____

   More accurate version: _____*I came on my own.*_____.

2. When talking about her parents, Marilena says:

   First few years I really miss them.

   Grammatical problem area(s): _____

   More accurate version: _____.

3. When talking about her brothers and sisters, Marilena says:

   No, they work all.

   Grammatical problem area(s): _____

   More accurate version: _____.

4. When talking about her new husband, Marilena says:

   I meet him when I divorce the first husband.

   Grammatical problem area(s): _____

   More accurate version: _*I met him after divorcing my* 1.hust.__.

5. When talking about all the procedures people used to have to follow in Romania to get a visa, Marilena says:

   and it was lots of procedures

   Grammatical problem area(s): _____

   More accurate version: _____.

6. When talking about what makes people attractive, Marilena says:

   I'm no pretty.

   Grammatical problem area(s): _____

   More accurate version: _____.

7. When talking about leaving her first husband in 2005, Marilena says:

   And I make a plan...

   Grammatical problem area(s): _____

   More accurate version: _____...

8. When talking about her sister in England, Marilena says:

   And she just organise, but she won't do it.

   Grammatical problem area(s): _____

   More accurate version: _____ _____ _____ .

9. When talking about the fact that Romanians used to need a visa to come to England, Marilena says:

   In that time we need visa.

   Grammatical problem area(s): _____

   More accurate version: _____ .

10. Still on the subject of visas, Marilena explains that:

   By 2007 we need visa.

   Grammatical problem area(s): _____

   More accurate version: _____ .

B Communication skills

When native speakers of a language interact with non-native speakers, or good non-native speakers interact with non-native speakers who speak the language less well, they all tend to do the same things, as we can see from this interview.

1. Speaking more slowly and clearly
   Listen how slowly and clearly the interviewer speaks at the start of the interview, before she knows how well Marilena can communicate:

   Interviewer: *OK. Um, Marilena, do you have a big family?*

2. Fronting – changing the conventional word order to bring key information to the start of a question to make it easier for the listener to understand. Look at these examples from the article:

   Interviewer: *Are they all older than you, your brothers and sister?*
   Interviewer: *Um, your mum and dad, are they still alive?*
   Interviewer: *And er, are the rest of them, they're all in Romania?*
   Interviewer: *What about um, grandparents? Are any of your grandparents alive?*
   Interviewer: *Um, with your um, brother and your two sisters, do any of them have children?*

Interviewer: *And her husband, does he earn good money, or...*
Interviewer: *Your grandparents, did they live in the countryside?*

3. Rephrasing to check understanding

The listener says the same thing as the speaker, but rephrases it, i.e. uses different words to check he or she has understood correctly. Look at these examples from the article:

Example 1

Marilena: *It's nice, but we fight!*
Interviewer: **When you say 'fight', you mean 'argue'...**

Example 2

Marilena: *And I think people they discriminate each other. But here... maybe they do, but they do nicely. Maybe. Maybe they...*
Interviewer: **So you don't see a big class difference?**

Example 3

Marilena: *And finally, yeah, I agree. But slowly, slowly. Hard. I said 'Oh, shall I? Shall I not? You know?*
Interviewer: **So he was asking and asking you and you weren't sure?**
Marilena: *Yes, he was asking, yeah, yeah.*

4. Seeking clarification

Look at how the interviewer seeks clarification when communication breaks down:

Interviewer: **And what was your sister? I couldn't hear.**

5. A) Correcting the speaker and B) helping out with lexis

On various occasions the interviewer and Jill either correct Marilena or supply lexis to help her. Look at these examples from the interview:

A) Correcting:

Example A1

Marilena: *My brother is oldest than me - five years oldest.*
Interviewer: *Five years **older,** OK.*

Notice how Marilena picks up on that correction in her next utterance when she says: And er, sister are **younger** than me.

Example A2

Interviewer: *OK. Um, with your um, brother and your two sisters, do any of them have children?*
Marilena: *More of them they have children.*
Interviewer: ***All** of them?*

Example A3

Marilena: *...they eat what they grow up.*
Jill: *Mmm.*
Marilena: *They...*
Jill: ***Eat what they grow** in the ground.*

B) Helping out with lexis

Example B1

Marilena: *Plus Romanian people who, who get rich they don't work hard. They work... They get rich from...*
Jill: ***Using other people.***

Example B2

Marilena: *And I have a friend which she know many mans and said she to...*
Jill: *Introduce you.*
Marilena: *...introduce us, yeah.*

Example B3

Marilena: *He's more religious and he won't do what in Bible say*

'Don't do it.' You know, something with rules in the, in the Bible, 'Don't do this, don't do this, don't do this.'

Jill: So he **obeys** the rules.

Marilena: Yes.

Example B4

Marilena: In our country we have er, some kind of part of country they're more religious, more...

Jill: **Orthodox.**

Example B5

Interviewer: So what does he do? What's his job?

Marilena: He was in, in co... in my country he is qualified as a counter.

Jill: **Accountant.**

Marilena: Yeah, accountant, yes.

Example B6

Marilena: She... No, yeah, she likes to organise something. She say er, like 'Can you do some cleaning?' Whatever. And she just organise, but she won't do it. (laughs)

Interviewer: I see. So a little bit **bossy,** maybe?

Example B7

Marilena: The prices of food are er, no like here...

Interviewer: Mmm.

Marilena: ...but no...

Interviewer: Not **cheap,** cheap.

Jill: Not cheap.

Marilena: Not cheap.

Example B8

Marilena: ...they eat what they grow up.

Jill: Mmm.

Marilena: They...

Jill: Eat what they grow in the ground.

Marilena: Exactly. They... yeah.

Jill: Yes. **Subsistence farming** is the official word, I think.

6. Helping out by making assumptions so that the speaker doesn't have to make so much effort

Look at these examples from the interview and notice in the first example how Marilena corrects the interviewer's assumption rather too strongly:

Example 1

Interviewer: *Um, did you and your sister come over from Romania together?*
Marilena: *No, I came in [sic – on] my own. And she came five months later.*
Interviewer: *Right. **Because you wanted her to...***
Marilena: *No, no, no. It was her option.*

(One 'no' would have been enough!)

Example 2

Interviewer: ***You felt more among the poor.***
Marilena: *Mmm, I don't feel poor, but... I don't like discrimination...*

Example 3

Marilena: *And he's working as a constru... in construction... As a builder. No big, high position, but he is a good man.*
Interviewer: *Yeah. And the money is quite good in construction.*
Marilena: *Is good yeah, yeah, yeah.*
Interviewer: *I mean it's hard - hard work and **he probably starts early and finishes early.***
Marilena: *No, start 8 o'clock and finish 6 o'clock.*
Interviewer: *That's, that's a long day, though. **But he must be very strong. Lots of muscles.***
Marilena: *No! He's thinner than me! (laughs)*

C Listener response 1: Signalling that you're paying attention

There are a number of different ways to signal to the speaker that you are paying attention and these are particularly useful on the telephone.

1. Mmm, hmm or Mmm.
2. Right.
3. Yeah.
4. OK.
5. Uh, huh.

Look at this excerpt from the interview:

Interviewer: *But when you say 'fight', you mean 'argue', you...*
Marilena: *Yeah, no, no, no (sound of fist hitting hand). (laughs)*
Interviewer: *Not physical?*
Marilena: *No.*
Interviewer: ***Right.*** *That would be terrible.*
Marilena: ***Mmm,*** *no.*
Interviewer: ***Yeah. OK.*** *Um, did you and your sister come over from Romania together?*
Marilena: *No, I came in [sic – on] my own.*
Interviewer: ***Mmm, hmm.***
Marilena: *And she came five months later.*
Interviewer: ***Right.*** *Because you wanted her to...*

Now have some short conversations with your fellow students and practise these signals.

D Communication and grammatical accuracy: Part 2

As mentioned before, it is interesting to note that although Marilena makes a number of grammatical errors, none of these have any impact on communication – the speaker understands exactly what she means. Imagine once again that Marilena has asked you to help her with her English.

Here is a list of the main grammar areas Marilena has problems with:

A   Comparatives and superlatives
B   Second conditional
C   Confusing the simple past and the present perfect simple
D   Definite and indefinite articles
E   It was/There were
F   Negatives
G   The passive

H   Plurals
I   Possessive and personal pronouns
J   Prepositions
K   The present perfect simple
L   3rd person final –s
M   The simple past
N   Word order

As in Exercise A, first identify the problem area(s) in these excerpts from the interview using the codes above, then try to make each excerpt more accurate.

1. When talking about her brother, Marilena says:

    My brother is oldest than me – five years oldest.

    Grammatical problem area(s): _____

    More accurate version: _____.

2. When talking about missing her parents, Marilena says:

    At that time when I talk about them I crying.

    Grammatical problem area(s): _____

    More accurate version: _____.

3. When talking about her brother, Marilena says:

    My brother have two daughters.

    Grammatical problem area(s): _____

    More accurate version: _____.

4. When talking about her sister and brother-in-law in Romania, Marilena says they live in:

    Bucharest, which is capital.

    Grammatical problem area(s): _____

    More accurate version: _____.

5. When talking about her new husband, Marilena says:

    He is of Romania, yeah.

    Grammatical problem area(s): _____

    More accurate version: _____.

6. When talking about her brother, Marilena says:

   My brother is policeman.

   Grammatical problem area(s): _____

   More accurate version: _____.

7. When talking about her husband's slim figure, Marilena says:

   Because he wasn't train as a builder.

   Grammatical problem area(s): _____

   More accurate version: _____.

8. The interviewer asks Marilena if she and her sister argue about things like who's cooking dinner. Marilena replies:

   No about dinner.

   Grammatical problem area(s): _____

   More accurate version: _____.

9. When talking about her two sisters, Marilena says:

   And sister are younger than me.

   Grammatical problem area(s): _____

   More accurate version: _____.

10. When talking about her new husband, Marilena says:

    He never been married.

    Grammatical problem area(s): _____

    More accurate version: _____.

11. When talking about her sister, Marilena says:

    She's train as...

    Grammatical problem area(s): _____

    More accurate version: _____...

12. When talking about her sisters' children, Marilena says:

    And sister from Romania have a daughter and sister from England have one daughter.

    Grammatical problem area(s): _____

    More accurate version: _____.

E The different uses of the word 'so'

The word 'so' is one of the most common words in English and it has a number of different uses. Can your students identify what three of these uses are by looking at the following extracts from the interview?

Use 1

So it's two sisters?
So he obeys the rules.
So you're sort of in the middle.
So in this house you've got you and your sister...
So you don't get stressed?
So a little bit bossy, maybe?
So you don't see a big class difference?
So it was quite easy for you to divorce?

Use 1: _____.

Use 2

So how many brothers and sisters have you got?
So is he from Romania?
So tell me about him.
So what does he do?

Use 2: _____.

Use 3

So she's in the same town as my parents.
And she's off, so we'll be able to do stuff together.

Other examples:

'I've got an exam on Thursday, so I can't come on Wednesday.'
'She's allergic to shellfish, so we can't have prawns.'
'He's got a new job, so he's over the moon.'

Use 3: _____.

F Listener response 2: Exclamations

Look at these listener responses in context:

M: *I have a sister with me in England er...*
I: **Oh, you do?**
M: *Yeah. Living with her...*
I: **Oh, that's nice.**

J: Yes. So er, yes, she's grand. I'm going to see them tomorrow, so that'll be really nice. And she's off, so...

M: **Oh, good.**

M: And I tried to run away from my husband. I, we couldn't divorce because he wa... he didn't agree to divorce.

I: **I see.**

M: And I make a plan, a secret plan to run away from him.

I: **Wow!**

I: OK, right. So tell me about him, please. Have you met him, Jill?

J: No. They had a do where he came, but of course I was in North Wales then.

I: **Oh, that's a shame.** So is he from Romania?

M: Er, yeah. But in my country basically we have... My sister is a nurse, have £200 a month. The living is...

I: **Really?**

I: And they built all these very modern, concrete houses.

M: Yeah, that... high blocks and...

I: Yeah. Do they live in something like that?

M: Yeah.

I: **Oh, dear.**

M: ...and they eat what they grow up.

J: Mmm.

M: They...

J: Eat what they grow in the ground.

M: **Exactly.** They... yeah.

J: Yes. Subsistence farming is the official word, I think.

Now have some short conversations with your fellow students and practise these responses.

G Features of a Romanian accent

Although Romanian is, of course, a Romance language, Marilena's spoken English contains many of the features typical of native speakers of Slavic languages – those languages spoken in the neighbouring countries of Ukraine, Moldova, Hungary, Serbia and Bulgaria. You and your fellow students may share some of these features.

Imagine that Marilena has asked you to help her with her pronunciation as she has an English exam in a few days' time.

1. Listen to how Marilena pronounces the initial letter /h/ sound of following words in these extracts from the interview:

    here   **him**   **he**

    Now listen to how a native English speaker pronounces the /h/ sound in these words.

    a) What is Marilena doing which is different from the native English speaker?
    b) What advice can you give her?

    A good language learner, when talking with a non-native speaker of English, will realise that when the speaker produces one non-standard pronunciation feature, the speaker is likely to produce this feature in all other words in English containing that sound.

    How might Marilena pronounce the following words before you help her?

    hard   hungry   hurt   heel   hear

2. Listen to how Marilena, and then a native English speaker, pronounce these words from the interview:

    mother   father

    a) What is Marilena doing which is different from the native English speaker?
    b) What advice can you give her?

    How might Marilena pronounce the following words before you help her?

    breathing   leather   feather   whether

3. Listen to how Marilena, and then a native English speaker, pronounce the highlighted words in these excerpts from the interview:

    to **visit** them   who are **rich**   to run away from **him**   Don't do **it**.   **pretty**

    a) What is Marilena doing which is different from the native English speaker?
    b) What advice can you give her?

How might Marilena pronounce the following words before you help her?

tip   fib   hill   tin   fit   bit

4. Listen to how Marilena, and then a native English speaker, pronounce the word yes:

a) What is Marilena doing which is different from the native English speaker?
b) What advice can you give her?

How might Marilena pronounce the following words before you help her?

best   less   west   mess   chest

5. Listen to how Marilena, and then a native English speaker, pronounce the /r/ sound in the highlighted words in these excerpts from the interview:

*And I have a **friend**...*
*When I'm going **there** to visit them, I feel my life is **here**. I can't stay **there**.*
*people who are **rich or poor***

a) What is Marilena doing which is different from the native English speaker?
b) What advice can you give her?

How might Marilena pronounce the following words before you help her?

doctor   waiter   crater   porter   more   tractor

A Dictation 1

 to

At times in the interview Marilena, Jill and the interviewer speak very quickly and consequently some words are not pronounced clearly. Work with a partner. First listen to the excerpts from the interview and write down how many words there are in each item. Then listen and write down the words you hear. After that check your answers with another pair.

1. (___ words) _____
2. (___ words) _____
3. (___ words) _____
4. (___ words) _____
5. (___ words) _____
6. (___ words) _____
7. (___ words) _____
8. (___ words) _____
9. (___ words) _____
10. (___ words) _____

B Fluency Practice 1 – Linking Part A

As we saw in the previous unit, linking occurs when the end of one word runs_into the start_of the next word. It is very common in informal spoken English, but less so in more formal English, such as speeches or lectures.

Look at the following extracts from the interview and predict where linking will occur. Then listen and check your answers against the recording.

1. *Um, your mum and dad, are they still alive?*
2. *Um, did you and your sister come over from Romania together?*
3. *All of them?*
4. *Do they live in a nice part of Romania?*

Now repeat each phrase or sentence after the interviewer, imitating her delivery.

Linking often occurs with the final letter –s of a word running into the start of the next word. The reason this happens so frequently is that the final letter –s is a marker for plurals and the 3rd person present simple.

Look at the following extracts from the interview and predict where linking will occur. Then listen to check your answers against the recording.

1. Are they all older than you, your brothers and sister?
2. So how many nephews and nieces have you got?
3. She moved a couple of years ago.
4. In your family, do you have anybody who employs other people?
5. Another sister is a nurse in Romania.
6. He probably starts early and finishes early.
7. That's a long day, though.
8. Is it who's going to cook dinner, or...?
9. 'It's all right. There's another day.'
10. It's all quite exciting, really.

Now repeat each phrase or sentence after the speaker, imitating the speaker's pronunciation.

C Weak Forms: Part 1

As we saw in the previous unit, the words between the stressed content words are known as grammatical (or function) words. These are the words which bind the speaker's content words together and they are a major contributing factor to the rhythm of English speech. These grammatical/function words tend to be unstressed, which makes them difficult to distinguish.

The following sentences contain the following weak forms:

and	*are*	*do you*	*from*	*have*
it's	*of*	*she's*	*that*	*the*	*your*

Listen and fill in the missing grammatical/function words, using capitals where necessary, then listen again and discuss how the pronunciation of these words has changed from how they sound in isolation.

NB Because this is a listening training exercise don't try to predict the answers before you listen!

1. So _____ two sisters?
2. Um, _____ mum _____ dad, _____ they still alive?
3. And er, are the rest _____ them, they're all in Romania?
4. Um, did you and _____ sister come over _____ Romania together?

5. So how many nephews _____ nieces _____ you got?
6. _____ _____ know much about Jill's family?
7. But she moved a couple _____ years ago
8. _____ dog's called Teddy _____ _____ lovely.
9. Is _____ up in North Wales?
10. Yes, _____ happy enough. She's working in a care home, actually.

D Dictation 2

At times in the interview Marilena, Jill and the interviewer speak very quickly and consequently some words are not pronounced clearly.
At other times they talk over each other. Listen to these excerpts and try to transcribe the missing words, working together in pairs.

76

1. Interviewer: Do you know much about Jill's family?
   Marilena: A little bit about her parents.
   _____, if she...

77

2. Jill: I mean there's lots of aunties and uncles around, but... you...
   Marilena: _____.
   Jill: No, you don't, really.

78

3. Marilena: ...I think it's another kind of life
   – _____
   _____ ...

79

4. Marilena: _____ who, who get rich, they don't work hard.

80

5. Marilena: And I make a plan, a secret plan to run away from him.
   Interviewer: Wow!
   Marilena: (laughs)
   Interviewer: To, to England?
   Jill: _____.
   Marilena: (laughs) Yes, yes.

81

6. Interviewer: But we, we all do that. I mean, I try to live like that. I'm sure you try to live like that.
   _____.
   Marilena: Yes, he's more... (laughs)
   Interviewer: He ne... He never does anything bad.

82

7. Marilena: And she just organise, but she won't do it. (laughs)
   Interviewer: Yes, so a little bit...
   Jill: Marilena _____.
   Marilena: (laughs)

8. Marilena: Yes, yes. And me, because we grow up, I'm the oldest one. We grew up - I should be bossy. (laughs) _____

_____! (laughs)

           Interviewer: OK. (laughs)

           Jill: She's quite laid-back...

           Interviewer: _____.

           Jill: ...at work. And she says 'Oh, it's all right. There's another day'. always, if something goes

_____.

           Marilena: (laughs)

9. Interviewer: So how, how does she manage? Do... _____

_____?

           Marilena: With her husband.

E Fluency Practice 2 – Linking Part B

Linking can also occur between the final letter –s and consonants, as well as vowels, where the /s/ sound merges with the next word, as in these examples:

Oh, that's_nice.
And she came five months_later.
That's_quite sad.

Look at the following extracts from the interview and predict where linking will occur. Then listen to check your answers against the recording.

1. No, she's not.*
2. It's life.
3. How many's that?
4. Do you know much about Jill's family?
5. The dog's called Teddy and he's lovely.
6. She's working in a care home, actually.
7. I mean there's lots of aunties...
8. So what does he do? What's his job?
9. Is it who's going to cook dinner, or...?
10. She's quite laid-back.

Now repeat each phrase or sentence after the speaker, paying attention to linking between the final letter –s and the next consonant.

*This linking between **he's_not, it's_not** and **she's _not** is common in informal spoken English. It's amusing, however, that the word 'snot' is a *slang word meaning mucus coming from the nose and is very impolite. However, because of the linking between **he's not**, **it's not** and **she's not**, we actually say 'snot' a lot, without realising it.*

F Weak Forms: Part 2

As we saw in Exercise C and in the previous unit, the words between the stressed lexical, or content, words are known as grammatical, or functional, words which bind the speaker's words together. These grammatical words tend to be unstressed, which makes them difficult to distinguish.

The following sentences contain the following weak forms:

about	*and*	*couldn't*	*for*	*I'm*	*it*	*of*
that'll	*the*	*them*	*to*	*was*	*we'll*	*what*
what's	*will*	*with*	*your*	*you're*		

Listen and fill in the gaps, using capitals where necessary.

NB This a listening training exercise, so don't try to predict your answers first.

88

1. _____ going _____ see _____ tomorrow, so _____ be really nice.
2. And she's off so _____ be able to do stuff together.
3. _____ you see the rest _____ _____ family while _____ up there?
4. _____ _____ _____ _____ sister? I _____ hear.
5. _____ _____ the reason you came here?
6. So _____ _____ quite easy _____ you _____ divorce?
7. You were saying _____ _____ sister and you fight _____ your sister, or you argue _____ your sister...
8. I feel sorry _____ _____ sister now.

Now listen again and discuss how the pronunciation of these words has changed from how they sound in isolation.

89 to **96**

1. **I'm** going **to** see **them** tomorrow, so **that'll** be really nice.
2. And she's off so **we'll** be able to do stuff together.
3. **Will** you see the rest **of your** family while **you're** up there?
4. **And what was your** sister? I **couldn't** hear.
5. **What was** the reason you came here?
6. So **it was** quite easy **for** you **to** divorce?
7. You were saying **about your** sister and you fight **with** your sister, or you argue **with** your sister...
8. I feel sorry **for your** sister now.

A Gap-Fill

Fill in the blanks in these new sentences with words you heard during the interview with Marilena and Jill. The words are listed in the box to help you.

> agree   couple   crying   guilty   knocked   miss
> mortgage   organise   religious   rest   rules   secret
> shame   slim   terrible   wages

1. Would anyone like the _____ of the spinach? It seems a shame to waste it.
2. Tom can't make it. He's got a _____ cold.
3. I lived in Sweden for a _____ of years when I was younger.
4. I feel really _____ that Simon was in hospital for a fortnight and I didn't visit him once, but I was really busy.
5. We can't _____ on what colour to paint the kitchen. I want terracotta and Chris wants primrose yellow.
6. Yasmin's parents don't approve of Mark so they have to meet in _____.
7. It's a _____ John's moving to Bath. I'll really _____ him.
8. I love watching football, but I don't really understand the _____. I mean, what's 'offside' all about, for example?
9. My neighbour's very _____ - she goes to church every Sunday.
10. I spend half my _____ on food these days.
11. I can't believe I used to be _____ enough to fit into this dress!
12. I think a surprise party's a great idea, but who's going to _____ it?
13. My son wants to get his own place, but he can't get a _____ because he's only been working a year.
14. There used to be a beautiful old cinema there, but then they _____ it down and replaced it with a car park.
15. Please stop _____! I didn't mean to upset you.

B Transformations

Change the word in each bracket that appeared in the interview to form a word that fits the gap, if necessary.

Here's an example to help you:

Example: I can make you a sandwich if you're (hunger) __hungry__.

1. She has quite a hard (alive) _____, being a single mother with three young kids.

2. Look, I don't want another (argue) _____.
3. Are safety belts (option) _____ in the UK or do you have to wear them?
4. My grandmother's in a (nurse) _____ home and I want to go and see her tomorrow, but I don't know the (visit) _____ hours.
5. My cousin is studying (engineer) _____ at Bath University.
6. This is one of the (sad) _____ songs I know.
7. What do the letters 'PG' stand for on a DVD? Is it (parent) _____ Guidance?
8. This is Steve's third (married) _____, so let's hope it works out this time.
9. You know what they say – (proud) _____ comes before a fall.
10. The National Health Service is one of the biggest (employs) _____ in Europe.
11. The problem with Andy is he doesn't know his own (strong) _____.
12. I really like Julie, but she's very (opinion) _____, don't you think?
13. What type of (organise) _____ does he work for?
14. Economic (grow) _____ in the UK nearly came to a standstill last year.
15. I think Sophie's finding her new job a bit (stressed) _____. That's why she's always too tired to come out these days.

C Prepositions and adverbs

Put the correct preposition or adverb into the gaps in these sentences based on the interview.

1. Could you call back later, please? I'm _____ the middle _____ a crisis.
2. Would you like a biscuit _____ your coffee?
3. Do you mind if I have the rest _____ the potatoes? I'm starving.
4. Why don't we go and sit _____ there _____ the shade?
5. Everyone went _____ an emergency site visit last week so I was in the office all _____ my own.
6. I originally trained _____ a teacher, but then I changed careers and became a police officer.
7. Do you know anything _____ getting rid _____ wasp nests? We've got one in the attic and we don't know what to do.
8. I loved Bali. In fact I'm planning to go _____ there _____ a couple _____ years.

9. I used to live in Aberdeen, _____ in the north _____ Scotland.

10. I'm _____ tomorrow so we could do something together if you like.

11. My parents are getting _____ a bit, so I try to get to see them as much as I can.

12. The people I work _____ are great, but our line manager's a nightmare.

13. I've just heard you passed your driving test first time! You should feel very proud _____ yourself!

14. My brother works _____ construction, so if you need any building work done, he's your man.

15. After I've paid my rent I only have £60 a week to live _____.

NB Because this is an English as a Lingua Franca unit, the following transcript is verbatim. Many of the grammatical errors it contains form the basis of earlier exercises.

I: OK. Um, Marilena, do you have a big family?

M: Yes, I do.

I: Mmm, hmm.

M: Um, mother, father... obviously. Therefore if it wasn't them, I wasn't here. *(laughs)*

I: *(laughs)*

M: And a brother...

I: Mmm, hmm.

M: ...and two sisters.

I: Mmm. Are they all older than you, your brothers and sister?

M: My brother is oldest than me – five years oldest.

I: Five years older, OK.

M: And er, sister are younger than me.

I: Mmm. So it's two sisters?

M: Yeah.

I: And they're younger than you. So you're sort of in the middle.

M: Yes.

I: OK. Um, your mum and dad, are they still alive?

M: Yes, they are, thank God. *(laughs)*

J: Mmm.

I: And er, are the rest of them, they're all in Romania?

M: I have a sister with me in England er...

I: Oh, you do?

M: Yeah. Living with her...

I: Oh, that's nice.

M: It's nice, but **(1) we fight!** *(laughs)*

J: They, they, they live together.

I: Oh, you do?

M: We don't fight every day either.

I: No. But when you say 'fight', you mean 'argue', you...

M: Yeah, no, no, no (sound of fist hitting hand). *(laughs)*

I: Not physical fighting?

M: No.

I: Right. That would be terrible.

M: Mmm, no.

I: Yeah. OK. Um, did you and your sister come over from Romania together?

M: No, I came in my own.

I: Mmm, hmm.

M: And she came five months later.

I: Right. Because you wanted her to...

M: No, no, no. **(2) It was her option.** And she came in other side. She came in **(3) Kent**...

I: Mmm, hmm.

M: ...around of London.

I: I see. South-east London.

M: Mmm, hmm.

I: Right. Is she also a nurse?

M: No, she's not. She's a... She's train as a engineer agriculture? Agriculture engineer.

I: Oh, OK, right. Mmm, hmm. What about um, grandparents? Are any of your grandparents alive?

M: No, they're not. Unfortunately no.

I: OK.

M: They're not. Um, grandparents from my father died when I was many years young – I don't remember them.

I: Mmm, hmm.

M: And er, grandparents from my mother died five years ago?

I: Oh, right, yeah. Oh, that's quite sad.

M: Yeah, it is sad. It's life.

I: OK. Um, with your um, brother and your two sisters, do any of them have children?

M: More of them they have children.

I: All of them?

M: Yeah.

I: OK.

M: *(laughs)*

I: So how many nephews and nieces have you got?

M: Er, my brother have two daughters.

I: Uh, huh.

M: And er, sister from Romania have a daughter and sister from England, in London, have one daughter.

I: OK. So in this house you've got you and your sister...

M: Mmm, hmm.

I: ...and your sister's daughter.

M: Yes.

I: Yeah, and...

M: Her husband.

I: Her husband, OK.

M: My husband.

I: And your husband.

M: Yeah.

I: Yeah. How many's that? One, two, three, four.... Five.

M: Five.

I: Five in the house. OK. Do you know much about Jill's family?

M: A little bit about her parents. I haven't heard about any sister – if she...

J: I have one sister. She's just... She used to live in Kent, also, but she moved a couple of years ago...

I: Mmm.

J: ...back up to er, home town, so she's in the same town as my parents.

M: Mmm, hmm.

J: Married. With a dog, no kids. The dog's called Teddy and he's lovely.

I: Is that up in North Wales?

J: Yes. Yeah.

I: Oh, OK. Right.

J: Yeah, she's happy enough. She's working in **(4) a care home**, actually.

M: Is she **(5) a care assistant?**

J: Mmm?

M: Is she care assistant?

J: Yes. So er, yes, she's grand. I'm going to see them tomorrow, so that'll be really nice. And **(6) she's off**, so...

M: Oh, good.

J: ...**(7) we'll be able to do stuff together**.

I: Yeah. Will you see the rest of your family while you're up there?

J: Mum and dad, obviously.

I: Mmm, hmm.

J: I mean there's lots of aunties and uncles around, but... you...

M: You don't have time.

J: No, you don't, really. No. And they're, you know, **(8) they're getting on a bit** and **(9) I feel quite guilty**, but um, you know. **(10) It's rare**.

I: What about you, Marilena? 'Cos you're, you're over here and most of your family's back at home. Do you miss them a lot?

M: I miss them when I came first. For a... First few years I really miss them. When I... At that time when I talk about them I crying. **(11) I was really sensitive**. But

now... When I wa... when I'm going there to visit them I feel my life is here. I can't stay there.

I: Right. Why, why do you feel that?

M: What happened there er... I think it's another kind of life – obviously because it's another country and er... It's different people who are rich or poor. And I think people **(12) they discriminate each other**. But here... maybe they do, but they do nicely.

J: Mmm, mmm.

M: Maybe. Maybe they...

I: **(13) So you don't see a big class difference?**

M: Mmm, mmm, mmm, mmm. Yes.

I: Yeah. The people you work with or...

M: Yes and I think people there who are rich, they, they like to be more proud of them.

I: Mmm. OK. So you didn't feel...

M: I don't like that.

I: No. You felt more among the poor.

M: Mmm, I don't feel poor, but... I don't like discrimination some....

I: Mmm, hmm. Right.

M: Plus many people who, who get rich, they don't work hard. They work... They get rich from...

J: Using other people.

M: Yes, and I don't like this.

I: Mmm. In your family, do you have anybody who employs other people - any people with their own businesses?

M: No, they work all as I work. My sister, she's... Another sister is a nurse in Romania and my brother is policeman. They can't employ other people!

J: No.

I: OK. Policeman... Oh, OK. And what was your sister? I couldn't hear.

M: Nurse.

J: Nurse.

I: Nurse.

M: From, from my country.

I: In... She's a nurse in Romania. Yeah. What, what's the reason you came here? Why, why...

M: *(laughs)* I don't think, I don't think we have enough time!

I: OK.

M: I was married in Romania and er, I wasn't happy in my marriage.

I: Mmm.

M: And I tried to run away from my husband. I, we couldn't divorce because he wa... he didn't agree to divorce.

I: I see.

M: And I make a plan, a secret plan to run away from him.

I: Wow!

M: *(laughs)*

I: To, to England?

J: It's all quite exciting, really.

M: *(laughs)*

I: Wow!

M: Yes, yes. And I came to England.

I: **(14) And it worked?**

M: It worked, yeah.

I: He didn't come after you?

M: Er, he couldn't. In that time we need visa.

I: Oh, I see.

M: When... Because I left in 2005 and we.... By 2007 we need visa, and it was lots of procedures to... And he couldn't find me anyway. And during two years he find somebody else.

I: Oh, OK. So it was quite easy for you to divorce?

M: No... Ah, yes, because I was away.

I: Mmm. And Jill was saying you got married a few weeks ago.

M: *(laughs)* Yes!

I: Fantastic, isn't it?

J: *(laughs)*

M: Yes!

I: Tell me about your partner, or your husband.

M: My husband, I meet him when I er, divorce the first husband, when I didn't know him, but I was in freedom. I said 'I don't want any man in my life.' I thought no, no way. And I have a friend which she know many mans and said she want me to...

J: Introduce you.

M: ...introduce us, yeah. 'I don't want it! Leave me alone!' She went 'No all, no all of man are the same. Try to...'

I: Mmm.

M: And obviously I try because she introduce me a few man! *(laughs)*

I: OK.

M: And then I... When I met this one I said 'Oh, he's nice, but I don't want to get married.' Because I was frighten from my past.

I: Yep.

M: And then finally, yeah, I agree. But slowly, slowly. **(15) Hard**. I said 'Oh, shall I? Shall I not?' You know?

I: So he was asking and asking you...

M: Yes, he was ask...

I: ...but you weren't sure.

I: OK, right. So tell me about him, please. Have you met him, Jill?

J: No. **(16) They had a do** where he came, but of course I was in North Wales then.

I: Oh, that's a shame. So is he from Romania?

M: He is of Romania, yeah. He never been married. He's, he's a good mad *[sic – man]*. Mostly he's frighten of God. I don't know if you know what I mean.

I: No.

M: He's more religious and he won't do what in Bible say 'Don't do it'. You know, something with rules in the, in the Bible, 'Don't do this, don't do this, don't do this.'

J: So he obeys the rules.

M: Yes. He was... In our country we have er, some kind of part of country they're more religious, more...

J: **(17) Orthodox**.

M: They don't do... No Orthodox. Everyone is Orth... most of them are Orthodox. But they are most... more... Um, follow some rules. They don't do to affect from others.

I: So they're very moral, if you like. They don't, they don't do bad things.

M: Yes, yes.

I: OK. What would, would we call that? **(18) God-fearing?**

J: God-fearing? I, I don't know.

M: They, they, they believe, or they believe if, if you do something bad to, to a person...

I: Mmm, hmm.

M: ...latest you will get worst. You know what I mean?

I: OK, yeah.

J: **(19) Karma**.

I: Sort of like karma?

M: Yeah, something like that.

J: Mmm.

I: But we, we all do that. I mean, I try to live like that. I'm sure you try to live like that. But he's a bit more extreme.

M: Yes, he's more... *(laughs)*

I: He ne... He never does anything bad.

M: Yes, he won't do that.

I: Oh, OK. Right. Very honest.

M: Yeah, yeah, yeah, yeah.

I: So what does he do? What's his job?

M: He was in, in co... in my country he is qualified as a counter.

J: **(20) Accountant.**

M: Yeah, accountant, yes.

J: Mmm.

I: OK.

M: Er, yeah. But in my country basically we have... My sister is a nurse, have £200 a month. The living is...

I: Really?

M: This is the wages...

I: Yeah.

M: What can I say. And he try to other ... And he's working as a constru... in construction...

I: Mmm.

M: As a builder. No big, high position, but he is a good man.

I: Yeah. And the money is quite good in construction.

M: Is good yeah, yeah, yeah.

I: I mean it's hard – hard work and he probably starts early and finishes early.

M: No, start 8 o'clock and finish 6 o'clock.

I: That's, that's a long day, though. But he must be very strong. Lots of muscles.

M: No! He's thinner than me! *(laughs)*

J: *(laughs)*

M: Because he wasn't train as a builder!

I: Oh, dear!

M: He was train as a counter, to count the money! *(laughs)*

J: I've seen pictures. He is quite **(21) a slim man**.

M: He is slim, yeah.

I: Is he handsome?

J: Yes.

M: Handsome? I no... I don't think...

J: He's quite handsome.

M: Yes.

J: Quite good-looking, I would say.

M: No, I think people... I'm not pretty, but I think people, the, the pretty came from inside of the heart, in my opinion.

I: Right.

M: It's not... Because I can see people very pretty outside...

I: Mmm, hmm.

M: ...but they're horrible inside – of the heart, you know.

I: Yes. Mmm, mmm. And he's, he's both.

M: Yes, he is.

I: Quite nice-looking....

M: **(22) In equilibration, yeah.**

I: Oh, that's... that's really good.

M: Mmm.

I: OK. You were saying about your sister, and you fight with your sister, or you argue with your sister. What, what do you argue about? Like when you go home tonight...

M: Ah, not tonight.

I: ...what, what, what could, what could you argue about? Is it who's going to cook dinner or...

M: No about dinner because we're, we're not er... We are really um, finding a good idea. If we don't have any cook... to... If no one want to cook - order pizza, whatever, no...

J: Mmm.

M: No, fight about...

J: Silly...

M: She... No, yeah, she likes to organise something. She say er, like 'Can you do some cleaning?' Whatever. And she just organise, but she won't do it. *(laughs)*

I: Yes, so a little bit...

J: **(23) Marilena ends up doing it**.

M: *(laughs)*

I: I see. So a little bit **(24) bossy**, maybe?

M: Yes, yes. And me, because we grow up, I'm the oldest one. We grew up – I should be bossy. *(laughs)* And I'm not! *(laughs)*

I: OK. *(laughs)*

J: **(25) She's quite laid-back**...

I: Relaxed.

J: ...at work. And she says 'Oh, it's all right. There's another day', always, if something goes horribly wrong.

M: *(laughs)*

J: 'It's all right!' Honestly!

I: So you don't get stressed?

M: Yeah - if I get stressed, for five minutes. I don't get... 'Cos I know if I get stressed, I will die then. Then to transport a dead body from here to Romania is too expensive. *(laughs)*

J: You have to think of these things! *(laughs)*

M: *(laughs)*

I: OK. **(26) I think on that happy note we shall stop.**

M and J: *(laughing)*

I: Thank you very much. **(27) That was great**.

I: You said your sister gets £200 a month. That's, that's nothing!

M: Yeah, but her... She has.... She, **(28) she bought her house in mortgage**, as I bought it, and er, she paying her mortgage every month £100...

I: Mmm.

M: ...which is...

I: So she has £25 a week to live on for food and...

M: Yes. And the food... The prices of food are er, no like here...

I: Mmm.

M: ...but no...

I: Not cheap, cheap.

J: Not cheap.

M: Not cheap.

I: No. So how, how does she manage? Do... does she do another job?

M: With her husband, yeah. No, she hasn't.

I: No. And her husband, does he earn good money, or...

M: She does... he, the same – £200. *(laughs)*

I: It's awful, Jill, isn't it?

M: It is.

J: Mmm. You don't think about it, do you, really?

I: No.

J: **(29) We are lucky here,** you know.

M: We are lucky because when I'm going there, I can't think to go for one, for two weeks with less than one thousand pounds. I can't go.

J: Mmm.

M: And in two weeks I can't say with one thousand pounds I have everything, just...

I: Mmm.

J: Yes.

I: Go, going out, having a cup of coffee, things like that. Not...

M: Yeah. And I think 'Oh, how... **(30) How she can manage**? How she...'

I: Mmm.

M: But they do manage.

J: Mmm. So would you if you went back. I mean because you can...

M: I did, I did manage as well, but now because **(31) I'm going to other level**, I come back, come back... I can't go back.

I: Mmm. No, you would find it too difficult, yeah. Hav... **(32) Having got used to this standard of living**...

M: Yeah.

I: ...and things. Yeah. Poor... I feel sorry for your sister now.

M: But they... Don't feel sorry for them! They are happy! *(laughs)*

I: OK.

J: They don't know any different, do they? It's just...

M: Yes.

I: No, so... Do they live in a nice part of Romania?

M: Bucharest, which is...

I: OK.

M: ...capital, which is...

I: Yeah. I've seen a...

J: Big city.

M: Big city.

I: ...documentary. It was... I think Ceausescu, he knocked down a lot of the big buildings, didn't he? And he made a big palace...

M: Yeah.

I: ...and a... avenue.

M: Yes, yeah.

I: And a lot of the old houses, they disappeared.

M: Yeah, yeah, yeah.

I: And they built all these very modern, concrete houses.

M: Yeah, that... high blocks and...

I: Yeah. Do they live in something like that?

M: Yeah.

I: Oh, dear. OK. Mmm. Do your gran... Your grandparents, did they live in the countryside?

M: Yes. What happened grandparents, what I remember, they didn't have a proper job. They were as a working farmer and they eat what they grow up.

J: Mmm.

M: They...

J: Eat what they grow in the ground.

M: Exactly. They... yeah.

J: Yes. **(33) Subsistence farming is the official word, I think**.

1   **we fight!** – we argue (in this case)
2   **It was her option**. – (unusual usage) It was her choice.
3   **Kent** – a county in the south-eastern corner of England which lies south-east of London
4   **a care home** – usually a home for elderly residents or people with special needs who are unable to look after themselves (as opposed to a nursing home where people need nursing care)
5   **a care assistant** – a person who works in a care home
6   **she's off** – she's free – she isn't working
7   **we'll be able to do stuff together** – we'll be able to do things together – go shopping, go for a walk, etc.
8   **they're getting on a bit** – they're getting older
9   **I feel quite guilty** – I feel quite bad (in this case) for not seeing them more often
10 **It's rare**. – It's very seldom that I see them.
11 **I was really sensitive**. – I was easily upset. (i.e. when she thought about her parents back in Romania)
12 **they discriminate each other** – they (in this case rich people) treat other people badly (in this case poor people)
13 **So you don't see a big class difference?** – We often talk about the class system in the UK, i.e. the upper class, the upper middle class, the lower middle class and the working class. However, Marilena hasn't noticed a difference between classes during her time in the UK.
14 **And it worked?** – (in this case) And your escape plan was successful?
15 **Hard**. – Difficult.
16 **They had a do** – they had a party, or some kind of social event to celebrate Marilena's marriage
17 **Orthodox**. – the Orthodox Church is part of the Christian Church found in Greece, Russia and many parts of Eastern Europe, including Romania
18 **God-fearing** – Someone who is God-fearing is very religious and tries to live a life that God would approve of.
19 **karma** – In the Buddhist and Hindu religions karma is the force produced by a person's actions in one of their lives which influences what happens to them in their future lives. Nowadays we often use karma to mean that if you do something good (or bad) to someone then something good (or bad) will happen to you. Another way of saying this is: What goes around, comes around.
20 **(an) accountant** – An accountant is a professionally trained person who keeps a record of money earned, paid out and owed to a company.
21 **a slim man** – 'slim' is positive; 'thin' is negative
22 **In equilibration, yeah.** – Here Marilena means that her husband is a good person and he's good-looking – the perfect balance or combination.
23 **Marilena ends up doing it**. – Marilena finds herself doing it in the end.
24 **bossy** – someone who is bossy is always telling other people what to do
25 **She's quite laid-back**... – She's quite relaxed – she doesn't get stressed easily.
26 **I think on that happy note we shall stop**. – I think this is a good place to stop, while we're all laughing.
27 **That was great.** – That was really good.

28 **she bought her house in mortgage** *[sic]* – she has a mortgage on her house (a mortgage is a loan used to buy a house, flat, etc.) NB We don't pronounce the letter –t- of mortgage.

29 **We are lucky here** – We are very fortunate here

30 **How she can manage?** – (in this case) How can she succeed in living on such a small amount of money?

31 **I'm going to other level** *[sic]* – I've gone up a level

32 **Having got used to this standard of living**... – Having got used to having a certain amount of money to live on (i.e. more than you had in Romania...)

33 **Subsistence farming is the official word, I think.** *[sic]* – Subsistence farming is the correct expression, I think.

UNIT 3 Randy

1.Pre-Listening Comprehension

Randy is a trained actor, musician and composer from Montana who is currently living in London. He has a strong American accent, despite having lived in the UK since 1999, first in London, then Edinburgh and then back in London. Here he talks about his family.

Warning! *This interview was recorded in a large Victorian pub during one afternoon in early summer and there is a lot of background noise (music, people talking and calling out, etc.), so you will probably find this unit very challenging. It is a good example, though, of real life listening.*

A Schema building – predicting which words will come up

Which 10 of these 20 words do you expect to hear during the interview?

a tray, a newspaper, grew up, yoghurt, cowboys, wheels, to raise, steam, polish, retire, planned, a tip, birth, a rug, kids, a cloud, alive, married, a label, a relationship

B Discussion

Discuss these questions in pairs or small groups and share your answers with the class:

1. Why do you think Randy moved to the UK?
2. What do you know about Montana?
3. How do you think Randy's family back in the USA feel about Randy moving to the UK?

C Normalisation 1: Features of an American accent

Listen first to how Randy pronounces the words and phrases below, then compare his accent with that of the speaker from England:

Montana   to get around
the Rocky Mountains   doing the exact same job
ranchers   I was on a plane...
and wanted space on their own   and one Italian
flood disasters

Now repeat these words and phrases after the two speakers.

D Normalisation 2 – Anticipating the next word

This exercise is designed to help you get used to Randy's voice.

Listen to Track 100. There is a word missing from the end of each excerpt. Try to guess the missing word and write it down. Then listen to Track 101 to check your answers. How well did you guess?

1. _____
2. _____
3. _____
4. _____
5. _____
6. _____
7. _____
8. _____
9. _____

E Normalisation 3: Questions

Randy talks about where he comes from. Listen and answer the questions.

1. How many US states does Randy mention in the first couple of sentences?
2. For how many years did he live in Montana?
3. Which famous mountains does he mention?
4. Which three types of people is Montana famous for, according to Randy?
5. Which famous film was set in Montana, according to Randy?

Glacier National Park, Montana

2. Listening Comprehension

A True/False

(103)

Randy talks about his parents and his two brothers. Answer true or false. Be prepared to give reasons for your answers.

1. _____ Randy's mother and father both had a close relationship with their families.
2. _____ The gap between Randy's older and younger brother is 22 years.
3. _____ Randy was still living at home when his younger brother was born.
4. _____ Randy's mother wasn't expecting to get pregnant again.
5. _____ Randy's mother was seriously ill after giving birth to his younger brother.

B Gap–Fill

(104)

Randy talks about his brothers and his father.

Before you listen, try to predict which words, or which types of words (nouns, adjectives, prepositions, parts of verbs, etc.) will fill the gaps. Listen and check your answers.

1. Randy's older brother's full name is _____ _____ Smartnick Jr.
2. His younger brother is _____ _____ Smartnick.
3. Randy says his father was _____ military.
4. His father fought in _____ and then trained as a National_____.
5. Randy's father _____ at the age of 54.

C True/False

(105)

Randy talks about the National Guard. Answer true or false. Be prepared to give reasons for your answers.

1. _____ People sign up to the National Guard to get financial help with their education.
2. _____ You have to train one day a week.
3. _____ The basic initial training period for the National Guard is less than for the military.
4. _____ The National Guard are called in to supplement local police in emergencies.

D Questions

Randy talks some more about his parents and his brothers. Listen and answer the questions.

1. What paid employment did Randy's mother used to have?
2. What have Randy's parents been unable to do?
3. What type of firm does Randy's dad work for?
4. What kind of things does his firm deliver in the north-west of the USA?
5. Why does Randy laugh when the interviewer asks him about his older brother's job?
6. Who is Randy's older brother married to?
7. How far does Randy's older brother live from his parents?
8. What is the population of Boulder?

E Gap-Fill

Randy talks about why his parents have moved around Montana so much and his younger brother.

As with Exercise B, try to predict your answers before you listen.

1. Randy says his parents _____ in four different _____ in Montana before the one they live in now.
2. He and his family moved to Boulder when he was _____.
3. Before that his parents moved around a _____ because of his father's _____.
4. Randy's younger brother is still in _____ _____.
5. He's really keen on _____ and he enters the _____ championships every year.

F True/False

Randy talks some more about his younger brother and his mother and father's families. Answer true or false. Be prepared to give reasons for your answers.

1. _____ Randy says his younger brother is less interested in music than the other four family members.
2. _____ Randy's younger brother pays the trombone, but only for his own pleasure.
3. _____ Randy recently went back to the States for a visit.
4. _____ Randy knows exactly how many cousins he has on his mother's side of the family.
5. _____ Randy's mother comes from a family of five children.
6. _____ Randy's aunts on his father's side both have children.
7. _____ Randy's father's family are based in Pennsylvania.

G Questions

Randy talks about his grandparents. Listen and answer the questions.

1. Why does Randy remember his father's father's funeral so well?
2. Why wasn't Randy particularly upset?
3. What do you think the expression 'open casket' means in relation to a funeral?
4. Did Randy attend his father's mother's funeral?
5. Did Randy's brothers attend her funeral?
6. Which of Randy's grandparents is still alive?
7. Which word does Randy use to describe this topic?

H Gap-Fill

Randy talks about his own life in London.

As with Exercises B and E, ask your students to try to predict their answers before they listen.

1. Randy says he's '_____ and _____ _____' at the moment.
2. He's had three _____ _____ so far, but not one of them lasted _____ _____.
3. He's _____ had an _____ girlfriend.
4. His previous girlfriends were _____, _____ and _____.
5. The interviewer asks if Randy found it difficult to make _____ when he first came to _____.
6. Randy says he's quite a _____ person.
7. He says it doesn't _____ him long to relax and _____ out with people.
8. He believes he's quite a good _____ of _____.
9. He doesn't _____ his energy with people he doesn't like.
10. Sometimes four months go by before he catches _____ with someone who lives on the other _____ of London, but he generally finds when he meets them that nothing's _____.

A American English versus British English

Randy uses a number of American terms in the interview. Here are the most useful, together with their British English equivalents:

1. **Mom/mom** (AmE)
    Mum/mum (BrE)

2. **to raise their family** (AmE)
    to bring up their family (BrE)

3. **a trucking firm** (AmE)
    a haulage firm (BrE)

4. **gas** (AmE)
    petrol (BrE)

5. **his high school sweetheart** (AmE)
    his girlfriend from secondary school/his girlfriend from sixth form (England and Wales)

6. **They live three blocks from my parents.** (AmE)
    They live just down the road from my parents./They live a couple of streets away from my parents. (BrE)

7. **sixth grade** (AmE)
    a student aged 11 to 12

8. **a junior** (AmE)
    a student in the 11th grade in high school, i.e. aged 16 to 17, or in their third year of college or university in the US

9. **a sophomore** (AmE)
    a student in the 10th grade in high school, i.e. aged 15 to 16, or a student in their second year of college or university in the US

10. **I haven't gotten to meet her yet.** (AmE)
    I haven't had a chance to meet her yet. (BrE)

11. **Grandma Smartnick passed five, six years ago maybe?** (AmE)
    Grandma Smartnick passed away (i.e. died) five, six years ago maybe? (BrE)

12. **I heard tell of it.** (AmE)
    Someone/They told me about it. (BrE)

B Classic intonation patterns

As Adrian Underhill has pointed out in his excellent book *Sound Foundations*, the classic intonation patterns listed in most books on phonology can vary depending on factors such as how well the speakers know each other and the topic they are discussing. However, the following three classic intonation patterns are all found in this interview:

1. Falling intonation for statements

    Randy: *I grew up in Montana.*

    Randy: *No. Number three was not planned.*

    Remember, though, that the voices of young British people, as well as New Zealanders, Australians and many more will often rise at the end of a statement. For this reason it may be more useful to look at the second purpose of falling intonation: to indicate that the speaker has finished what he or she wanted to say.

2. Rising intonation for Yes/No questions

    There is a tendency for the speaker's voice to rise at the end of questions to which the answer will be Yes or No:

    Interviewer: *Do you think number three was planned?*

    Interviewer: *Is your dad still alive?*

    Interviewer: *Have you got lots of cousins?*

3. Falling intonation for Wh- questions

    There is a tendency for the speaker's voice to fall at the end of *Wh-* questions:

    Interviewer: *So um, Randy, where are you from?*

    Interviewer: *So why did you end up in Montana? Why did they want to move there?*

    Interviewer: *What does your father do?*

C 'um' and 'er'

We often use 'um' or 'er' to give ourselves time to think. These sounds indicate to the listener(s) that we are thinking and so no one should interrupt us. Look at these examples from the interview:

1. Interviewer: *So **er**, brothers and sisters?*
    Randy: *Um, I have an older brother **er**, three years older than myself and **er**, my younger brother is 19 years younger...*

2. Randy: *Er, my dad was career military. **Um**, fought in Vietnam and **er**, then trained as a, trained as a National Guardsman **er**, up until... He was 54 when he retired.*

3. Interviewer: *And **um**, your older brother - what does he do?*
    Randy: *Er, he works **er**, for a competing trucking firm...*

4. Interviewer: *Have you ever been in a long-term relationship?*
    Randy: *Um, I've had three serious relationships at this point in my life. None of them lasting very long.*
    Interviewer: *Were they all with American girls?*
    Randy: *Er, never.*

D Simplification of individual words

When we are speaking quickly we often reduce the number of syllables in words, as in these highlighted examples from the interview:

both **families**	3 syllables >2 syllables
interesting	4>3
recovery	4>3
different	3>2
I **suppose**	2>1
I was **probably** seven.	3>2
policing force	3>2

4. Further Listening Practice

A Dictation

 to

At times in the interview Randy and the interviewer speak very quickly and consequently some words are not pronounced clearly.

Work with a partner. First listen to the excerpts from the interview and write down how many words there are in each item. Then listen and write down the words you hear. After that check your answers with another pair.

1. (___ words) _____
2. (___ words) _____
3. (___ words) _____
4. (___ words) _____
5. (___ words) _____
6. (___ words) _____
7. (___ words) _____
8. (___ words) _____
9. (___ words) _____
10. (___ words) _____

B Weak forms

As we saw in the previous units, the words between the stressed lexical, or content, words are known as grammatical, or functional, words which bind the speaker's words together. These grammatical words tend to be unstressed, which makes them difficult for you to distinguish.

Listen to these excerpts and fill in the following weak forms:

| and | for | from | of | to |

1. Mom _____ dad went back _____ Pennsylvania _____ the funeral, but I don't think any _____ the rest _____ the family made it back, sadly.

2. Mum's _____ Texas, dad's _____ Pennsylvania...

Can you hear the difference between these words in isolation and in a stream of speech?

The following sentences contain the following weak forms:

| about | an | around | at | for | have |
| than | that | wasn't | will | would | your |

Listen and fill in the missing grammatical/function words, using capitals where necessary, then listen again and discuss how the pronunciation of these words has changed from how they sound in isolation.

NB Because this is a listening training exercise don't try to predict the answers before you listen!

1. Um, I have _____ older brother er, three years older _____ myself...
2. OK. _____ you got a middle name?
3. And _____ younger brother?
4. We lived in four different towns in Montana before the one _____ they're in now.
5. But er, before _____ we moved _____ a lot _____ his work...
6. Yeah, he's done really well since he, since he started _____ three years ago...
7. ...which _____ be six, maybe?
8. I know I've seen them more recently _____ the ones in Pennsylvania...
9. I do remember questioning why I _____ upset _____ it...
10. I've had three serious relationships _____ this point in _____ life.

C Sentence stress

As we saw in Unit 1, it is important that you are able to recognise stressed words in a stream of speech because these are the words that carry the speaker's meaning. Each speaker stresses the words he, or she, feels are necessary to get his, or her, message across. Listen to these excerpts from Randy's interview and mark where the stressed words occur.

NB Unlike scripted listening passages, this exercise is not suitable as a predictive activity because the stressed words are personal to Randy and the interviewer and therefore cannot be predicted by looking at the written script in isolation.

1. Um, I have an older brother er, three years older than myself and er, my younger brother is 19 years younger...
2. Interviewer: *Do you think number three was planned?*
   Randy: *Um, no. Number three was not planned...*
3. Interviewer: *And he's fine – no health problems?*
   Randy: *Oh, nothing for him, no. It, it almost took her out, but um...*
4. Have you got a middle name?
5. What does your father do?

6. And when there's flood disasters or, you know, things go wrong and you need some kind of policing force that is extra and above what you would usually get, the National Guard are called in to deal...

7. He works er, for a competing trucking firm doing the exact, same job.

8. Yeah, 'cos mom had two sisters and two brothers.

9. Um, do you remember your grandparents, growing up?

10. That was a dark topic, wasn't it?

11. Yeah, I didn't know any of them because we grew up in Montana, you know...

12. Have you ever been in a long-term relationship?

13. Interviewer: *Did you find it hard to come to London - to make friends?*
    Randy: *I really don't feel that I have.*

14. We might not see each other for more than – you know, it might be every four months before I catch up with somebody who lives on the other side of London, but er, that's... when you catch up nothing's changed.

D Fluency practice 1 – elision

As we saw in Unit 1, when speaking quickly in English, a process called 'elision' often occurs, most frequently with words ending in –d and –t. This results in these sounds not being pronounced when the next word begins with a consonant. For example, a speaker will say *las' night* instead of *last night, jus' got here* instead of *just got here*, or *trie' to* instead of *tried to*.

Listen and repeat these excerpts from the interview, all of which contain examples of elision. Remember not to pronounce the highlighted letters.

1. Why di**D** they want to move there?
2. I ha**D** gone to university...
3. No. Number three was no**T** planned...
4. I don'**T** know what that means...
5. He's marrie**D** to his er, high school sweetheart...
6. We lived in four differen**T** towns in Montana before the one tha**T** they're in now.
7. I only have one cousin on tha**T** side....
8. Do you remember your gran**D**paren**T**s, growing up?
9. The firs**T** time I was on a plane...
10. I didn'**T** really know him tha**T** well, you know...
11. An**D** on my mom's side my gran**D**mother is still alive...
12. I also fin**D** myself quite a goo**D** judge of character...

E Fluency practice 2 – linking

As we saw in the previous unit, linking occurs when the end of one word runs_into the start_of the next word. It is very common in informal spoken English, but less so in more formal English, such as speeches or lectures.

Look at the following extracts from the interview and predict where linking will occur. Then listen and check your answers.

Next repeat each phrase or sentence after the speaker, imitating the speaker's pronunciation.

1. Family politics and wanted space on their own...
2. That's heck of a gap.
3. Yes, they both are still alive, yeah.
4. We lived in four different towns in Montana before the one that they're in now.
5. Have you got lots of cousins?
6. On my mom's side my grandmother is still alive.
7. Have you ever been in a long-term relationship?
8. I've had three serious relationships at this point in my life.
9. Yes, not at all...
10. We might not see each other...
11. when you catch up nothing's changed

A Gap-Fill

Fill in the blanks in these new sentences with words you heard during Randy's interview. The words are listed in the box to help you.

> basic   competing   cousin   exact   gap   honest   into
> kids   owns   raise   relax   rest   retired   serious
> single   space   trained   type   upset   wrong

1. We split up because I felt I needed my own _____.
2. I think it's much better to _____ a family in the country than in a city.
3. There's a _____ of five years between my brother and me.
4. Marc _____ to be a doctor, but then he gave up medicine and became a diver instead.
5. My father _____ when he was 55, but I'll be lucky to go before I'm 66.
6. What _____ of dog is he?
7. My French is very _____, but I know enough to get by.
8. I had a terrible day today – everything I did went _____!
9. Do you know who _____ that car parked over there?
10. Can I get past, please? My brother's _____ in this next race.
11. When you're measuring the ingredients for a recipe, you need to make sure you have the _____ amount of everything.
12. My _____ love going to McDonald's.
13. I'm not really _____ jazz. I prefer classical music.
14. I don't drink tea, to be _____. Could I have coffee instead?
15. My father's brother's son Mike is my favourite_____.
16. Sophie's a bit _____ at the moment because her mother's not well.
17. Would you mind if I had the _____ of your sandwich? I'm starving!
18. You have to tick the relevant box – married, civil partnership, _____, divorced or widowed.
19. He's never had a _____ relationship, but then he's only 20.
20. It's no wonder you've got high blood pressure – you work too hard. You need to _____ more.

B Phrasal verbs

Randy uses a number of phrasal verbs in his interview. Insert the correct preposition or adverb in the following sentences.

1. My brothers and I grew _____ in a little village near Cambridge.
2. I think you should give Maria a ring. She's really going _____ it at the moment.
3. I haven't seen you for ages! Why don't you come for dinner next week and we can catch _____.
4. Do you mind if I change the music? I'm not really _____ Abba.
5. We planned to have a picnic by the sea, but the weather was so bad we ended _____ having it in the car instead.
6. My boss has signed me _____ for a three-day course on customer care for some reason.

C Transformations

Change the word in each bracket that appeared in the interview to form a word that fits the gap, if necessary.

Here's an example to help you:

*Example: I can make you a sandwich if you're (hunger) **hungry**.*

1. Can I have your date of (born) _____, please?
2. Her son gave a very (move) _____ speech which had everyone in tears.
3. Rio Tinto is one of the biggest (miners) _____ companies in the world.
4. What are your (planned) _____ for the summer vacation?
5. You don't look very (health) _____. Perhaps you should take more exercise.
6. Has he (recovery) _____ from his operation yet?
7. We're going on a two-day (trained) _____ course next week, so that'll make a nice change.
8. Economic (grew) _____ is at its lowest level since 1990.
9. What are you two (whisper) _____ about?
10. Would you be (interesting) _____ in our special offer on double-glazing?
11. What's the current (retired) _____ age for men in Japan?
12. I just need your (sign) _____ at the bottom, there.
13. He's (basic) _____ a nice man, but he's just really boring.
14. Camilla's got a job as a (reception) _____ in a legal firm, so she's really pleased.
15. My dad's just won first prize in a photographic (competing) _____. Not bad for 80, is it?
16. Love Story is the (sadly) _____ film I've ever seen.
17. The closest we have to a (social) _____ party in England is the Labour party.
18. It was a great holiday, but it wasn't very (relax) _____ because we went on loads of trips.

I: So um, Randy, where are you from?

R: Er, I grew up in Montana...

I: Mmm, hmm.

R: ...born in Pennsylvania, um... **(1) Mom's from Texas,** dad's from Pennsylvania and er, we moved out to Montana where I was three...

I: Mmm, hmm.

R: ...and I was there till I was 18.

I: Right.

R: So I grew up in the Rocky Mountains and...

I: Oh, wonderful. God!

R: ...around lots of **(2) cowboys, (3) miners, (4) ranchers.**

I: That, that's it, 'cos er, was it The Horse Whisperer – was that filmed in...

R: Yes, filmed in...

I: Montana?

R: Montana, yeah.

I: Yeah, brilliant. Now your dad's from Texas, you said?

R: Er, dad's from Pennsylvania.

I: Right. And your mum's from...

R: And mom's from Texas.

I: **(5) So why did you end up in Montana?** Why did they want to move there?

R: Um, well... *(laughs)* I think they just kind of wanted to get away from both er, both families, to be completely honest.

I: Oh, interesting.

R: Yes *(laughs).*

I: So...

R: Family politics and wanted space on their own and to, to raise their family, you know...

I: OK. So er, brothers and sisters?

R: Um, I have an older brother er, three years older than myself and er, my younger brother is 19 years younger, so...

I: **(6) That's heck of a gap.**

R: So I had gone to university...

I: Yeah.

R: ...and er, and along came number three. *(laughs)*

I: Do you think number three was planned?

R: Um, no. Number three was not planned, but seen as **(7) a great blessing,** so mom was 44 when she gave birth to Robbie and...

I: And he's fine – no health problems?

R: Oh, nothing for him, no. It, **(8) it almost took her out,** but um...

I: Really?

R: Yeah, about three years' recovery – **(9) pretty hard core from that delivery, but er...**

I: Goodness me.

R: Yeah. Everybody's healthy and happy now, so that's good.

I: Yes. *(laughs)*

R: Yeah.

I: OK. What's your older brother name, er, brother name!

R: My older brother's name is Ron.

I: Right.

R: Ronald Andrew Smartnick Junior.

I: Right.

R: Nice American – Junior, Senior.

I: OK. Have you got a middle name?

R: Er, yes, Randy Lee Smartnick.

I: OK. And your younger brother?

R: Er, Robert Charles.

I: Oh, very nice. OK.

R: Yeah.

I: Um, what does your father do? What's his job?

R: Um, **(10) my dad was career military.** Um, fought in Vietnam and er, then trained as a, trained as a National Guardsman er, up until... He was 54 when he retired. And er...

I: I don't know what that means – National Guardsman.

R: National Guard are... Boy, **(11) I don't know how to equate that over here.** Um, people will sign up for the Guard **(12) to get assistance with um, schooling** or... or it's kind of a part-time type of job where you train one weekend a month with the National Guard.

I: Is it, is it military? It's not police? It's...

R: Ah, it's military. You'll go through, you'll go through your six-week basic training, same as you would for the military.

I: Right.

R: And then er, then you only work like one weekend a month. And when there's flood disasters or, you know, things go wrong and you need some kind of policing force that is extra and above what you would usually get, the National Guard are called in to deal...

I: OK. So it is, it is national – it's not just a state thing?

R: No, it is, it is national, yeah.

I: OK. And your mum?

R: Er, mom was pretty much a er, full-time, raising the kids most of the time. She did a lot of reception work for a physical therapist...

I: Mmm.

R: ...um, as I was growing up and er, now she owns a, a small kind of dollar-type, get everything that you need store in a little town of two thousand...

I: Like **(13) a pound store** over here. OK. Right. Um, is your dad still alive?

R: Yes, they both are still alive, yeah.

I: So how old are they now?

R: Er, dad's 62; mom will be 60...

I: OK.

R: Yeah. And dad....

I: So quite young.

R: Yeah. Um, either one of them - neither one of them were able to retire, so um, so dad works for **(14) a trucking firm** now. He basically is **(15) a despatch** for one of the bigger north-west trucking firms to get **(16) cattle, (17) gas** – whatever it takes to get around and...

I: Right. And um, your older brother – what does he do?

R: Um, he works er, for a competing trucking firm *(laughs)* doing the exact same job, if you believe that, yeah. **(18) He's married to his er, high school sweetheart** and er, **(19) they live three blocks from my parents...**

I: Mmm.

R: ...in the lovely town of 2,000 that I come from. And er, and yeah, two kids there, so two nephews, and...

I: So your mum and dad never moved after they got to Mantan... Montana.

R: No, we lived in four different towns in Montana before the one that they're in now.

I: Oh, I see.

R: And that's where er, **(20) from the time I was in sixth grade**, so probably from the time I was 12 we lived in Boulder.

I: OK.

R: But er, before that we moved around a lot for his work and...

I: I see. And your younger brother? What's he?

R: He's er, still in high school, so he's **(21) a junior** this year, **(22) sophomore** this year. Yeah. Um, does a lot of **(23) wrestling**. He's a really good wrestler. **(24) He's er, topping up on the state champions every year** and er...

I: Really?

R: Yeah. He's done really well, since he, since he started about three years ago and.... **(25) He's not as into music as er, as some of us in the family were**. He plays trombone um, in the band and he's got a lovely girlfriend. I haven't gotten to meet her yet 'cos it's been a while since I've been home, but, no, he seems pretty healthy and happy...

I: How old is he, then?

R: Er... 15.

I: Fifteen. And he's got a girlfriend already?

R: Er, 16 now, sorry. I missed a year there.

I: Sixteen. OK. All right.

I: Um, going back to your family...

R: Mmm, hmm.

I: ...you've got your mum, your dad and your two brothers. Have you got lots of cousins?

R: Um, not really, to be honest. I have... On my mum's side, I suppose, has, I have the most cousins on, which would be six, maybe? All of them would be out of high school at this point. Um... Yeah, 'cos mom had two sisters and two brothers, so hers was the bigger family.

I: Right.

R: My dad had two sisters and I only have one cousin on that side, so...

I: OK. So...

R: ...first cousins, anyway.

I: ...you... So you're not very close, it seems, with your mother's...

R: Um, neither side of the family, to be completely honest, yeah. I, I guess mom's, mom's side we're, we're a bit closer with. Um...

I: Mmm.

R: I know I've seen them more recently than, than the ones in Pennsylvania, but er...

I: OK.

I: Um, do you remember your grandparents, growing up?

R: I do. Um... the first time I was on a plane was for my dad's dad's er, **(26) funeral**. *(laughs)* So I remember that! Um, I do remember questioning why I wasn't upset about it, but I suppose that's because I didn't really know him that well, you know...

I: Mmm.

R: ...um, but it was also the first **(27) open–casket** funeral I'd ever seen which was...

I: Really? A bit scary.

R: ...a bit disturbing.

I: Yes.

R: I was probably seven.

I: Ah.

R: Um...

I: Was his wife still alive or...

R: Yes, er, Grandma Smartnick **(28) passed** five, six years ago, maybe? Um, **(29) I heard tell of it** and mom and dad went back to Pennsylvania for the funeral, but I don't think any of the rest of the family made it back, sadly. Um, and on my mom's side my grandmother is still alive, but my grandpa died once again when I was quite young – um, probably eight, nine.

I: OK. Um... *(laughs)*

R: Yeah, sorry! That was a dark topic, wasn't it? *(laughs)* Death, death, death. Yeah, I didn't know

any of them 'cos we grew up in Montana! You know... *(laughs)*

I: Um, have you got a girlfriend?

R: I do not. I am, I am single and loving life.

I: OK.

R: *(laughs)*

I: Have you ever been in a long-term relationship?

R: Um, I've had three serious relationships at this point in my life. None of them lasting very long.

I: Were they always American girls?

R: Er, never.

I: Really?

R: *(laughs)*

I: OK.

R: *(laughs)* Yes, not at all.... um, other nationalities. Er, one Welsh, one Scottish and one Italian.

I: Oh, right. You don't think you could do Welsh, Scottish, English and Northern Irish? That would have been quite interesting.

R: *(laughs)* Yeah, I've missed out on the Northern Irish so far, but...

I: Yes. *(laughs)* OK. So you're not with anybody at the moment?

R: No.

I: No. Um, did you find it hard to come to London – to make friends?

R: I really don't feel that I have. I'm, I'm quite a social person and it doesn't take long for me to relax and **(30) chill out with people** and I'm quite a... I also find myself quite a good judge of character, so I don't waste my energy on a lot of people...

I: Mmm, hmmm.

R: ...**(31) and the people that I find I spark with,** that's it. They're friends, you know.

I: Right.

R: **(32) We're in there.** We might not see each other for more than – you know, it might be every four months before I catch up with somebody that lives on the other side of London, but er, that's... when you catch up nothing's changed, you know. And, and it's good to have that support, yeah.

1 **Mom's from Texas (AmE)** – Mum's from Texas (BrE)
2 **cowboys (AmE)** – a cowboy is someone, especially in the western US, who takes care of cattle and who generally rides a horse
3 **miners** – people who work in mines, a hole or system of holes in the ground where gold, coal etc. are removed by digging
4 **ranchers (AmE)** – a rancher is someone who works on a ranch (AmE), i.e. a very large farm, particularly in North and South America, on which animals are kept
5 **So why did you end up in Montana?** – So how did you come to live in Montana?
6 **That's (a) heck of a gap.** – That's a huge age difference.
7 **a great blessing** – something which is extremely lucky which brings you happiness
8 **it almost took her out** – it almost killed her
9 **pretty hard-core from that delivery (AmE)** – she became extremely ill as a result of giving birth (If something is 'hard-core' it means intense.)
10 **my dad was career military (AmE)** – my father was a professional soldier or member of the armed forces
11 **I don't know how to equate that over here.** – I don't know what the British equivalent would be.
12 **to get assistance with um, schooling** – to get financial assistance with educational fees
13 **a pound store (BrE)** – a shop where everything costs one pound
14 **a trucking firm (AmE)** – a haulage firm (BrE) which transports goods in trucks (AmE), i.e. lorries (BrE)
15 **a despatch(er)** – the person who tells the truck drivers what to transport in their trucks and where they have to drive to make a delivery
16 **cattle** – the plural of large farm animals (generally cows, bullocks and bulls) kept for their milk, meat or for breeding
17 **gas (AmE)** – petrol (BrE)
18 **He's married to his er, high school sweetheart** – He's married to a girl he met at high school, i.e. somewhere between the ages of 14 and 18.
19 **they live three blocks from my parents (AmE)** – they live just down the road, or a couple of streets away, from my parents
20 **from the time I was in sixth grade** – from the time when I was about 12
21 **a junior (AmE)** – a student in the 11th grade in high school, i.e. aged 16 to 17, or a student in their third year of college or university in the US (The four years of study post-18 are known as Freshman, Sophomore, Junior and Senior years.)
22 **(a) sophomore** – a student in the 10th grade, i.e. aged 15 to 16, or a student in their second year of college or university in the US
23 **wrestling** – a sport where two people fight and try to throw each other to the ground (NB we don't pronounce the letter –t– of wrestling)
24 **He's topping up on the state champions every year…** – Here the meaning is he is building up quite a collection of trophies and titles every year at the Montana state wrestling tournament.
25 **He's not as into music as er, as some of us in the family were.** – He's not as interested in music as some of us in the family were.
26 **(a) funeral** – a ceremony held when someone dies
27 **open-casket (AmE)** – where the lid is left off the coffin (BrE)
28 **passed (AmE)** – passed away (BrE), i.e. died

29 **I heard tell of it (AmE)** – someone/they told me about it (BrE)
30 **(to) chill out with people** – to relax in the company of other people
31 **and the people that I find I spark with** – and the people that I find I hit it off with, i.e. get on well with straight away
32 **We're in there**. – We're solid. i.e. We're good friends.

UNIT 4 Eileen

Eileen was born in Watford in north-west London, but she now lives in Walthamstow in east London with her husband and two children. She has a strong east London accent.

A Discussion

Discuss these questions in pairs or small groups and share your answers with the class:

1. What are the advantages and disadvantages of growing up with lots of brothers and sisters as a child?

2. What are the advantages and disadvantages of having lots of brothers and sisters as an adult?

B Normalisation – Questions

This exercise is designed to help you get used to Eileen's voice.

Eileen talks about her brothers, sisters and her parents. Listen and answer the questions.

1. How many names can you distinguish?
2. In which year was the youngest child born?
3. In which city was Eileen's mother born?
4. Where is Croydon?

Leeds Civic Hall

A Aural Gap-Fill

Eileen talks some more about her parents and growing up in a large family.

You will only hear the following extract, not see it. It contains eight pauses. Write down what you think the missing word is after each pause.

1. _____
2. _____
3. _____
4. _____
5. _____
6. _____
7. _____
8. _____

Now listen and check your answers.

B Questions

Eileen talks about her aunt and cousin. Listen and answer the questions.

1. Which medical condition resulted in the death of Eileen's mother's sister when she was just three months old?
2. Where did Eileen's Uncle George meet his wife?
3. When did Eileen's cousin Linda pass away?

C True/False

Eileen talks about her aunts. Answer true or false. Be prepared to give reasons for your answers.

1. _____ One of Eileen's uncles was a Cabinet minister.
2. _____ Both Eileen's uncles were very talkative.
3. _____ As a child, Eileen rarely saw her uncles.
4. _____ Eileen's cousin Maureen has Down's syndrome.
5. _____ Eileen's Auntie Erika and Auntie Reenie are dead now.
6. _____ It seems Auntie Erika liked being in charge.
7. _____ Auntie Reenie believed a woman's place was to look after the men in her life.
8. _____ Eileen didn't like her aunts very much.

D Questions

Eileen talks about her father's family. Listen and answer the questions.

1. Where did Eileen's father's family live?
2. Who prevented Eileen and her brothers and sisters from seeing her father's family?
3. Did Eileen's father see much of his family?

E Aural Gap–Fill

Eileen talks some more about her cousins and then her nephews and nieces.

You will only hear the following extract, not see it. It contains 11 pauses. Write down what you think the missing word is after each pause.

1. _____
2. _____
3. _____
4. _____
5. _____
6. _____
7. _____
8. _____
9. _____
10. _____
11. _____

Now listen and check your answers.

F Tick the correct statement

Eileen talks about the financial challenge of buying presents for her 10 brothers' and sisters' children for Christmas, birthdays, etc.

Tick (✓) which of these statements are correct.

The children of Eileen's 10 brothers and sisters only receive presents from their uncles and aunts

_____ when they are born.
_____ on their first birthday.
_____ for their first Christmas.
_____ on their 18th birthday.
_____ on their 21st birthday.
_____ on their 25th birthday.
_____ when they get engaged.
_____ when they get married.
_____ on their first wedding anniversary.
_____ when they get their first job.
_____ when they get their first home.

G Calculation questions

Eileen lives in Walthamstow in north-east London. Here she talks about where her 10 brothers and sisters have ended up.

Try to work out how many people live in each of these places.

1. How many live in Norfolk? _____
2. How many live in Northampton? _____
3. How many live in Leeds? _____
4. How many live in Watford, where they were born? _____

A Four features of an east London accent

1. Dropping the initial letter *h–*

A typical feature of an east London accent is for the speaker not to pronounce the initial letter *h–* at the start of words such as *'ouse, 'ad, 'appy,* etc.

Listen to these examples from the interview:

> She *'ad* two younger brothers, Jack and George.
> and that's where *'e* met *'is* wife
> always made *'er* own meals

A good language learner, when talking with a non-native speaker of English, will realise that when the speaker produces one non-standard pronunciation feature, the speaker is likely to produce this feature in all other words in English containing that sound.

How would a person with an east London accent say the following sentences?

> **1.** We're hoping to buy a new house.
> **2.** I hope he comes home soon.
> **3.** How was your holiday?

2. Dropping the final *–d* of *and*

Another typical feature of an east London accent is for the speaker not to pronounce the final *–d* of the word *and*.

Listen to these examples from the interview:

> June was born in June, 1942 *an'* there's actually 22 years between June *an'* the youngest child, who's Lynn.
> My mum was born in Leeds *an'* my father was born in south London - Croydon.
> they set them up with jobs *an'* houses

3. The glottal stop

Another feature of an east London accent is the *glottal stop*. This happens when the speaker tightens his or her throat and very briefly stops the air from getting through. This results in the /t/ sound at the end of words such as *got* or *lot*, or the /t/ sound in words such as *bottle* or *kettle* not being fully pronounced. This can make it difficult for you to recognise words containing this feature.

Listen to these examples from the interview:

*My dad was a lorry driver, so he used to go away a **lot**...*
*and **that's** where he **met** his wife*
*and they **get** on very well*
***Not** all of them!*
*there's a **lot** of them*
*that's **what** we agreed*
*They see each other **quite** a **lot.***

How would a person with an east London accent say the following sentences?

1. We've got a new cat.
2. Could you put the kettle on, please?
3. Cup of coffee?

4. Using the letter **v** instead of the /ð/ sound

   Another typical feature of an east London accent is to use the /v/ sound instead of the /ð/ sound found in **other, mother, bother,** etc.

   Listen to these examples from the interview:

   *My mum moved down **with** her **father** in 1933.*

   *My **grandfather** and **grandmother** actually lived around the corner.*

   *...and they live quite close **together**. And they're, they're actually quite close. They see each **other** quite a lot...*

   How would a person with an east London accent say the following sentences containing the four features listed above?

   1. Can I have another bottle of Coke, please?
   2. I haven't decided yet.
   3. I'll see him later.
   4. My daughter's just had a little girl.
   5. I'm gutted Kate's got married to Harry. *

   The meaning of *gutted* is 'extremely upset'.

B There's + plural

Although we should use *there're + plural*, it is quite common in spoken US and British English to hear *there's + plural*. This is probably because it is far easier to say *there's* than *there're* in a stream of speech. Listen to these excerpts from the interview:

There's June, Anne, Derek, John, Billy, David, myself – Eileen, Joyce, Sue, Jan and Lynn.

there's actually 22 years between June and the youngest child, who's Lynn

We made a deal because there is so many of us, um...

C actually

The adverb actually is used far more often in spoken English than in written English. In this interview Eileen uses actually to mean that she is giving the exact and real truth of her family's situation, as opposed to what people might assume to be the truth.

Look at these examples from the interview:

*and there's **actually** 22 years between June and the youngest child, who's Lynn*

*He **actually** came from a family of nine.*

*so the British Legion **actually** moved quite a few northern people down into outer areas*

*My grandmother and grandfather **actually** lived around the corner.*

Notice how the word *actually* sounds more like *'ak-shi'* in a stream of speech.

D *do + verb stem* for emphasis

We use do + verb stem when we wish to emphasise something.

Look at these examples from the interview:

*So I think I've got 24 nephews and nieces. Um, (laughs) yes, quite a few, and I **do know** their names!*

*Yeah, I **do get** on with my nephews and nieces...*

*Hannah is 20 and Andrew is 18, and they **do see** their cousins.*

*I **do know** their birthdays, but I do get them mixed up, 'cos there's a lot of them.*

*But we **do see** them and we **do spend** time with them.*

A Gap-Fill

Fill in the blanks in these new sentences with words you heard during Eileen's interview. The words are listed in the box to help you.

actually	agreed	bossy	carpenter	common	deal
get	gorgeous	made	mix	mixed	obviously
plumber	quiet	shortage	side	spend	vicar

1. I've never _____ been to Paris. I just know a lot about it.
2. There's a major _____ of lithium batteries at the moment, for some reason.
3. One of the most _____ birds in the garden these days is the blue tit.
4. My brother's friend is a _____. He's just made me a fitted wardrobe and he did a great job. Do you want his number?
5. Can you kids keep _____, please? I'm trying to concentrate.
6. That dress is _____! It really suits you.
7. My older sister used to be really _____ when I was growing up. She was always telling me and my brother what to do.
8. I haven't _____ anything for dinner because I had to work late. Do you mind if we have a takeaway?
9. We're a bit worried about our son. We think he's started to _____ with the wrong sort of people.
10. We got some new taps for our bathroom last week for just under £50, but then we had to pay the _____ £60 to fit them.
11. Sophie's _____ in love with Tom. You can tell by the way she looks at him.
12. I don't really know my cousins on dad's _____ of the family because they all live in Australia.
13. The _____ at my brother's wedding was excellent. He made everyone feel at ease.
14. I'm really lucky because I _____ on really well with my girlfriend's parents.
15. My boyfriend and I made a _____ this Christmas that we wouldn't spend more than £50 on each other.
16. My parents have _____ to let me have a party at home for my birthday. Isn't that great?
17. I always get _____ up with my left and my right so I'm rubbish at following directions.
18. I really should _____ more time studying and less time enjoying myself.

B Transformations

Change the word in each bracket that appeared in the interview to form a word that fits the gap, if necessary.

Here's an example to help you:

Example: I can make you a sandwich if you're (hunger) __hungry__.

1. Would you mind (tell) _____ me how much you paid for it?
2. We're having a party next week to celebrate the (born) _____ of our first grandchild, so I want to get a new suit.
3. This is the (actually) _____ spot where I was standing when Andy proposed to me.
4. The food was wonderful but the (serve) _____ was very slow.
5. Jake's feeling a bit (depression) _____ because he's just split up with Fiona.
6. My father's busy (set) _____ up a new company supplying flowers to hotels.
7. It quickly became (apparently) _____ that we should have worn warmer clothes.
8. My grandfather had his own (carpenter) _____ firm by the time he was 25.
9. I'm not very good at (plumber) _____ so I usually get a professional in when I need something doing.
10. There was another student from New Zealand on the course so the two of us (pair) _____ up.
11. They say a little (know) _____ is a dangerous thing.
12. My son's not very (communication) _____, I'm afraid. He spends most of his time sitting in front of the computer.
13. You need special (authoritative) _____ to park here.
14. We were (burgle) _____ last month so we now have new locks on all our doors and windows.

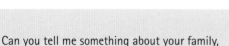

I: Can you tell me something about your family, please?

E: Hello, yes. Um, I come from a family of 11.

I: Eleven children?

E: Eleven children, yes. Um, June is the eldest. There's June, Anne, Derek, John, Billy, David, myself – Eileen, Joyce, Sue, Jan and Lynn. June was born in June, 1942 and there's actually 22 years between June and the youngest child, who's Lynn. Um, my mum was born in **(1) Leeds** and my father was born in south London – **(2) Croydon**. He actually came from a family of nine. *(laughs)*

I: *(laughs)* Such, such large families!

E: My mum *(laughs)* Um, my mum moved down with her father in 1933. Um, he was in **(3) the British Legion**, having served in the First and Second World War. Um, there was like a depression – there was a very... great shortage of work, so the British Legion actually moved quite a few northern people down into outer areas, which is why they moved to **(4) Watford**. And, um, **(5) they set them up with jobs and houses**. Um, my, my grandfather and grandmother actually lived around the corner. Um, my mum and dad lived up the road and they had all 11 children in the house. Um, there was actually several families in our road with large, well, you know, with large families so it wasn't really a problem in that area. Um, my dad was a lorry driver, so he used to go away a lot...

I: Um, so your, your father had nine... well, eight brothers and sisters.

E: Mmm.

I: And your mother? How many brothers and sisters did she have?

E: Oh, she just had a sister and then two brothers. And her sister died.

I: Oh, dear. Did, did she die very young?

E: Um, about three months old...

I: OK.

E: ...which was I think quite common in... Um, 1922 she was born and they used to get like **(6) a twisted gut**, which was apparently... was quite common in those days, so she died quite small. Um, she had two younger brothers, Jack and George. Um, my, my Uncle George actually served in Germany, um, with the **(7) National Service** in the '50s and that's where he met his wife, um, Erika. And they had two children, Sylvia and er, Linda (she died a couple of years ago) er, Sylvia and Linda. Um, Uncle Jack had one daughter, Maureen. But um, Dad's family... there was a lot of them. Er, there was eight or nine. Lots of aunts and uncles.

I: I think you said before your mother had two brothers and one sister. What were the names of the brothers?

E: Jack and George.

I: Jack and George. And what did they do for a living?

E: Uncle George was **(8) a carpenter**. Um, used to make **(9) cabinets** and various things. He was very... very quiet. He didn't really talk much to be quite honest. Um... *(laughs)* And Uncle Jack was **(10) a plumber** for many, many years so...He was also very... the pair of them were very, very quiet. Actually didn't really talk a lot at all. I actually don't know a lot about them at all. Just that they came down at Christmas and um, George had the two girls, Sylvia and Linda. And Uncle Jack had **(11) a Down's syndrome daughter**, Maureen, who is absolutely gorgeous and we love her to bits. And so basically they were like the main communication really, the two aunts. Auntie Erika was very authoritative... er, very **(12) authoritative** and quite **(13) bossy** actually. And Auntie Reenie um, was a northern lady. She actually came from **(14) Bridlington** and very much typical northern per... woman, I would say, very homemaker, always made her own meals and **(15) the menfolk**, she always talked about the menfolk, what the menfolk needed and what they didn't. So they, they were very nice, but no, actually, when I think about it

I don't actually know a lot about them. Just that they were very nice people.

But my Dad's family... We didn't actually see them very often um, because they, they lived in south London um, we didn't really know them very well because my mum just said that they were... that they were... A couple of them had been in (16) **burglaries** and that, and they, they weren't the sort of people she wanted us to mix with, to be quite honest.

I: So she tried to keep you children away...

E: Yeah.

I: ...from that side of the family?

E: And my Dad, *(laughs)* to be quite honest, so we, we stayed in Watford where she felt it, it was a nicer area and we mixed with nicer people. We liked them, obviously.

I: Um, are you... So you're not really very close with your cousins, apart from...

E: Not on my Dad's side, no. Just on my mum's side. The two... Well, um, Linda unfortunately died about five years ago um, and left two boys. Um, she died actually of (17) **lupus,** I think she got lupus and died. Um, she was 32. Um, Sylvia has actually moved back up north. She's got four children. Her husband's (18) **a vicar** um, so he's got (19) **a parish** up there, so they live up there. So we actually don't see them very often. But um, we do have... Where I have like the 10 brothers and sisters, obviously they're all married and they all have children and now their children have children, so I think I've got 24 nephews and nieces. Um, *(laughs)* yes, quite a few, and I do know their names! *(laughs)* And um, and I think David, Paul, Michael have children as well, so we have sort of great... so I'm actually a great aunt as well. And there's... So we have a lot there. Yeah, (20) **I do get on with my nephews and nieces well** and my two children... 'cos I'm married, I have two children, Hannah and Andrew. Hannah is 20 and Andrew is 18, and they do see their cousins. They do see my brothers' and sisters' kids and they get on very well, so it's, it's quite nice.

I: Do you remember the birthdays of all your nieces and nephews? Do you remember to send them a card?

E: Not all of them! *(laughs)* Um, (21) **we made a deal** because there is so many of us um, what with weddings, anniversaries, birthdays... and obviously us brothers and sisters are on the, the 4-0s, the 5-0s and the 6-0s, um, we agreed that we would do their first birthday, their first Christmas, their 18th and their 21st and their weddings because there was just too many, it's just too many. I do know their birthdays, but I do get them mixed up, 'cos there's a lot of them.

I: Yes.

E: So that's, that's what we agreed, so at least they get those (22) **decent presents** then. But we do see them and we do spend time with them.

I: That's nice.

I: Your um, brothers and sisters, do they all live in the London area?

E: Um, no, no. I'm the only one that lives in London.

I: Oh, really?

E: *(laughs)* Um, Ann lives in um, (23) **North Walsham,** which is in Nor... um, (24) **Norfolk,** and that's very nice down there. I've got two brothers and a sister in er, Northampton and they live quite close together. And they're, they're actually quite close. They see each other quite a lot and they're up in Northampton area. And the rest actually... Um, no, Billy lives in Leeds. He moved back to Leeds. And the rest of them live in Watford.

1   **Leeds** – a large city in West Yorkshire in the north-east of England
2   **Croydon** – a town nine miles south of central London which is part of Greater London
3   **the (Royal) British Legion** – a charity which provides help and support to members and ex-members of the armed forces and their families
4   **Watford** – a town 20 miles (32kms) north-west of central London
5   **they set them up with jobs and houses** – they provided them with jobs and somewhere to live
6   **a twisted gut** – the long tube through which food moves during digestion was twisted in on itself and the food couldn't get through
7   **National Service** – the period from 1949 until 1963 when healthy men aged 17 to 21 were expected to serve in the armed forces for 18 months
8   **a carpenter** – a person whose job is making and repairing wooden objects
9   **cabinets** – a cabinet is a piece of furniture with shelves or drawers used for showing or storing things, e.g. a china cabinet
10 **a plumber** – a person whose job is to supply and connect, or repair, water pipes, sinks, taps, toilets, baths, etc.
11 **a Down's syndrome daughter** – Down's syndrome is a chromosomal condition which affects cognitive ability and physical growth
12 **authoritative** – someone who is authoritative is naturally good at managing people and telling them what to do
13 **bossy** – someone who is bossy is always telling other people what to do
14 **Bridlington** – a seaside resort in East Yorkshire on the north-east coast of England
15 **the menfolk** – an old-fashioned word for men
16 **burglaries** – a burglary is the crime of illegally entering a building and stealing things
17 **lupus** – an autoimmune disease – a type of self-allergy
18 **a vicar** – a priest in the Church of England in charge of a church and the spiritual needs of people in the surrounding area, i.e. the parish
19 **a parish** – the surrounding area of a church
20 **I do get on with my nephews and nieces well** [sic – I do get on well with my nephews and nieces] – I do have a good relationship with my nephews and nieces
21 **we made a deal** – we decided something together; we came to an agreement that we would do something
22 **decent presents** – good quality (and expensive) gifts
23 **North Walsham** – a market town in Norfolk
24 **Norfolk** – a low-lying county on the east coast of England famous for the Broads, a network of rivers and lakes which is a popular tourist destination

UNIT 5 Hannah and Luke

Hannah (aged 20) and Luke (aged 18) are the daughter and son of Judy in Unit 1. As with a lot of young people they speak very quickly.

A Schema building – predicting which words will come up

Discuss these questions in pairs or small groups and share your answers with the class:

1. What are the advantages and disadvantages of being the only girl with three younger brothers?

2. What must it be like for Hannah to move back home for the holidays after living away from home when she's at university?

B Normalisation 1 (Luke): Freestyle listening comprehension

This listening activity is designed to help you get used to Luke's voice.

While the interviewer and Luke are waiting for Hannah to arrive, Luke reminds the interviewer of an embarrassing incident which occurred during her last visit. Can you work out what happened?

The first two lines of this extract are as follows:

Interviewer: *Can you cook spaghetti bolognese now?*
Luke: *Can you put sugar in your tea now? (laughs)*

C Normalisation 2 (Hannah): Gap-Fill

This listening activity is designed to help you get used to Hannah's voice.

The interviewer asks Hannah and Luke how the four children get on.

Before you listen, try to predict which words, or which types of words (nouns, adjectives, prepositions, parts of verbs, etc.) will fill the gaps. Listen and check your answers.

1. Hannah points out that she'd been away _____ university so it's _____ for her.
2. Luke's coping strategy is to _____ himself to himself and get _____ with his _____.
3. He says 'I get on _____ when I _____ to – if I _____ something.'
4. Hannah says that because the boys are all teenagers now, it is quite _____ and _____ at home.
5. She expects things to improve once all the _____ have _____.
6. Luke agrees and says this is probably the _____ _____ of the children's development.

A Gap-Fill

Hannah talks about being away at university.

Before you listen, try to predict which words, or which types of words (nouns, adjectives, prepositions, parts of verbs, etc.) will fill the gaps. Listen and check your answers.

1. Hannah initially says it's a lot _____ at university than at home.
2. She then qualifies this by saying that she's been _____ in a very _____ hall of _____.
3. This means she hasn't _____ _____ at university either.

B Aural Gap-Fill

Hannah talks about how difficult she finds it to be living back at home again after being away.

This is a challenging exercise as you will only hear the following excerpt, not see it. It contains 11 pauses. Write down what you think the missing word is after each pause.

1. _____
2. _____
3. _____
4. _____
5. _____
6. _____
7. _____
8. _____
9. _____
10. _____
11. _____

Now listen and check your answers.

3. Interesting Language Points

A Use of tenses

1. The simple future

    We use the simple future to make predictions. Look at these two examples from the interview:

    Hannah: *I think **it'll** get better when all the hormones have faded.*

    Hannah: *I probably **won't** be done till midnight.*

2. The present perfect simple and the present perfect continuous

    We use the present perfect simple to talk about things we have done during a period of time leading up to the present. Look at this example from the interview:

    Interviewer: *That's why **I haven't been** back for two years*

    We use the present perfect continuous to talk about something we have been doing in a period of time leading up to the present. Look at this example from the interview:

    Hannah: ***I've been living** in very loud halls of residence, so **I haven't been sleeping** at university either.*

B There would have been no point doing something

We use this structure when we are talking about something that didn't happen for a good reason. Look at this example from the interview:

Hannah: *And **there would have been no point me getting** out of bed in the morning because then I won't be able to last until midnight.*

Here are some more examples:

'There would have been no point going to the seaside yesterday because it rained all day.'

'There would have been no point giving her flowers for her birthday because she's got a garden full of them.'

'There would have been no point taking him to hospital because he obviously hadn't broken anything.'

C The glottal stop

As we heard in Units 1 and 4, an important feature of informal spoken English is the *glottal stop*. A glottal stop happens when the speaker tightens his or her throat and very briefly stops the air from getting through. This results in the /t/ sound at the end of words such as *got* or *lot*, or the /t/ sound in words such as *bottle* or *kettle* not being fully pronounced. This can make it difficult for students to recognise words containing this feature.

Listen to these examples of the glottal stop taken from the interview:

Interviewer: *Do you **get** on well?*

Hannah: *I've been **at** university, so **it's different**.*

Luke: *I keep myself to myself – **get** on with my work. I **get** on well when I need to.*

Interviewer: *But gen... generally, would you say you, you... as a family you **got** on well?*

Hannah: *It's three teenage boys so I would say **it**, **it** is **quite** argumentative and loud **at** the **moment**.*

A Gap-Fill

Fill in the blanks in these new sentences with words you heard during the interview. The words are listed in the box to help you.

> argumentative   bunch   changed   definitely   embarrassed
> faded   hard   last   obviously   plant
> point   stage   way

1. I'll be ready in five minutes. I just need to get _____ out of my work clothes.
2. He was really _____ when he went to introduce me because he'd _____ forgotten her name.
3. Let's get your mum a _____ of flowers to cheer her up.
4. Do you think this _____ is dead, or is it supposed to look like that?
5. I like my new manager, but some people find her a bit _____. She certainly likes to make sure she always the last word.
6. I had a wonderful suntan when we came back from Crete, but it's _____ now.
7. What's the next _____ in the process?
8. I find it really _____ to get up in the winter.
9. We _____ said we were going to meet at seven.
10. Stop looking at me in that _____!
11. There's no _____ leaving yet. Her train doesn't get in for another hour.
12. Have we got enough milk to _____ till I can go shopping on Saturday?

B Transformations

Change the word in each bracket that appeared in the interview to form a word that fits the gap, if necessary.

Here's an example to help you:

Example: I can make you a sandwich if you're (hunger) **_hungry_**.

1. It was really (embarrassed) _____ going through the security gate because I forgot they sometimes ask you to take your shoes off and both my socks had holes in them.
2. Thanks for (remember) _____ my birthday.
3. What do you (food) _____ your dog on?
4. Will you kids please stop (argumentative) _____! I can't hear myself think.
5. You need a good (imagine) _____ to write children's books.
6. Passing my driving test was the (hard) _____ thing I've ever done.
7. There seems to be a general (assuming) _____ that if you're deaf then you're stupid.
8. That (waitress) _____ over there is really handsome, isn't he?

I: Can you cook spaghetti bolognese now?

L: Can you put sugar in your tea now? *(laughs)*

I: I forgot about that. That's why I haven't been back for two years, **(1) I was so embarrassed.**

L: Do you remember that?

I: Yes, I do remember that, actually.

L: *(laughs)*

I: Every time I get a bunch of flowers and there's some plant food I remember that.

L: *(laughs)*

I: Sigh!

Part 2   **I:** Interviewer   **H:** Hannah   **L:** Luke

I: OK. Um, so there's the four of you. **(2) Do you get on well?**

H: Well, I haven't been around. I've been at university, so it's different.

I: Uh, huh.

L: **(3) Just keep myself to myself** – get on with my work.

H: You don't work, do you?

L: I get on well when I need to – if I want something. *(laughs)*

H: *(laughs)*

I: But gen... generally, would you say you, you... as a family you got on well?

L: Er...

H: Um, no.

I: *(laughs)*

L: No, it's...

H: It, it's three teenage boys, so I would say it, **(4) it is quite argumentative** and loud at the moment. But I think it'll get better **(5) when all the hormones have faded.**

L: This'll probably, this'll probably be the worst stage when all three of the boys are teenagers.

I: Yes, I can imagine. Your poor mum! And Hannah, it must be fantastic being away.

H: Yeah, it is a lot quie... well, not quieter, as I said. I've been living in very loud **(6) halls of residence,** so I haven't been sleeping at university either.

I: What was it like coming home after being away at university, having all that freedom?

H: Yeah, it's hard because obviously mum and dad tell me what to do all the time and I'm not used to that because I always had... I had **(7) a gap-year** as well.

I: Oh, that's right.

H: So I was in Africa for six months. So I def... definitely know how to look after myself. But it's just mum and dad are used to talking to the boys in a certain way, assuming they're not going to do something, so they talk to me in the same way. I'm happy, I'm happy to do it, but it's the whole like getting out of bed in the morning. **(8) I'm not so great at that.** But that's 'cos at the moment I'm waitressing and I have to waitress. And tonight **(9) I probably won't be done till midnight...**

I: Mmm, hmm.

H: And there would have been no point me getting out of bed in the morning because then I won't be able to last until midnight.

I: I see. So you need your sleep.

H: Yeah. Generally the arguments are about me not getting up in the morning. Everything else I think I'm doing all right.

1   **I was so embarrassed** – I felt very uncomfortable at what I'd done
2   **Do you get on well?** – Do you have a good relationship with each other?
3   **Just keep myself to myself** – I don't have much to do with the others
4   **it is quite argumentative** – (unusual usage) If a person is argumentative it means they enjoy arguing. Here Hannah means that there are a lot of arguments.
5   **when all the hormones have faded** – Hormones are chemicals produced by the body which influence the development, growth and sex of a person or animal. Teenagers can be affected by hormones which may affect their behaviour. We use the verb **to fade** when, for example, a strong colour fades in direct sunlight. Here Hannah means that the four children will get on better once the boys are a bit older.
6   **halls of residence** – purpose-built accommodation for students
7   **a gap-year** – A lot of young people take a year off, or have a gap-year, between school and university, either to travel and see the world or to get some work experience and earn money.
8   **I'm not so great at that.** – I'm not very good at that.
9   **I probably won't be done till midnight** – I probably won't finish work until midnight.

A Typical Day

UNIT 6 Ingse

Ingse is a divorced mother of twin girls who lives in Bergen on the west coast of Norway, where she works for a large energy company. She speaks excellent English as she lived and worked in the UK for a number of years. She has a slight Norwegian accent combined with a slight Geordie accent which she acquired from living in Sunderland. Here she talks about a typical working day.

A Schema building

Which 10 of these 20 words do you expect to hear during the interview?

traffic, grass, cloudy, interviewing, ladder, department, sandy, earwax, colleagues, drawing, contract, sailing, canteen, chocolate, overtime, course, foam, pay, wasp, meetings

B Discussion

Discuss these questions in pairs or small groups and share your answers with the class:

1. If you had the chance to work flexitime, would you start early and finish early or start later and finish later? Why?
2. When you hear the word 'Norway', what things come into your mind?

C Normalisation 1: Anticipating the next word

This exercise is designed to help you get used to Ingse's voice.

Listen to Track 156. There is a word missing from the end of each excerpt. When you hear the beep sound, try to guess the missing word and write it down. Then listen to Track 157 to check your answers. How well did you guess?

1. _____
2. _____
3. _____
4. _____
5. _____
6. _____
7. _____

D Normalisation 2: Freestyle listening comprehension

How much do you learn about Ingse in this opening section? Listen and take notes.

A Questions

Ingse talks about what happens when she gets to work. Listen and answer the questions.

1. Why does Ingse say she likes to start work at 7am because 'you get a nice long afternoon in the sun' when she doesn't get home until 3.15pm or later?
2. Does Ingse have breakfast before she leaves home?
3. Which two words does Ingse use to describe the taste of Norwegian goat's cheese?
4. What does Ingse do while she has breakfast?

B True/False

Ingse talks about her office and the people she works with. Answer true or false. Be prepared to give reasons for your answers.

1. _____ There are partitions between Ingse and her work colleagues.
2. _____ Ingse shares the office with three colleagues.
3. _____ Ingse does similar work to her colleagues.
4. _____ Ingse finds it difficult to concentrate when her colleagues are on the phone.
5. _____ Ingse used to share an office with far more people.
6. _____ Ingse has a good relationship with her colleagues.
7. _____ Ingse is now on a permanent contract.
8. _____ Ingse and her colleagues are all around the same age.

C Cloze

Ingse talks about her lunch break. Read through this excerpt and predict the missing words. Then listen and check your answers.

I: So you're _____ all your work in the morning. Wha... what time do you _____ for lunch?

In: Er, 11.30.

I: That... That's very _____. You see in England we'd be stopping for our mid-morning _____ at 11.30.

In: *(laughs)* Yeah. Some people go for er, 10.30, but I think that's far too early for me. I've just finished _____ by then.

I: OK. *(laughs)*

In: Yes. *(laughs)* How I feel!

I: So do you have a restaurant at work, or a canteen?

In: Yes, a lovely canteen with hot and _____ food and... very, very good food. A salad _____ costing us a quid.

I: Really?

In: Or less than that, but more or less. Yes, a quid.

I: So the food's quite_____? And subsidy... subsidised?

In: Yes, subsidised food in the canteen, yes.

I: Uh, huh.

In: And they serve dinner, which is...

I: Really?

In: ...dinner at Norwegian _____, which is about 4 o'clock. *(laughs)*

I: Huh! *(laughs)*

In: So if you get there quarter past four it's _____! *(laughs)* And that's for the people doing _____, yeah.

D Questions

Ingse talks about a typical Norwegian lunch. Listen and answer the questions.

1. What is a typical Norwegian lunch?
2. Which two words does Ingse use to describe her kind of food?
3. Who tend to eat more at lunchtime – Norwegian or Swedish people?
4. What is one reason Ingse gives for the fact that Norwegians like to make their own lunch at home and then take it into work?

E True/False

Ingse talks about who she goes to lunch with and the advantages of flexitime. Answer true or false. Be prepared to give reasons for your answers.

1. _____ Ingse's colleagues in her office go to lunch before Ingse.
2. _____ Ingse's company runs confidence courses in a confidence centre.
3. _____ Ingse sometimes chooses to sit on her own for lunch.
4. _____ The location of Ingse's company is quite isolated.
5. _____ Ingse thinks flexitime is great.
6. _____ Ingse never stays out late during the working week.
7. _____ Flexitime means that people can start work at 11am and finish at 5pm.

F Cloze

Ingse talks about why she doesn't do overtime.

Read through the following excerpt and insert the words in the box into the gaps. Then listen and check your answers.

can't	double	evenings	eyes	front
meetings	pay	sit	tired	tiring

I: If you do work on a Saturday and Sunday do you get better _____?

In: 100 per cent, yes.

I: Yeah, so it's _____?

In: Yeah.

I: Yeah.

In: And I'm so _____ after eight hours...

I: Mmm.

In: ...in _____ of that computer I _____ do any work in the _____.

I: Mmm.

In: It kills me.

I: Right. *(laughs)*

In: No, but if you, if you do a different job – if you're interviewing, if you're going to _____ – and then you _____ down at the computer... But when you are in front of that computer for eight hours...

I: Mmm.

In: My neck and my _____... *(laughs)*

I: Yes. Very _____.

G True/False

Ingse talks about what she does when she leaves work. Answer true or false. Be prepared to give reasons for your answers.

1. _____ The average working week in Norway is 37½ hours.
2. _____ Ingse tries to start work earlier in the summer than in the winter.
3. _____ The interview took place in the spring.
4. _____ There is a lake between Ingse's home and her workplace.

H Questions

Ingse talks about relaxing after work and her flat. Listen and answer the questions.

1. Give two reasons why Ingse has recently stopped cooking an evening meal when she gets home from work.
2. What does Ingse prefer to do rather than watch television?
3. Who did Ingse look after until recently, besides her children?
4. When did Ingse's children leave home?
5. What is different about the flat now that the girls have left home?
6. What is the one thing Ingse would like to change about the flat?

A An important feature of Ingse's Norwegian accent

Many non-native speakers of English find the /ð/ sound representing the letters *th* in words such as *the, this* and *with,* very difficult to pronounce in English because they don't have that sound in their own language. French and German speakers tend to use the letters *'s'* or *'z'* instead, whereas Ingse, in common with other Scandinavian speakers of English, tends to use the letter *'d'.* This affects the following function words:

the – der, this – dis, they – dey, with - wid

Listen to these excerpts from the article:

*But in **the** summer I, I cycle.*
*which in **the** summer is marvellous*
*I wait till I turn on **the** computer...*

*So **this** one, **this** one is a, is a small one.*

***they** have moved out*
*And **they** serve dinner...*

*and I bring some er, bread **with** goat cheese**
*You can't cut it **with** a knife.*
*Yes, a lovely canteen **with** hot and cold food and...*

*[sic – goat's cheese, i.e. cheese made from the milk of a goat, rather than from a goat itself]

A good language learner, when talking with a non-native speaker of English, will realise that when the speaker produces one non-standard pronunciation feature, the speaker is likely to produce this feature in all other words in English containing that sound.

How might Ingse pronounce the following words?

another   these   breathing   leather   feather   whether

B Signalling that the person listening is paying attention

We use words such as 'OK', 'I see' and 'Right' to signal that we're paying attention to a speaker, as well as the sounds 'Mmm' and 'Mmm, hmm'.

Listen to these examples from the interview:

OK.	Interviewer:	So how many hours do you work a week?
	Ingse:	It's 40. Minus lunch – half-an-hour a day – so, 37 and a half.
	Interviewer:	**OK.**

I see.	Ingse:	The taste is so strong that all you want is just a thin slice...
	Interviewer:	**I see.**
	Ingse:	...on a slice of bread.
	Interviewer:	OK.
Right.	Ingse:	But I'm so tired after eight hours in front of that computer I can't do any work in the evenings.
	Interviewer:	Mmm.
	Ingse:	It kills me.
	Interviewer:	**Right.**
Mmm, hmm.	Ingse:	And I bring some er, bread...
	Interviewer:	**Mmm, hmm.**

C Expressing surprise when listening

We often use the word *Really?* or *Oh, really?* to express surprise. Listen to these excerpts from the interview:

Interviewer: In the summer, what, what time does the sun set, then?
Ingse: Eleven...
Interviewer: **Oh, really?**
Ingse: ...eleven-thirty.

Ingse: We have an open landscape...
Interviewer: **Oh, really?**

Ingse: A salad bar costing us a quid.
Interviewer: **Really?**

Interviewer: How long do you get for lunch?
Ingse: Half an hour.
Interviewer: **Oh, really?**

D D'you...? instead of Do you...?

In informal spoken English we often combine *Do you* or *do you* into one sound: *D'you* or *d'you*. Listen to how the interviewer asked these questions in the interview:

Interviewer: **Do you** have your own office?

Interviewer: And are your colleagues nice? **Do you** get on well with them?
Ingse: Very nice.

Interviewer: So, **do you** have a restaurant at work?

Interviewer: How long **do you** get for lunch?

Interviewer: How many hours **do you** work a week?

E The different uses of *so*

a) To signal a change of topic

1. Using So + comma at the start of a question to signal a change of topic. The interviewer does this at the start of the interviewer to signal to Ingse that the interview has begun:

Interviewer: *So, er, can you tell me about a typical day?*

TOP TIP!   *So + comma at the start of a question is also a very natural way to break a long period of silence. It makes the opening question softer and less interrogational.*

b) To make deductions based on what the speaker has said:

Ingse: *...and about mid-June er, my contract went out and they asked if I would like to stay on for another year.*
Interviewer: *So your, your contract expired.*
Ingse: *Yes.*

Interviewer: *If you do work on a Saturday and Sunday do you get better pay?*
Ingse: *100 per cent, yes.*
Interviewer: *Yeah, so it's double?*

c) To give explanations or reasons for something

Ingse: *I get up fairly early in the winter because it's er, er, heavy traffic – the traffic jam, so I want to start off before that.*

Ingse: *It's only four or five kilometres from where I live to, to the office so it isn't really heavy traffic, but to me it is.*

Ingse: *And I wasn't interested in all that going on, so that was just noise.*

d) As an intensifier:

Ingse: *the taste is so strong*

Ingse: *Well, I've been so lazy.*

Now ask your students to explain the function of the word **so** in the following extracts. The explanations are marked a – d after each occurrence.

1. Interviewer: So ( ) how many hours do you work a week?

2. Ingse: So ( ) if I'm in by seven I can leave by three o'clock...

3. Ingse: I use my bike because it's so ( ) close so ( ) it's nice to get some fresh air.

4. Interviewer: So ( ) the food's quite cheap?

5. Ingse: And there're no shops... so ( ) you have to take your car in if you want to go shopping or go to the bank or something.

6. Ingse: But this summer has been so ( ) nice so ( ) quite often I've er, taken a longer trip to get home...

7. Ingse: And then we just sit down and chat.
    Interviewer: Oh, that's nice. So ( ) you're not sitting on your own?

8. Ingse: I had an aunt I was looking after which took quite um, a lot of time. I went to Tae Kwon Do three times a week in the evenings. So ( ) I was quite busy.

9. Ingse: They have so ( ) much gear...

10. Ingse: And they serve dinner, which is dinner at Norwegian time, which is about 4 o'clock. So (c) if you get there quarter past four it's finished!

4. Further Listening Practice

A Dictation

 to

At times in her interview Ingse and the interviewer speak very quickly and consequently some words are not pronounced clearly.
Work with a partner. First listen to the excerpts from Ingse's interview and write down how many words there are in each item. Then listen and write down the words you hear. After that check your answers with another pair.

1. (___ words) _____
2. (___ words) _____
3. (___ words) _____
4. (___ words) _____
5. (___ words) _____
6. (___ words) _____
7. (___ words) _____
8. (___ words) _____
9. (___ words) Interviewer: _____
    (___ words) Ingse: _____

B Contractions

Contractions are very common in informal spoken English. Which contractions fit the gaps in these excerpts from the interview? Write down your answers and then listen and check them. How well did you do?

1. But in the summer I, I cycle. I use my bike because _____ so close _____ nice to get some fresh air.
2. And _____ got flexible hours. So if _____ in by seven I can leave at three o'clock...
3. _____ all working with the same things.
4. _____ typically Scandinavian, _____ it?
5. And _____ so tired after eight hours in front of that computer I _____ do any work in the evenings.
6. So you try to finish quarter past three. _____ done your eight hours...
7. _____ really lazy with that because I _____ like cooking.
8. And this autumn _____ been so lazy...
9. But _____ happy because _____ happy...
10. It _____ work out as well as it could have. _____ good friends though.

C Sentence stress

It is important that you are able to recognise stressed words in a stream of speech because these are the words that carry the speaker's meaning. Each speaker stresses the words he, or she, feels are necessary to get his, or her, message across. Listen to these excerpts from Ingse's interview and mark where the stressed words occur.

NB Unlike scripted listening passages, this exercise is not suitable as a predictive activity because the stressed words are personal to Ingse and the interviewer and therefore cannot be predicted by looking at the written script in isolation.

1. In the summer, what, what time does the sun set, then?
2. I get in to the office and what I normally do is, is have a coffee and I bring some er, bread with goat cheese, which is a Norwegian thing.
3. I think I tried some once. It tastes a little bit like chocolate.
4. You can't cut it with a knife.
5. The taste is so strong that all you want is just a thin slice on a slice of bread.
6. Do you have your own office?
7. we're all working with the same things
8. But I used to be in a department with engineers...
9. What are the ages in the office?
10. I've just finished breakfast by then.
11. A piece of bread with cheese and things but no top on it.
12. But in Norway they still bring their sandwiches from home.
13. It was like they take part of their home with them to the office.
14. And I'm so tired after eight hours in front of that computer I can't do any work in the evenings. It kills me.
15. Do you cook yourself dinner when you get home?
16. I read quite a lot.
17. But I've been so lazy. It's, it's all different because when I had the kids at home there was always something to do...
18. But I'm happy because they're happy...
19. I want my life and they want their life...

D Linking

Linking occurs when the end of one word runs_into the start_of the next word. It is very common in informal spoken English, but less so in more formal English, such as speeches or lectures.

The most common linking occurs between the consonant at the end of a word when the next word begins with a vowel, as in these examples from the interview.

There are just woods_and walks_and...
...to cut_it. You can't cut_it with a knife.
you get_on your bike and you cycle home
I get_up fairly early in the winter...

However, linking also occurs with other sounds, for example when one word ends in the same letter as at the start of the next word, as in these examples from the interview:

the taste is_so strong

Linking also occurs when the final letter –s merges with the start of the next word, as in this example:

I can hear things, but it's_not noise.

Mark where you expect linking to occur in these excerpts from the interview. Then listen and check your answers.

1. so I want to start off before that
2. it isn't really heavy traffic, but to me it is
3. because it's so close so it's nice to get some fresh air
4. So if I'm in by seven, I can leave at three o'clock...
5. No, we have an open landscape which is a new, a new thing in Norway at the moment.
6. if I hear a name or I hear decisions or I hear questions and answers
7. Eight hours altogether.
8. Well, soup is dinner, really...
9. It's all different because when I had the kids at home there was always something to do...
10. I had an aunt I was looking after...
11. I went to Tae Kwon Do three times a week...

Now read these phrases and sentences aloud. Remember to link words wherever possible.

A Gap-Fill

Fill in the blanks in these new sentences with words you heard during Ingse's interview. The words are listed in the box to help you.

bar	change	chat	contract	decisions
department	interested	jam	laugh	lazy
like	marvellous	neck	packed	straight

1. Sorry I'm late. I got caught in a traffic_____.
2. I've got some _____ news! Tom and I are getting married.
3. This cheese smells _____ my brother's socks!
4. Our managers never consult us even when they're making big_____.
5. I know which company she works for, but I don't know which _____ she works in.
6. I never knew you were so _____ in history, Dave!
7. Whenever I meet up with my old schoolfriends we always have a good _____.
8. You really shouldn't start work until you've signed a _____.
9. The salad _____ is over there, next to the waiter with the strange hair.
10. It was really embarrassing because I'd _____ my alarm clock in my suitcase and it went off just as we were landing.
11. Why don't we have a _____ about it over lunch? I'm sure we can sort something out.
12. I've hurt my _____ so badly that I can't even turn my head at the moment.
13. Could you come _____ home tonight? I need to talk to you about something.
14. I was really _____ yesterday. I didn't get up till twelve.
15. Why don't you come over to our place for a _____?

B Transformations

Change the word in each bracket that appeared in the interview to form a word that fits the gap, if necessary.

Here's an example to help you:

Example: I can make you a sandwich if you're (hunger) **_hungry_**.

1. We (typical) _____ get between 20 and 30 orders a day.
2. Which is (heavy) _____ – gold or silver?
3. I love it when he (flexible) _____ his muscles!
4. Have you got any (sweet) _____? I'm trying not to have sugar at the moment because I'm on a diet.

5. Looking back I think our children (benefit) _____ from being brought up in the country.
6. My sister studied civil (engineers) _____ at university.
7. They say (laugh) _____ is the best medicine.
8. We are (contract) _____ to work 37 hours a week, but I normally do around 45.
9. What's the (expired) _____ date on that cream? I don't want to give everyone food poisoning.
10. The EU used to give farmers (subsidised) _____ if they created areas for wildlife, but I'm not sure if they do any more.
11. I'm (boring) _____! Can't we go out?
12. I'm sorry, but I can't come out. I'm doing my (packed) _____. We're flying to New York tomorrow.
13. She certainly very (competence) _____, but her people skills need some work.
14. Stop (chat) _____, you two, and get on with your homework!
15. I've just had a (thinking) _____. Isn't Val a vegetarian?

C Phrasal verbs

All these phrasal verbs cropped up in the interview. Put the appropriate preposition or adverb in the gaps.

1. Karl started _____ the meeting, but then Chloe carried _____ because he had to take an important phone call.
2. Come and sit _____ by the fire and warm yourself up – it's freezing out there.
3. I'm very lucky because I get _____ with both my brothers.
4. I find it much more difficult to get _____ in the winter than in the summer.
5. Would you mind looking _____ our cat this weekend? We're going away.
6. They were married for five years, but it didn't work _____ because he wanted kids and she wanted to concentrate on her career.

D Accuracy and communicative competence

Although Ingse speaks fluent English, she does make a number of grammatical errors. However, these do not affect comprehension – it is still clear to the listener what she is talking about.

Try to make the following excerpts from the interview more accurate.

1. you get a long, nice afternoon in the sun

   _____ _____ _____ _____ _____

2. It's only four people in there.

   _____ _____ _____ _____ _____

3. My contract went out.

   _____ _____ _____ _____ _____

4. In Sweden I think they have full lunch now.

   _____ _____ _____ _____ _____

5. In some places you get paid lunch.

   _____ _____ _____ _____ _____

6. And there're no shops – nothing around in nearby.

   _____ _____ _____ _____ _____

7. And the house is tidy and clean for a change.

   _____ _____ _____ _____ _____

Geiranger fjord, Norway

I: So er, can you tell me about a typical day?

In: Yes, um, I get up fairly early in the winter because it's er, er, heavy traffic – the traffic jam...

I: Mmm.

In: ...so I want to start off before that.

I: Mmm.

In: Er, it's only four or five kilometres from where I live to, to the office so it isn't really heavy traffic, but to me it is.

I: OK.

In: But in the summer I, I cycle. I use my bike...

I: OK.

In: ...because it's so close, so it's nice to get some fresh air.

I: Mmm.

In: Get in to the office...

I: Oh, I'm sorry. You said you, you get up quite early. What, what time do you get up?

In: At six o'clock.

I: Oh, dear!

In: Yeah, to be in the office by seven.

I: Uh, huh.

In: And we've got **(1) flexible hours.**

I: Mmm, hmm.

In: So if I'm in by seven I can leave at three o'clock and can be home by quarter past three, half-past three.

I: Mmm.

In: Which in the summer is marvellous because you get a long, nice...

I: Mmm.

In: ...um, afternoon in the sun, when it's not raining.

I: In the summer, what, what time does the sun set, then?

In: Eleven...

I: Oh, really?

In: ...eleven-thirty. Yes.

I: That's absolutely fantastic. OK...

In: So back to...

I: Yes.

In: Yeah. I get in the office and what I normally do is, is have a coffee and I bring some er, bread...

I: Mmm, hmm.

In: ...with goat cheese, which is a Norwegian thing. Brown cheese from, yeah, goat cheese which I enjoy very much.

I: Right.

In: And er, my job is...

I: I think I tried some once. It tastes a little bit like chocolate.

In: It's sweet, yes.

I: Yes, very sweet.

In: And you use a... You need a, **(2) a cheese–slicer** to er, to cut it.

I: Mmm, hmm.

In: You can't cut it with a knife.

I: Mmm. OK.

In: And that would be far too much to eat as well. I mean the str... the taste is so strong...

I: Mmm.

In: ...that all you want is just a thin slice...

I: I see.

In: ...on a slice of bread.

I: OK. So that's your, your breakfast. You don't have breakfast at home?

In: No. I, I wait 'till I turn on the computer and sit down and read my mails.

I: Can, can you just tell me about your office? Do, do you have your own office and computer?

In: No, **(3) we have an open landscape**...

I: Oh, really?

In: ...which is a new, a new thing in Norway at the moment.

I: OK.

In: So this one, this one is a, is a small one.

I: Mmm.

In: It's only four people in there. And it's a quite good way of working because we're all working with the same things and we can hear – you know, if I hear a name or I hear decisions or I hear questions and answers – and I can benefit from that.

I: Mmm.

In: But I used to be in a department with engineers and we were about 20 or... to 30 people at... in one room.

I: Mmm.

In: And I wasn't interested in all that going on, so that was just noise.

I: Mmm, I see.

In: Whereas now I can, it, it, it's... I can hear things, but it's not noise.

I: And are your colleagues nice? Do you get on well with them?

In: Very nice. They're very nice. **(4) We have a good laugh** in there. And I ke.. that's why I stay. You know. Um, in the... it was about mid-June er, **(5) my contract went out...**

I: Mmm.

In: ...and they asked if I would like to stay on for another year.

I: So your, your contract expired then.

In: Yes...

I: Yeah.

In: ...expired then, so um, I said 'Yes' because we have a good laugh.

I: Mmm. OK.

In: Yes.

I: Is it, is it men and women in the office?

In: Three women and a man – one man. *(laughs)*

I: Does he have a hard time?

In: *(laughs)* I think he's here enjoying it! *(laughs)* Gunnar... Gunnar and his ladies! *(laughs)* Yeah.

I: And what are the ages in the office?

In: Er, about my age.

I: Uh, huh.

In: Yeah, 40, 50.

I: OK.

In: Yeah.

I: So you're doing all your work in the morning. Wha... what time do you stop for lunch?

In: Er, 11.30.

I: That... That's very early. You see in England we'd be stopping for our mid-morning break at 11.30.

In: *(laughs)* Yeah. Some people go for er, 10.30, but I think that's far too early for me. I've just finished breakfast by then.

I: OK. *(laughs)*

In: Yes. *(laughs)* How I feel!

I: So do you have a restaurant at work, or a canteen?

In: Yes, a lovely canteen with hot and cold food and... very, very good food. **(6) A salad bar costing us a quid.**

I: Really?

In: Or less than that, but more or less. Yes, a quid. And...

I: So the food's quite cheap? And subsidy... subsidised?

In: Yes, **(7) subsidised food** in the canteen, yes.

I: Uh, huh.

In: And they serve dinner, which is...

I: Really?

In: ... dinner at Norwegian time, which is about 4 o'clock. *(laughs)*

I: Huh! *(laughs)*

In: So if you get there quarter past four it's finished! *(laughs)* And that's for the people doing overtime, yeah.

I: Right. So... there, there's no point to take your own lunch in. You just go to the canteen?

In: Yeah, I do. Former... In, in other jobs I would have...

I: Mmm.

In: ...I have brought my lunch, which is an open sandwich.

I: Mmm. Right.

In: Very boring, but...

I: That's a... That's typically Scandinavian, isn't it? A... something like....

In: Yeah.

I: ...a piece of bread with cheese and things, but no top on it.

In: Yeah.

I: OK.

In: Just very simple. And that's... I heard somebody saying that's... in Norway, more than in, in Sweden, I think... In Sweden I think they have full lunch now.

I: Mmm.

In: But in Norway they still bring their sandwiches from home.

I: Mmm, hmm.

In: Packed lunch. And it... Somebody said it was part of... It was like they take part of their home with them...

I: Mmm.

In: ...to the office.

I: That's a nice way of thinking about it.

In: Yes, yeah.

I: Ah. OK, the... Do you, do you all stop at the same time for lunch – you and your three colleagues?

In: No, they go at 11 – er, 10.30 or 11 o'clock – and I go with the consultants.

I: Mmm.

In: And some people from... er, we have a competence course and competence centre and I go with them.

I: Right.

In: And we always find a table. We know that 11.30 we can go down. Somebody will be there that I know.

I: That's nice.

In: And then we just sit down there and chat.

I: Oh, that's nice. So you're not sitting on your own?

In: No, I wouldn't.

I: OK. Um, how long do you get for lunch?

In: Half an hour.

I: Oh, really?

In: Yeah.

I: OK.

In: And there're no shops – nothing around in nearby. There are just woods and walks and...

I: Mmm.

In: Yeah, so you have to take your car in...

I: Mmm. To... to...

In: ...if you want to go shopping or go to the bank or something.

I: Right. And then you carry on the same work in the afternoon till...

In: Till three or four or five.

I: Mmm.

In: Because of the flexible hours – which I think is marvellous.

I: Yeah.

In: Because if I've been out late one night...

I: Mmm, hmm.

In: ...too much to drink – you can just stay on and go to work at 9 o'clock.

I: But nine o'clock's the latest...

In: Yeah.

I: ...you can start work.

In: Nine to three is the... you have to be there by nine.

I: Mmm.

In: Between nine and three.

I: OK.

I: If you do work on a Saturday and Sunday do you get better pay?

In: 100 per cent, yes.

I: Yeah, so it's double?

In: Yeah.

I: Yeah.

In: And I'm so tired after eight hours...

I: Mmm.

In: ...in front of that computer I can't do any work in the evenings.

I: Mmm.

In: It kills me.

I: Right. *(laughs)*

In: No, but if you, if you do a different job – if you're interviewing, if you're going to meetings – and then you sit down at the computer... But when you are in front of that computer for eight hours...

I: Mmm.

In: My neck and my eyes... *(laughs)*

I: Yes. Very tiring.

In: Yes.

I: Mmm. So how many hours do you work a week?

In: It's 40. Minus lunch – half-an-hour a day – so, 37 and a half.

I: OK.

In: It's normal working hours.

I: Right. And is that normal for Norway, those hours?

In: I think so, yes, yeah. Somewhere... Some... In some places you get paid lunch...

I: Mmm.

In: Yeah.

I: OK. Um, so you finish sort of quarter past three in the summer.

In: Mmm, hmm...

I: Yeah.

In: Yes.

I: What time in the winter?

In: The same.

I: The same.

In: Yeah.

I: So you try to finish quarter past three. You've done your eight hours, which is...

In: Yeah.

I: ...half an hour lunch, but...

In: Yeah.

I: ...seven and a half hours working.

In: Yeah.

I: Eight hours altogether. And then do you... you get on your bike and you cycle home?

In: Yeah.

I: Yeah.

In: Sometimes I go straight home which is about... between five and seven kilometres, I think. But this summer has been so nice, so quite often I'm er, taking a longer trip to get home...

I: Mmm.

In: ...just to get the exercise, the fresh air and stop at a lake or go for a swim or something.

I: That sounds really nice.

In: And go home in the evening, yeah.

I: Do you cook yourself dinner when you get home?

In: I do normally, yes, but now that **(8) the kids** are moving out... they have moved out I'm... because of that good lunch I get at work...

I: Mmm.

In: ...I don't, I do not always need a dinner when I get back home.

I: OK. So you just have a sandwich or...

In: Yeah.

I: ...something.

In: Soup. Well, soup is dinner, really, but... *(laughs)*

I: OK.

In: I'm really lazy with that because I don't like cooking, you know. No.

I: You never have?

In: No, not really.

I: OK um, um, watch television?

In: I read quite a lot.

I: OK.

In: I like to do... Well, I've been so lazy. It's, it's all different because when I had the kids at home there was always something to do...

I: Mmm.

In: To get organised and I have... I had an aunt I was looking after which took quite um, a lot of time. I went to **(9) Tae Kwon Do** three times a week in the evenings. So I was quite busy. And this autumn I've been so lazy, doing so little – reading, doing Sudokus, going for walks. Just being lazy. And the house is tidy and clean for a change.

I: *(laughs)* Hah! Do you miss the girls?

In: Yeah, I do. Yes, it's er.... But I'm happy because they're happy, so... And, and the flat is too small for the three of us, really. I realised that in the summer. **(10) They have so much gear** and... I want my life and they want their life and... It didn't work out...

I: OK.

In: ...as well as it could have. We're good friends though, yes.

I: Right. OK. Thank you very much.

7. Words and Phrases

1 **flexible hours –** (BrE – flexitime; AmE flextime) A system of working in which you have to be at work during a set time period, e.g. 9am to 3pm, but which allows you to start work earlier or later, as long as you work a certain number of hours a week.

2 **a cheese-slicer –** a special kitchen implement, popular in Scandinavia, with a sharp blade which you slide across a lump of hard cheese, thereby cutting a slice

3 **we have an open landscape –** The expression 'open landscape' is an emotional one for Scandinavians as it refers to the fact that you can walk anywhere in the countryside, even on private land, as long as you don't damage anything. Here Ingse equates an open landscape with an open-plan office.

4 **We have a good laugh... –** We get on really well together...

5 **my contract went out** *[sic]* **–** my contract ran out; my contract expired

6 **A salad bar costing us a quid.** *[sic]* **–** A salad bar which only costs us a quid. (A quid is slang expression for one pound sterling.)

7 **subsidised food –** food which is cheap because the company pays part of the cost

8 **the kids –** a slang word for children

9 **Tae Kwon Do –** a type of martial art originating in Korea

10 **They have so much gear... –** They have so many things – clothes, books, etc.

UNIT 7 Dorah and Jill

Dorah and Jill both work as operating theatre nurses in two different London hospitals. Dorah is a black South African who came to work in the UK in 1998. She specialises in operations on eyes. Jill comes from North Wales but moved down to London in 1987. She specialises in orthopaedics, i.e. operations involving bones. Both Dorah and Jill have marked accents. Here they talk about a typical working day.

A Schema building

Based on your own knowledge of nurses and hospitals, what can you predict about Dorah and Jill?

a) their personalities/characters
b) the hours they work
c) the type of work they do

B Discussion

Discuss these questions in pairs or small groups and share your answers with the class:

1. Would you like to work as a nurse? Why/Why not?
2. How do you feel about the sight of blood?
3. How do you feel about eye operations?

C Normalisation 1 (Jill): True/False

This exercise is designed to help you get used to Jill's voice.

Here Jill talks about her work in the trauma theatre. Answer true or false. Be prepared to give reasons for your answers.

1. _____ The normal working week for a nurse is supposed to be 37½ hours in theory, but not in practice.
2. _____ The trauma theatre has always run seven days a week.
3. _____ The trauma theatre operates on patients of all ages.
4. _____ Someone who has just fallen down and broken their arm would be operated on in the orthopaedic theatre.

D Normalisation 2 (Dorah): Sentence completion

Dorah talks about work at her hospital.
Before you listen, try to predict which words, or which types of words (nouns, adjectives, prepositions, parts of verbs, etc.) will fill the gaps. Listen and check your answers.

1. Dorah has only been working regular hours _____ _____.
2. Sometimes she has to work _____ _____.
3. This is to reduce the number of patients on the NHS waiting _____.
4. Dorah says she is supposed to be paid extra for the extra work, but she doesn't seem very _____.
5. The responsibility for reducing waiting times is supposed to be being taken over by an _____.

A Sentence completion

Dorah talks some more about proposed changes at her hospital.

Before you listen, try to predict which words, or which types of words (nouns, adjectives, prepositions, parts of verbs, etc.) will fill the gaps. Listen and check your answers.

1. The agency is proposing to pay staff less than the _____.
2. The agency wants to pay staff on a weekly basis rather than a

    _____ _____.
3. This means the extra money will no longer be included in Dorah's

    _____.

B Questions

Dorah and Jill talk about the extra hours they have to work. Listen and answer the questions.

1. Why does Dorah say: *I'm lucky if I go off at 5?*
2. Did she have to work longer or shorter hours in her last job?
3. Why do Jill and Dorah often work longer hours than they are contracted to?

    a. Because they are ordered to.
    b. Because they feel obliged to.
    c. Because they need the money.

C True/False

Dorah talks some more about working extra hours. Answer true or false. Be prepared to give reasons for your answers.

1. _____ Dorah sometimes works at the weekend, as well as during the week.
2. _____ Sometimes she has to work through the night.
3. _____ Once last week it took Dorah nearly two hours to get home.
4. _____ According to Jill, anyone who works beyond 8pm gets paid twice the normal hourly rate.

D Cloze

Jill and Dorah talk some more about working extra hours. As with Exercise A, try to predict your answers before you listen.

I: Interviewer   **J:** Jill   **D:** Dorah

I: But your job – you finish at... You start at 8 and you finish at 6 those four days and, and _____ it.
J: Mmm.

I: You don't have to work any extra?

J: Well, you _____. It's the _____ as Dorah, really. You, you know, you _____ just stop your _____.

D: Mmm.

J: If it's over-running then you have... you have to _____ on, of course. And um, _____ to see that recovery people are all _____ and what have you.

I: So the same thing. You can't... You _____ you can't just _____ away.

D: No.

J: That's _____.

D: You can't take your _____ and say 'Oh, my shift is 5. I'm going _____!'

J: '_____ you!' *(laughs)* You can't do that.

D: You can't do _____.

E True/False

(193)

Jill talks about people finishing work on time. Answer true or false. Be prepared to give reasons for your answers.

1. _____ Jill says it's generally impossible to leave work on time, unless you have a specific appointment.

2. _____ She gets angry when people tell her they have to leave on time.

3. _____ Jill says sometimes people try to leave work on time without a valid reason, but they don't succeed.

F Questions

(194)

Jill and Dorah talk about what they do for lunch. Listen and answer the questions.

1. Who has a longer lunch break, Jill or Dorah?
2. Which three lunch options are there for staff at Dorah's hospital?
3. What must you do if you decide to leave the hospital premises for lunch?
4. What must theatre staff do before they go to the canteen at Jill's hospital?
5. Where is the canteen in Jill's hospital in relation to her operating theatre?

G Gap-Fill

(195)

Jill and Dorah talk about the Waiting List Initiative, i.e. a Government measure to bring down waiting times for operations. As with Exercises A and D, try to predict your answers before you listen.

1. Jill works around one Saturday in_____.
2. Dorah is generally asked to work extra shifts if there is a _____ of staff or an extra _____.
3. She says most of the _____ lists are done on Saturdays.

4. The Waiting List Initiative has been brought in to encourage hospitals to get through the _____ of operations.

5. No one should currently wait longer than _____ _____ for an orthopaedic operation in England.

H Cloze

Jill and Dorah talk some more about working extra hours. As with Exercises A, D and G, try to predict your answers before you listen.

I: Interviewer   **J:** Jill   **D:** Dorah

I: So um, what about when you get home, the two of you. What do you do? What's the _____ thing you do when you _____ home, Dorah?

D: *(laughs)* If I do get home! *(laughs)* Well, it _____. If I'm _____ – if I'm really, really _____, I just go in, _____ and just _____. Don't do anything... Because if I, I get home at... Let's say, for _____, at quarter-past 11.

I: Mmm.

D: You can't even _____. By the time you _____...

I: Mmm.

D: ...it's past 12 to 1. And then you're _____ to be up at half-past five.

I: God!

D: So I'm... It depends what time I get home.

I: Uh, hum. Right.

D: If I come home _____ then I can, you know... You know, relax. Have a _____.

I: Cook a nice _____.

D: Yeah, have a nice meal, _____ whatever.

I: Uh, huh.

D: But if I get home late I just don't _____. I just want to _____ _____.

I: What about you, Jill? What do you do when you come home? What's the first thing you do?

J: Um, generally I will _____...

I: Mmm, hmm.

J: ...which is all right. I find that quite relaxing. And then er, eat it. Have a _____ or something like that.

I: Mmm.

J: Either watch _____ _____ _____ television or go _____. Meet some _____.

I: Mmm.

J: Yeah, that kind of thing.

I: Where do you go out?

J: The _____, normally.

I: OK. *(laughs)*

J: This local pub _____ _____ _____.

I: I see.

A Imprecision in spoken English

1. **stuff**

    We often use *stuff* to refer to objects or things in informal spoken English when we do not need to be precise. Look at these examples from the interview:

    When talking about lunchtimes Jill says:

    > *Most people bring their own **stuff** in anyway...*

    Here the meaning is: Most people bring in their own lunch – sandwiches, etc.

    Later the interviewer asks what the difference is between the trauma theatre and the orthopaedic theatre. Jill replies:

    > *Orthopaedics is generally elective **stuff**...*

    Here the meaning is: Orthopaedics is to do with planned or elective operations.

2. **sort of and sort of like**

    We use *sort of* to describe something approximately as in this example:

    'My new car's a sort of bluey-grey colour.'

    We also use *sort of* or *sort of like* when asking questions. Here the effect is to make the question less interrogational. Look at these examples from the interview:

The interviewer asks Jill:	*Do you have regular hours? Do, do you **sort of like** do 9 to 6?*
The interviewer asks Dorah:	*Do you have regular hours – **sort of like** 8 to 6, like Jill, or...?*

    We also use *sort of* to make an answer less abrupt, as in this example from the interview:

Interviewer:	*But why are you saying 'elective'? 'Cos it's not like you've chosen to do it. Why's it called 'elective'?*
Jill:	*Well, you **sort of** have, haven't you, really?*

B Using the verb DO + main verb stem for emphasis

We often use do + main verb to emphasise or stress something, as in these examples from the article:

Interviewer: *Do you have regular hours – sort of like 8 to 6, like Jill, or...?*
Dorah: *Yeah, now, since um, since Monday I **do** have regular hours...*

Interviewer: *OK. But er, I mean in an eye hospital, surely you were just working during the day – you weren't working evenings or weekends.*
Dorah: *We **do** work weekends.*

Interviewer: *What's the first thing you do when you get home, Dorah?*
Dorah: *(laughs) If I **do** get home! (laughs)*

C Increasing fluency 1 Using the word JUST

The word *just* is one of the most common words in informal spoken English. It has a number of meanings. Here we will focus on two taken from the interview.

1. *just* meaning **only**

    Look at these examples from the interview:

    Interviewer: *But er, I mean in an eye hospital, surely you were **just** working during the day – you weren't working evenings or weekends.*

    When talking about her lunch break Dorah says: *It's **just** 45 minutes.*

2. *just* meaning **simply**

    Look at these examples from the interview:

    *you can't **just** stop your list*
    *You feel you can't **just** walk away.*
    *If I'm exhausted – if I'm really, really tired, I **just** go in, change and **just** sleep.*
    *But if I get home late I **just** don't care. I **just** want to sleep and rest.*

D Increasing fluency 2
Using the word SO

The word so is also an extremely common word in informal spoken English. It has various uses, as demonstrated in the interview.

1. Using *So + comma* at the start of a question to signal a change of topic. It is a gentle way to signal to the speaker that you would like to talk about something else. The interviewer does this towards the end of the interview after Jill and Dorah have been talking about the Waiting List Initiative.

    Interviewer: ***So*** *um, what about when you get home, the two of you. What do you do?*

    TOP TIP!   *So + comma* at the start of a question is also a very natural way to break a long period of silence. It makes the question softer and less abrupt or interrogational.

2. Using *so* a) to make deductions and b) to check that we've understood something correctly.

    Jill: *My hours are 8 to 6, generally.*
    Int.:   *Right.*
    Jill: *Four days a week.*
    Int.:   *Oh,* ***so*** *you get one day off because you're doing more than 37 hours, is that right?*

Later Jill talks about the difference between orthopaedic theatre and trauma theatre, to which the interviewer replies:

> *Right.* ***So*** *orthopaedic would be planned operations? You know you're going to have an operation hopefully that day?*

Later Jill and Dorah explain that it's impossible to leave work on time, to which the interviewer replies:

> *So you're not in a position where you can say 'no'?*

When talking about her lunch break, Dorah says: *It's just 45 minutes.*

The interviewer replies: *So that doesn't give you very long, really, to go to lunch.*

3. Using *so* to refer back to something that has already been said

When asking about Dorah's new post the interviewer says:

> Um, you said now you're, you're doing regular hours, **so** what, **so** what are those hours?

Dorah explains that she and her colleagues have been working extra hours to bring down waiting times. The interviewer says:

> OK, **so** do you get paid extra for that – doing the backlog?

4. Using *so* to give an explanation

The interviewer asks: *What does trauma mean? Is that broken bones?*
Jill replies: *Well, it is in our hospital, yes. **So**, **so** whatever – road traffic accidents, old lady falling down, you know, broken arms, little kids...*

Jill then goes on to say:

> Orthopaedics is generally elective stuff which is... **So** that would be like a, a, a total knee replacement, total hip replacement.

Dorah says: *...they have introduced um, some extra hours, **so** we're doing the backlog of, of the, the NHS list.*

Later, when Dorah talks about the low pay the agency is proposing she says:
> But the rates are very small, **so** we didn't sign anything...

Later, when Jill explains that she only gets 30 minutes for lunch and it takes her 10 to 15 minutes to walk to the canteen she says:

> **So** it's not worth it, really.

E Listener response

1. Signalling agreement

Obviously we can indicate to the speaker that we agree by using words like *yes* and *yeah*. But another very common way of signalling agreement is to make the sound Mmm. Look at these examples from the interview:

Interviewer: *Jill and Dorah, you both work as nurses.*
Jill: ***Mmm.***

Interviewer:	*You're not in a position where you can say 'no'.*
Dorah:	**Yeah.**
Interviewer:	*You feel you have to say 'yes'.*
Dorah:	*Yeah.*

Jill:	*It's the same as Dorah, really. You, you know, you can't just stop the list.*
Dorah:	**Mmm.**
Jill:	*If it's over-running then you ha... you carry on, of course.*
Dorah:	*You can't.*

2. Signalling that you are paying attention

As in the interview with Ingse, the interviewer used words such as *OK* and *Right* to signal that she is paying attention to the speaker, as well as the sound Mmm, hmm. Listen to these examples from the interview:

Jill:	*We tend to do more than 37½ hours anyway.*
Interviewer:	**OK.**

Jill:	*My hours are 8 to 6, generally.*
Interviewer:	**Right.**
Jill:	*Four days a week.*

Jill:	*I do the occasional Saturday.*
Interviewer:	**Mmm, hmm.**

Another way of showing you are paying attention is to repeat the speaker's words, as in this excerpt:

Dorah:	*I'm supposed to do 8 to 5.*
Interviewer:	**8 to 5.**

F Fillers

1. *ums* and *ers*

As your students are probably aware, we use *um*, and *er*, as fillers – words which the speaker uses to give him or herself time to plan what they are going to say next. The fact that they are making a noise at the same time indicates to the other speaker(s) that they shouldn't interrupt. Listen to these examples from the interview:

Interviewer: *And do you, do you have regular hours – sort of like 8 to 6 like Jill, or...*

Dorah: *Yeah, now, since um, since Monday I do have regular hours, though now they have introduced um, some extra hours...*

Interviewer: *Do you, do you get paid double or triple time?*

Dorah: *Er, yeah, there are those um, er, doubles and one-and-a-halves and...*

2. Well...

We often use **Well + comma** when we start to answer a question, again to give ourselves time to think. Another use of **Well + comma** is to contradict the speaker politely, as in the third example.

Interviewer: *Oh, so you get one day off because you're doing more than 37 hours, is that right?*

Jill: ***Well**, yes. We tend to do more than 37½ hours anyway.*

Interviewer: *What does trauma mean? Is that broken bones?*

Jill: ***Well**, it is in our hospital, yes.*

Interviewer: *But why, why are you saying 'elective'? 'Cos it's not like you've chosen to do it. Why's it called 'elective'?*

Jill: ***Well**, you sort of have, haven't you, really?*

G Classic intonation patterns

As Adrian Underhill has pointed out in his excellent book **Sound Foundations**, the classic intonation patterns listed in most books on phonology can vary depending on factors such as how well the speakers know each other and the topic they are discussing. However, the following three classic intonation patterns are all found in this interview:

1. Falling intonation for statements

Dorah: *I'm supposed to do 8 to 5.*

Jill: *It is 18 weeks.*

Dorah: *It depends what time I get home.*

Remember, though, that the voices of young British people, as well as New Zealanders, Australians and many more will often rise at the end of a statement. For this reason it may be more useful to look at the second purpose of falling intonation: to indicate that the speaker has finished what he or she wanted to say.

2. Rising intonation for Yes/No questions

There is a tendency for the speaker's voice to rise at the end of questions to which the answer will be Yes or No:

Interviewer: *Do you have regular hours?*
Interviewer: *Do you both get an hour for lunch?*
Interviewer: *And then did you have to work the next day?*

3. Falling intonation for *Wh-* questions

There is a tendency for the speaker's voice to fall at the end of Wh- questions:

Interviewer: *What does trauma mean?*
Interviewer: *What was so bad about that?*
Interviewer: *What about when you get home, the two of you? What do you do? What's the first thing you do when you get home, Dorah?*

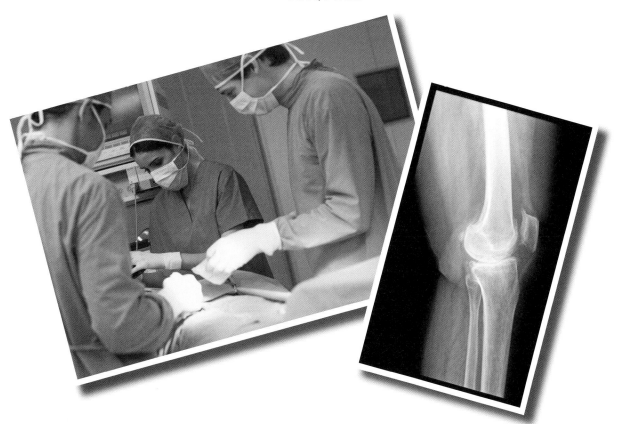

A Dictation

 to

At times in the interview Jill, Dorah and the interviewer speak very quickly and consequently some words are not pronounced clearly. Work with a partner. First listen to the excerpts from the interview and write down how many words there are in each item. Then listen and write down the words you hear. After that check your answers with another pair.

1. (___ words) _____
2. (___ words) _____
3. (___ words) _____
4. (___ words) _____
5. (___ words) _____
6. (___ words) _____
7. (___ words) _____

B The glottal stop

The glottal stop happens when the speaker tightens his or her throat and very briefly stops the air from getting through. This results in the /t/ sound at the end of words such as *got* or *lot*, or the /t/ sound in words such as *bottle* or *kettle* not being fully pronounced. This can make it difficult for you to recognise words containing this feature. Both the interviewer and Jill use the glottal stop in this interview.

Try to fill in the gaps before you listen and then listen and check your answers.

Can you imitate the glottal stop?

1. broken arms, _____ kids
2. 'Cos it's _____ _____ you've chosen to do it...
3. Is _____ in London?
4. So do you get paid extra for _____...
5. You don't sound very _____.
6. _____ was so bad about _____?
7. You're _____ in a position where you can say 'no'.
8. If you work over 8 o'clock you _____ a _____ more money...
9. Do you both _____ an hour for lunch?

C Sentence stress

As we heard in the previous unit, it is important that you are able to recognise stressed words in a stream of speech because these are the words that carry the speaker's meaning.

Listen to these excerpts from the interview and mark where the stressed words occur.

NB Unlike scripted listening passages, this exercise is not suitable as a predictive activity because the stressed words are personal to Dorah, Jill and the interviewer and therefore cannot be predicted by looking at the written script in isolation.

1. And they do extra lists on a Sunday at the moment.
2. So that would be like a, a, a total knee replacement, total hip replacement...
3. But why, why are you saying 'elective'? 'Cos it's not like you've chosen to do it.
4. Well, you sort of have, haven't you, really?
5. It's an elective list as opposed to something you can't help. You... Trauma is accidents, isn't it?
6. So orthopaedic would be planned operations.
7. Are you doing orthopaedics as well, Dorah?
8. So do you get paid extra for that?
9. We do work weekends.
10. And then did you have to work the next day?
11. But there are varying rates, although not much.
12. What about when you get home, the two of you?

D Fluency practice 1 linking

As we heard in the previous unit, linking occurs when the end of one word runs_into the start_of the next word. It is very common in informal spoken English, but less so in more formal English, such as speeches or lectures.

Look at the following extracts from the interview and predict where linking will occur. Then listen and check your answers.

After this listen and repeat each phrase or sentence after the speaker.

1. you both work as nurses
2. My hours are eight to six, generally. Four days a week.
3. It is in our hospital.
4. 'Cos it's not like you've chosen to do it.
5. It's the same as Dorah, really.
6. That's not bad.

7. So it's not worth it, really.
8. How often is that?
9. Once every six weeks or so.

E Fluency practice 2 – elision

In fast spoken English a process called 'elision' often occurs, most frequently with words ending in –d and –t. This results in these sounds not being pronounced when the next word begins with a consonant. These excerpts from the interview all contain examples of elision. Listen and repeat them without pronouncing the highlighted letter.

1. And then I was home by quarter pasT twelve.
2. AnD then did you have to work the nexT day?
3. You can'T jusT stop your list.
4. MosT people bring their own stuff in anyway.
5. And then you're supposeD to be up at five.
6. But if I get home late I jusT don'T care.
7. They don'T really.
8. It useD to be included in our salary.
9. I'm supposeD to do eighT to five.

F Fluency practice 3 – weak forms

The words between the stressed lexical, or content, words are known as grammatical, or function, words which bind the speaker's words together. These grammatical words tend to be unstressed, which makes them difficult to distinguish.
Listen to these excerpts and repeat them. Can you hear what has happened to the highlighted words in a stream of speech?

1. **Do you** have regular hours?
2. My hours **are** 8 **to** 6 generally.
3. So orthopaedic **would** be planned operations?
4. You know you're **going to** have an operation hopefully that day?
5. Do you have regular hours? Sort **of** 8 to 6, like Jill, or...
6. You're not in a position where you **can** say 'no'.
7. 'I'm sorry I can't stay today because such and such.' **And that's** fine.
8. So that **doesn't** give you very long, really, **to** go **out for** lunch.
9. **Is it** 18 weeks, or **something** like that?
10. **What's the** first thing **you** do when **you** get home, Dorah?

G Three features of Dorah's South African accent

These three features of Dorah's accent could potentially cause misunderstandings:

1. /æ/ (bad) – /e/ (bed)

   Listen to how Dorah pronounces the /æ/ sound in *happy*.

   *We as nurses are not **hAppy** about what they're proposing to give us.*

   A good language learner, when talking with a non-native speaker of English, will realise that when the speaker produces one non-standard pronunciation feature, the speaker is likely to produce this feature in all other words in English containing that sound.

   How might she pronounce the following words?

   salary, rates, that, relax

   Now listen to check if you were correct.
   (NB The word **salary** sounds more like **celery**.)

2. /i:/ (sheep) – /I/ (ship)

   Listen to how Dorah pronounces *sleep* in the extract:

   *I just go in, change and just **slEEp**.*

   How might she pronounce the following words? **seat, feet, steep**
   (NB The word **sleep** sounds more like **slip**.)

3. /I/ (ship) – /i:/ (sheep)

   Conversely listen to how Dorah pronounces the word *list*.

   *Or if there's an extra **lIst** to do.*

   How might she pronounce the following words? **fist, kissed, missed**
   (NB The word **list** sounds more like **least**.)

H People talking over each other

In real life, as opposed to coursebooks, it is very common for two or more people to talk over each other at the same time. Fill in the missing words in these excerpts from the interview where the participants are talking at the same time.

Please note this is a very difficult task that many native speakers would find tricky!

I: Interviewer   **D:** Dorah   **J:** Jill

Excerpt 1

I: But why, why...
J: ...arthroscopies...
I: ...are you saying 'elective'? 'Cos it's not like you've chosen to do it. _____?
J: Well, you sort of have, haven't you, really?

Excerpt 2

J: ...so... Most people bring their own stuff in anyway because by the time you've changed and gone to the canteen...
D: Mmm.
J: ..._____ and er, come back then there's 10...
D: 10 minutes **left**.
J: ...10, 15 minutes gone, yes. So it's not worth it, really.

Excerpt 3

D: If I come home early then I can, you know... You know, relax. _____.
I: Cook a, cook a nice meal.
D: Yeah, have a nice meal, watch whatever.

5. Further Language Development

A Gap-Fill

Fill in the blanks in these new sentences with words you heard during the interview. The words are listed in the box to help you.

backlog	bones	canteen	compared	confident	generally
hip	hopefully	included	off	overtime	paid
quite	salary	shortage	tend	well	whole

1. We _____ to eat mainly salads in the summer.
2. I _____ go to my parents on Sunday for lunch.
3. The hotel was _____ nice, but very expensive.
4. The problem with the chicken biryani here is that it's got _____ in it.
5. My mum's going into hospital for a _____ replacement next Monday, so I've taken the week _____ work.
6. We had to work _____ last week to clear the _____ of customer orders.
7. My daughter needs three grade As to go to university, but she seems pretty _____ that she'll make it.
8. My _____ gets _____ into the bank on the last Thursday of the month.
9. I think Paris is really expensive _____ to London.
10. My parents are coming to stay this weekend so I've got to clean the _____ house.
11. Would you like another slice of cake as _____, Toni?
12. Is the service charge _____ in the bill?
13. You must never sign a contract without checking it through.
14. We've organised a big party for my parents' silver wedding anniversary so _____ my mum will be out of hospital by then.
15. I used to eat in the _____ at work, but they closed it last month to save money.
16. There's a _____ of qualified teachers at the moment, so class sizes are getting bigger.

B Colloquial English

Fill in the blanks in these new sentences with words you heard during the interview. The words are listed in the box to help you.

bit	care	help	even	hard	kids
lucky	OK	quite	supposed	surely	worth	up

1. Once the _____ have left home we're going to sell this place and buy somewhere smaller.
2. Oh no! I was _____ to be home 10 minutes ago.

3. It's _____ you brought your umbrella. Look at the rain!
4. You're _____ not going to walk home at this time of night!
5. It's _____ working such long hours, but I do enjoy my work.
6. Could I have a _____ more cake, please? I'm starving.
7. You should have seen his last girlfriend – she was _____ taller!
8. I can't _____ feeling bad about what I said to Kim last night.
9. Are you _____ with this music or shall I put something else on?
10. I'm not _____ sure if we can park here.
11. We're meeting at seven, so it's not _____ going home first.
12. I was so angry with him I couldn't _____ speak.
13. I don't _____ what time it is. I'm tired and I want to go to bed.
14. We're really lucky living here because there's a wonderful pub just _____ the road.

C Transformations

Change the word in each bracket that appeared in the interview to form a word that fits the gap, if necessary.

Here's an example to help you:

Example: I can make you a sandwich if you're (hunger) **hungry**.

1. My husband has a (tend) _____ to snore if he lies on his back.
2. Yesterday I (accidents) _____ ran over a woman's foot with my shopping trolley. You should have heard what she called me!
3. You've got a (choose) _____ of cabbage, sweetcorn or peas – which do you fancy?
4. When our last manager retired they (replacement) _____ him with a 24-year-old straight out of university, but he didn't last long.
5. Don't bother reading the (introduce) _____ – it's quite boring.
6. She's very good at her job, but she just lacks (confident) _____.
7. I have to say that merging the two departments was a (logistics) _____ nightmare.
8. The Government's new (proposing) _____ is to freeze public sector pay for two years.
9. I can assure you that isn't my (sign) _____.
10. We did a price (compared) _____ on some website and this policy was definitely the cheapest.
11. This is the (bad) _____ cup of coffee I've ever had!
12. They don't accept credit card (paid) _____ so we'll have to pay in cash.
13. We don't go out every Friday. It (varying) _____.
14. I told you (specific) _____ to be home by midnight.
15. My cousin has just been (appointment) _____ chief marketing officer at JB Cunningham, so we're going out tonight to celebrate.
16. I enjoy gardening, to be honest. I find it very (relax) _____.

I: Jill and Dorah, you both work as nurses.

J: Mmm.

I: Do you have regular hours? Do, do you sort of like do 9 till 6? Does, does that happen with you, Jill?

J: I do. My hours are 8 to 6, generally.

I: Right.

J: Four days a week.

I: Oh, so you get one day off because you're doing more than 37 hours, is that right?

J: Well, yes. We tend to do more than 37 and a half hours anyway.

I: OK.

J: So yes, which is quite nice. I do the occasional Saturday...

I: Mmm, hmm.

J: And they do extra (1) **lists** on a Sunday at the moment. Er, (2) **trauma** – they're trying to do trauma as in um, a seven-day a week thing.

I: OK. What does, what does trauma mean? Is that broken bones?

J: Well, it is in our hospital, yes. So, so whatever – road traffic accidents, old ladies falling down, you know, broken arms, little kids....

I: Well, how is that different from (3) **orthopaedic theatre**?

J: Orthopaedics is generally (4) **elective stuff** which is... You're doing that, Letta, aren't you, at the moment as well?

L: Yeah.

I: What, what... But...

J: So that would be like a, a, a total knee replacement, total hip replacement...

I: But why...

J: ...(5) **arthroscopies**...

I: ...why are you saying 'elective'? 'Cos it's not like you've chosen to do it. Why's it called 'elective'?

J: Well, you sort of have, haven't you, really? You, you needed to come in. It's an elective list as opposed to something you, you can't help. You... Trauma is accidents, isn't it?

I: Right. So orthopaedic would be planned operations? You know you're going to have an operation hopefully that day?

J: Yes, yes. Planned. OK, yes.

I: Oh, right. Um, are you doing orthopaedics as well, Dorah?

D: No, it's an eye hospital.

I: Oh, OK. Is that in London?

D: Yeah.

I: And do you, do you have regular hours – sort of like 8 to 6 like Jill, or...

D: Yeah, now, since um, since Monday I do have regular hours, though now they have introduced um, some extra hours, so we're doing (6) **the backlog** of, of the, (7) **the NHS list**.

I: OK, so do you get paid extra for that – doing the backlog?

D: We're, we're supposed to.

I: You don't sound very confident.

D: Yeah, because they're a lot of um, um, (8) **logistics**.

I: Really?

D: Do you know... They're still negotiating the cost. We, as nurses, are not happy about what they're proposing to give us...

I: Mmm.

D: ...and um, we'll see. They're still negotiating. They haven't yet... It, it... They... There's an agency that's supposed to take over...

I: Right.

D: ...this, this extra job that we're going to do.

I: Mmm, hmm.

D: And er, the... What they're supposed to pay us we are not happy because it's even less than what the hospital was going to pay us.

I: Oh, I see.

D: The difference is now the, the, they want to pay us on weekly basis *[sic – on a weekly basis]*.

I: Instead of per hour...

D: On monthly basis. Inc... It would be... It used to be included in our salary...

I: Mmm, hmm.

D: ...but now with this agency work we're supposed to be paid on weekly basis *[sic – on a weekly basis]*. But the rates are very small so we didn't sign anything, we didn't do anything....

I: Oh, OK.

D: ...so...

I: You said now you're, you're doing regular hours, so what, so what are those hours?

D: I'm supposed to do 8 to 5.

I: 8 to 5.

D: And I'm lucky if I go off at 5.

J: Mmm.

D: But it's still OK compared to where I was working before, you know. *(laughs)*

J: Yeah.

I: What, what was so bad about that? What kind of hours were you doing there?

D: Um...

I: Was it still 35 hours a week, or...

D: Yeah. It er...

I: Mmm.

D: I'm intended to work up to 37½ hours...

I: Mmm.

D: ...but you... They put you in your, in your corner. *[They put you in a corner.]* You know, you, you are somehow... You somehow find yourself doing the extra hours...

I: Mmm, hmm.

D: ...because um...

J: You can't not. You can't leave it, can you? That's the...

D: You know... It's, it's, it's the very...

J: They know you can't do that.

D: No, **(9) they tie you down**. You can't...

I: So you're not in a position where you can say 'No'.

D: Yeah.

I: You feel you have to say 'Yes'.

D: Yeah.

J: Mmm.

I: OK. But er, I mean in an eye hospital, surely you were just working during the day – you weren't working evenings or weekends.

D: We do work weekends.

I: Oh, really?

D: And er, of course it's evening, even if it's not the whole night. I mean some time, like last week, we went off at er, half-10 and then I was home by er, quarter past 12.

I: At night?

J: Oh, dear.

I: And then did you have to work the next day?

D: Yes.

I: Yeah. That's, that's, that's hard, isn't it? But you got overtime for the extra hours.

D: Um, yeah, but you get paid.

I: Mmm. Do you, do you get paid double or triple time?

D: Um, yeah, there are those um, er, doubles and one-and-a-halves and, and all those things.

J: You, you get paid I think sort of... If you work over eight o'clock you get a bit more money...

I: Mmm.

D: Mmm.

J: ...up to whatever time.

D: Mmm.

J: I'm not quite sure what they are. But **(10) there are varying rates**, although not much.

I: But your job – you finish at... You start at 8 and you finish at 6 those four days and, and that's it.

J: Mmm.

I: You don't have to work any extra?

J: Well, you do. It's the same as Dorah, really. You, you know, you can't just stop your list.

D: Mmm.

J: If it's over-running then you have... you carry on, of course and, and um, check to see that **(11) Recovery people** are all right and what have you.

I: So the same thing. You can't... You feel you can't just walk away.

D: No.

J: That's right.

D: You can't take your bag and say 'Oh, **(12) my shift** is 5. I'm going home', and take my bag.

J: 'See you!' *(laughs)* You can't do that.

D: You can't do that. *(laughs)*

I: Doesn't anyone ever try to do that?

J: They don't really. Some people will but if, if they've got a specific appointment or something...

D: Mmm.

J: ...but they already let you know – 'I'm sorry, I can't stay today...

D: Mmm.

J: ...because such and such.' And that's fine.

I: Uh, huh.

J: **(13) Some will try it on, of course, but they don't get very far.**

I: I see. Do you, do you both get an hour for lunch?

J: I don't.

D: *(laughs)* Well, I do get my, my er... We get er, 45 minutes.

J: Do you?

D: Mmm, hmm.

J: OK.

I: That's not bad. Do you take food in or do you eat at the hospital?

D: I bring my, my lunch with me.

I: OK. Right.

D: But there is, of course, canteen *[sic – a canteen]* or even you can go outside, whatever.

I: Mmm, hmm.

D: It's just 45 minutes.

I: Right. So that doesn't give you very long, really, to go out for lunch.

D: No. As long as you let people know where you are...

I: Mmm, hmm.

D: You know, that I'm going out and...

I: Mmm, hmm. Right. What about you?

J: We... Our official is half-an-hour...

I: Right.

J: ...so... Most people bring their own stuff in anyway because by the time you've changed and gone to the canteen...

D: Mmm.

J: ...which is the other end of the hospital and er, come back then there's 10...

D: 10 minutes left!

J: ...10, 15 minutes gone, yes. So it's not worth it, really.

I: OK. Do you, do you have... You said you have to work sometimes on a Saturday.

J: Yes.

I: How often is that?

J: Er, once every six weeks or so? Something like that.

I: Right. And Dorah, do you regularly work weekends, or has that stopped with this...

D: Mmm. Most of the time I'm asked to work if there's maybe a shortage...

I: Mmm, hmm.

D: ...or if there's an extra list...

I: Right.

D: ...to do.

I: Yeah.

D: But we do work weekends, you know. And most of **(14) the Initiative Lists**, um, especially at the big hospital, they do them on Saturday.

I: Right. What, what? I don't know what that means – Initiative Lists? Oh, trying to get through the backlog...

D: Yeah.

I: ...of operations.

J: The Waiting List Initiative, it's called.

I: And that's a Government thing – to push through...

D: Yeah.

I: ...operations.

J: Yes.

I: 'Cos I think you have to have an operation within a certain time – is it...

J: Yeah.

I: ...18 weeks or something like that?

D: Mmm.

J: It is 18 weeks.

I: So um, what about when you get home, the two of you. What, what do you do? What's the first thing you do when you get home, Dorah?

D: *(laughs)* If I do get home! *(laughs)* Well, it depends. If I'm exhausted – if I'm really, really tired, I just go

D: in, change and just sleep. Don't do anything... Because if I, I get home at... Let's say, for instance, at quarter-past 11.

I: Mmm.

D: You can't even eat. By the time you relax...

I: Mmm.

D: ...it's past 12 to 1.

I: Mmm.

D: And then you're supposed to be up at half-past five.

I: God!

D: So I'm... It depends what time I get home.

I: Uh, hum. Right.

D: If I come home early then I can, you know... You know, relax. Have a bath.

I: Cook a nice meal.

D: Yeah, have a nice meal and watch whatever.

I: Uh, huh.

D: But if I get home late I just don't care. I just want to sleep and rest.

I: What about you, Jill? What do you do when you come home? What's the first thing you do?

J: Um, generally I will cook...

I: Mmm, hmm.

J: ...which is all right. I find that quite relaxing. And then er, eat it. Have a bath or something like that.

I: Mmm.

J: Either watch a bit of television or go out. Meet some friends.

I: Mmm.

J: Yeah, that kind of thing.

I: Where do you go out?

J: The pub, normally.

I: OK. *(laughs)*

J: This local pub up the road.

I: I see. OK.

1   **lists** – Here the specific meaning is the lists of patients waiting to have an operation.

2   **trauma** – Here the specific meaning is the operating theatre in a hospital which deals with patients who have had an accident and broken one or more bones and as a result require surgery.

3   **orthopaedic theatre** – the operating theatre dealing with planned operations such as hip replacements, broken wrists, etc.

4   **elective stuff – i.e. elective operations.** – Operations which are planned in advance, i.e. they are not the result of a trauma.

5   **arthroscopies** – An arthroscopy is a surgical procedures where a miniature digital camera is inserted into the patient's body to find out what is wrong.

6   **the backlog** – Here the specific meaning is the number of patients waiting for elective surgery, i.e. planned operations.

7   **the NHS list** – the National Health Service list of patients waiting for elective surgery, i.e. planned operations

8   **logistics** – the organisation of something which is complicated so that it runs smoothly. (In this case transferring some of the backlog of the NHS patients requiring an operation to a private agency.)

9   **they tie you down** – they limit your freedom, i.e. by not allowing you to leave work on time

10 **there are varying rates** – the money paid per hour varies

11 **Recovery people** – The nursing staff who look after a patients who have had an operation in a quiet room near the operating theatre until they are well enough to be returned to the ward.

12 **my shift** – the fixed period of work that I am contracted to do

13 **Some will try it on, of course, but they don't get very far.** – Some people will try to pretend that they have an appointment, but I generally know when they're lying.

14 **the Initiative Lists** – These lists are part of The Waiting List Initiative, a measure introduced by the Government to reduce the number of patients waiting for planned operations by paying extra money to hospitals that have successfully reduced waiting lists (for example, by carrying out operations at weekends) and fining those that haven't.

UNIT 8 Randy

We heard Randy talking about his family in Unit 3. Randy is a trained actor, musician and composer from Montana in the USA and currently lives in London. In this unit he talks about how he manages to juggle earning a living with his theatre work.

A Schema building – predicting which words will come up

Which 10 of these 20 words do you expect to hear during the interview?

a show, a flight, wallpaper, a piano, cream, a rehearsal, brakes, a script, a vest, dandruff, tunes, sunburnt, composed, buttons, lines, a hedgehog, an audition, artistic, foam, music

B Discussion

Discuss these questions in pairs or small groups and share your answers with the class:

1. Why do you think Randy moved to the UK to pursue a career in the theatre?
2. What do you know about Montana?
3. How do you think Randy makes a living when he isn't performing in a play or a musical?

C Normalisation 1: Anticipating the next word

This exercise is designed to help you get used to Randy's voice.

There is a word missing from the end of each excerpt. Try to guess the missing word and write it down. Then listen to Track 225 to check your answers. How well did you guess?

1. It was too easy over there to fall into a menial job that, you know, would pay the _____.
2. I spend about three hours a morning scanning for jobs and applying for things that I find _____.
3. Most actors pay the er, pay the bills with barwork and er, waiting some_____
4. So I get up in the morning and er, I go for my run and then I come back and _____...
5. And he works during the day so I make sure I sing during the day so he's not there and not too late at _____.
6. But how can you make enough money with barwork? I didn't think that was very well _____.
7. There are days where I will hibernate and 14 hours later my eyes will open up and life will be _____ _____.

D Normalisation 2: True/False

Randy talks about why he moved to the UK. Answer true or false. Be prepared to give reasons for your answers.

1. _____ Randy's parents didn't want him to leave the USA.
2. _____ Randy didn't feel he would be sufficiently challenged if he stayed in the USA.
3. _____ The American pronunciation of Edinburgh is the same as the Scottish pronunciation.
4. _____ Randy found it hard to find theatre work in Scotland.
5. _____ He says there are more opportunities in the theatre in Scotland than in New York.
6. _____ Randy has taught music at university level in the USA.
7. _____ It is impossible to teach at an American university without a post-graduate degree.
8. _____ Randy says generally music programmes in schools receive less funding than sports programmes in the USA.

2. Listening Comprehension

A Sentence completion

Randy talks about how he makes ends meet.

Before you listen, try to predict which words, or which types of words (nouns, adjectives, prepositions, parts of verbs, etc.) will fill the gaps. Listen and check your answers.

1. Randy is a freelance actor and writer so he spends a lot of time
_____-_____.

2. It's difficult to find work at the moment because of the _____
_____.

3. Randy spends three hours every morning scanning the Internet and theatrical papers looking for work which is _____.

4. He's posted a few photos (i.e. put up some advertisements) for individual _____.

5. To give music lessons you need a place to teach that contains a
_____.

6. To make ends meet (i.e. to survive financially) Randy sometimes waits tables or does _____.

B Questions

Randy talks about his daily regime. Listen and answer the questions.

1. What does Randy do to keep fit every morning?
2. What does he do for three hours after his shower?
3. What is he having to learn for his next show?
4. What does he do for at least two hours every afternoon?
5. Who may get annoyed by this?

C Correcting mistakes

Randy talks about where he lives. Correct the mistake in each statement.

1. Randy lives in a house with two bedrooms.
2. He shares with a man from Ireland.
3. The other man is unemployed.
4. The piano was already there when Randy moved in.
5. The piano is an antique.
6. Randy usually eats out.
7. He's only just moved in.
8. Randy and his friend don't get on with their landlord.

D Gap-Fill

Randy talks about his evenings. As with Exercise A, try to predict your answers before you listen.

1. Randy does a lot of _____-_____ work in the _____.
2. If he's not working he tries to _____ _____ with friends.
3. Randy says he is _____ on the _____-_____ for new things to do.
4. The interviewer asks how Randy can make enough money just by doing _____.
5. She doesn't think this kind of work is well _____.
6. She asks Randy how he can afford to pay the _____.
7. Randy says this is one of the _____ why he lives _____ of the_____.
8. It's _____ to rent in south London than in central or north London.
9. Randy and his friend made sure they found somewhere to live that they could _____.
10. Randy and his friend are very careful about how much they spend on _____ _____.

E True/False

Randy talks about combining barwork with his theatre work. Answer true or false. Be prepared to give reasons for your answers.

1. _____ Randy is trying to make as much money as possible at the moment.
2. _____ Randy explains that bar staff are usually paid a flat rate per hour.
3. _____ The expression 'strapped for cash' means well off.
4. _____ Randy restricts himself to just doing barwork.
5. _____ Randy believes customer service is far better in the US than London.
6. _____ Randy is often asked to work extra hours.
7. _____ Randy never works more than five days a week.
8. _____ Randy only works in bars close to where he lives.
9. _____ No matter what time he finishes work, he always gets up for his morning run.

F Cloze

Randy talks about the bars he likes to visit.

As with Exercises A and D, try to predict your answers before you listen.

I: Um, have you ever worked anywhere really _____?

R: Oh, yes! *(laughs)* _____ we all! Oh, _____ do I begin?
     (laughs) I suppose for me the _____ _____ of bar jobs are
     just... It might sound a bit _____, but I, I do like the gastro bars
     and, and the places that do offer a little bit more _____ than
     some place you just walk in and _____ football on TV and, and
     drink pints out of _____ glasses. It drives me _____. I have
     a real _____ standard to what I offer as far as service and...

I: Mmm, hmm.

R: ...and I _____ _____ dirt and _____ and _____,
     you know. I, I like someplace that, that, it, you know, offers good
     _____ and offers _____ service and somewhere that you
     want to go in, but not because _____ going to get _____
     on a bottle of wine for £5. You're going to have a bottle of wine
     _____ £30 - £40 because it's _____ and you're going to
     _____ it with people and...

I: Mmm.

R: ...you know, have that _____ rather than just _____ it and,
     you know...

G True/False

Randy talks some more about his life after work. Answer true or false.
Be prepared to give reasons for your answers.

1. _____ The interviewer's local pub is clearly a very upmarket
   establishment.
2. _____ Randy never drinks in a downmarket bar.
3. _____ When Randy works late, he can't go to sleep as soon as he
   gets home.
4. _____ Randy does his best to get up at the same time every
   morning, even if he's worked late.
5. _____ Randy says he has lots of things going on at the moment.
6. _____ It seems Randy feels guilty if he has a lie-in.
7. _____ Randy sleeps less than four hours a night, on average.
8. _____ Randy say most people in England sleep longer in the
   winter.

A Four features of Randy's North American accent

Remember, a good language learner will realise that when a speaker produces one non-standard pronunciation feature, the speaker is likely to produce this feature in all other words in English containing that sound.

Listen first to how Randy pronounces the highlighted words in the following extracts and compare his accent with that of the speaker from England reading the same excerpt. Can you hear the differences in their accents? What are they?

1   get

It was too easy over there to fall into a menial job that, you know, would pay the bills and **get** you by.

2   during

He works **during** the day so I make sure I sing **during** the day so he's not there.

3   important

You just have to budget what's **important** and what's not and, you know...

4 can't

I **can't** stand dirt and grime and, and filth...

Now compare Randy's pronunciation of *can't* with *can*. Can you hear a difference?

I **can't** stand dirt and grime and, and filth...

so that, you know, you **can** enjoy having a life without slaving away at a job 50 hours a week...

B Colloquial language

Randy uses a lot of colloquial expressions in the interview. Here are the most useful in context:

to make sure

Make sure you remember to close all the windows when you go out.

to get by

I don't earn a lot, but I make enough to get by.

to push yourself

You really need to push yourself if you're going to pass your exams.

There's no way...

There's no way I'm going to the party if Alain's going to be there!

to catch up with people

I'm so busy these days that I never get chance to catch up with my friends.

to be strapped for cash

Could you lend me $20? I'm a bit strapped for cash at the moment.

can't stand

I get on really well with my cousin, but I can't stand her new husband.

to land on your feet

My sister's really landed on her feet. She got offered a fantastic job the week after she left university.

to keep on top of something

I'm finding it really difficult to keep on top of my work because two of my colleagues are on sick leave at the moment.

to wind down

The best way to wind down after a busy day is to have a hot bath.

Now try to write your own examples using these colloquial expressions.

C Could have done something

We use **could have + past participle** to show that something could have happened in the past, i.e. the opportunity was there, but it didn't actually happen. Look at this example from the interview:

I know I could have ended up happily in New York as well...

Here Randy is saying he would have been happy in New York, but he decided to come to the UK instead.

Here are some more examples of this structure:

> 'Her voice is so good she could have been a professional singer, but she became a police officer instead.'
> 'We could have gone to Jerusalem while we were staying on the Red Sea, but we ran out of time.'
> 'I could have gone to university when I left school, but I was fed up with studying.'

Now try to write your own examples.

D Would have done something

We use **would have + past participle** to show that we would have done something if it had been possible or if something hadn't prevented it happening.

Look at this example from the interview:

> *'I would have happily taught at a college or university, but as, as far as my parents' financial situation and mine, coming out of four years' private er, college, there's no way I could have gone to grad school...'*

Here Randy is saying he would have gone to grad school if his parents and he could have afforded it, but they couldn't.

Here are some more examples:

> 'I would have sent you a birthday card, but I don't have your new address.'
> 'My grandfather would have been a hundred this year, if he'd lived.'
> 'We would have invited Christian, but we thought he was still on holiday.'

Now try to write your own examples.

E The gerund

There are numerous examples of the gerund in the interview.

1. Verb + –ing form

   Randy says he sings for at least two hours a day because *that's something I enjoy doing.*
   Other verbs that take the –ing form include start, love, like, hate and prefer.

   Ask your students to come up with their own examples.

2. **Verb + object + preposition + -ing form**

*How did your family feel about you **coming** over to live in England?*

Here are some more examples of this structure:

> 'These flowers are to thank you for looking after the cat while I was away.'
> 'I'm sorry I accused you of using my milk yesterday.'
> 'Luckily the gap between our houses stopped the fire from spreading.'

3. **Preposition + -ing form**

Randy says he and his flatmate budget carefully *so you can enjoy having a life without **slaving** away at a job 50 hours a week.*

We often use the -ing form after prepositions. Here are some more examples:

> as a result of, in favour of, against, as well as, besides, without, what about, how about, in spite of, for, by, on

Ask your students to come up with their own examples using some of the above.

4. **To spend time doing something**

Randy says: *I spend about three hours a morning **scanning** for jobs and **applying** for things that I find interesting.*

Here are some more examples:

> 'Yesterday I spent nearly an hour down the market **looking** for ripe avocadoes.'
> 'We spent most of our holiday **lying** on the beach and relaxing.'
> 'Our neighbours spent most of the weekend **arguing** again.'

5. **To end up doing something**

Randy says: *My problem is if I get strapped for cash... I will end up **being** there 50, 60 hours a week.*

Look at these other examples:

> 'There were no buses, so I ended up walking home.
> 'My manager was off sick last week so I ended up doing her work as well as mine.'
> 'We were planning to have a barbecue but we'd run out of coals so we ended up getting a pizza delivered.'

This is a very common expression. Can your students think of some more examples?

6. **The problem with doing something**

Randy says: *The problem with working late nights um, is usually when you do get home it takes a couple of hours to wind down before you get to sleep.*

This is a very common expression. Can your students think of some more examples?

Now try to write your own sentences featuring the gerund.

A Dictation

 to

At times in the interview Randy speaks very quickly and consequently some words are not pronounced clearly.

Work with a partner. First listen to the excerpts from the interview and write down how many words there are in each item. Then listen and write down the words you hear. After that check your answers with another pair.

1. (___ words) _____
2. (___ words) _____
3. (___ words) _____
4. (___ words) _____
5. (___ words) _____
6. (___ words) _____
7. (___ words) _____

B Sentence stress

As we saw in the previous two units, it is important that you are able to recognise stressed words in a stream of speech because these are the words that carry the speaker's meaning.

Listen to these excerpts from the interview and mark where the stressed words occur.

NB Unlike scripted listening passages, this exercise is not suitable as a predictive activity because the stressed words are personal to Randy and the interviewer and therefore cannot be predicted by looking at the written script in isolation.

1. I'm so much more interested in this country than I ever was in the States.
2. And I first moved over here in '99.
3. It's not just bill-paying, you know.
4. You have to have the music and the piano ready, you know...
5. I get up in the morning and er, I go for my run and then I come back and shower and er, and search for a job.
6. And I spend a good three hours on that.
7. Did you have to buy that?
8. One of the reasons I live south of the river is because it's cheaper.
9. You just have to budget what's important and what's not...
10. You're always paid depending on experience in this industry...
11. It might sound a bit snobby, but I do like the gastro bars and...

C People talking over each other

In real life, as opposed to coursebooks, it is very common for two or more people to talk over each other at the same time. Fill in the missing words in these excerpts from the interview where the participants are talking at the same time.

Please note this is a very difficult task that many native speakers would find tricky!

R: Randy   I: Interviewer

Excerpt 1

R: Belt away to the... to the disgrace and dismay of the neighbours! *(laughs)*

I: So _____ a bedsit or a studio flat?

Excerpt 2

R: Um, it was a gift from a friend of mine that I composed a show with in... up in er, Scotland.

I: Oh, that's wonderful! Yeah.

R: So it's...

I: _____.

R: ...it's full 88 keys and it's digital...

Excerpt 3

R: ...the American experience of waiting...

I: Mmm.

R: ...and waiting tables and bartending, and the customer service is, you know, second to none. It's, it's...

I: So _____...

R: _____trained hard in the States.

I: I see.

Excerpt 4

R: I try to get up at half-seven every morning as well...

I: Do you? _____ _____ _____ _____ _____?

R: ...regardless of whether I've gotten up at six or not.* **

*gotten (US English) got (BrE)
** Here Randy makes a mistake. He meant to say '...regardless of whether I've gotten home at six or not.'

D Fluency practice 1 – linking

As we heard in the previous unit, linking occurs when the end of one word runs_into the start_of the next word. It is very common in informal spoken English, but less so in more formal English, such as speeches or lectures.

Look at the following extracts from the interview and predict where linking will occur. Then listen and check your answers.

After this listen and repeat each phrase or sentence after the speaker.

1. there's no way I could have gone to grad school
2. So it's words and music you're having to learn?
3. That's lucky, isn't it?
4. I try to socialise and catch up with people...
5. One of the reasons I live south of the river is because it's cheaper.
6. which works out well
7. You just have to budget what's important and what's not.
8. Does a lot of the barwork pay minimum wage?
9. the sun comes out in the summer

E Fluency practice 2 – elision

In fast spoken English a process called 'elision' often occurs, most frequently with words ending in –d and –t. This results in these sounds not being pronounced when the next word begins with a consonant. These excerpts from the interview all contain examples of elision. Listen and repeat them without pronouncing the highlighted letter.

1. AnD I firsT moved over here in '99.
2. AnD I was in London for six months before I wenT to Edinburgh for five and a half years.
3. Yeah, and in Scotland I jusT found that I, I was always constantly finding somebody to work with...
4. you finisheD your degree...
5. At the moment I am er, job-hunting , as always, as a freelancer musT do.
6. my nexT show
7. And I pretty habitually sing at leasT two hours a day jusT to keep my chords up.
8. seconD to none
9. Um, it mighT become a more afternoon/evening run.
10. AnD I can'T stanD dirt anD grime anD, anD filth...
11. don'T get me wrong

F Fluency practice 3 – weak forms

As we saw in the previous unit, the words between the stressed lexical, or content, words are known as grammatical, or function, words which bind the speaker's words together. These grammatical words tend to be unstressed, which makes them difficult to distinguish.

Listen to these excerpts and repeat them. Can you hear what has happened to the highlighted words in a stream of speech?

1. I spend about three hours a morning scanning **for** jobs and applying **for** things **that** I find interesting.
2. But how **can** you make enough money **with** barwork? I **didn't** think that was very well paid.
3. How **can** you make enough **to** pay the rent in London?
4. So what **are** you up to these days?
5. and all that kind **of** stuff
6. You **don't** need to. You **could** get up any time you want...
7. **Do you** have a piano in the flat?
8. you finished **your** degree

A Gap-Fill

Fill in the blanks in these new sentences with words and phrases you heard during Randy's interview. The words and phrases are listed in the box to help you.

bills	can't afford	cheaper	constantly
experience	financial situation	for a living	funded
hit a point	individual tuition	interested in	level
opportunities	pushed	end up	minimum wage
to check out	strapped for cash	to get by on	trained
definitely	hard	menial	spend

1. Anders and I have just _____ _____ _____ in our relationship where we both feel ready to get married.
2. I'm not very _____ Greek history. What's in the next room?
3. If you don't study _____ and pass your exams, you'll _____ in a _____ job just paying the _____.
4. So long as I earn enough money to pay the _____ I'll be happy.
5. He could have got a grade A if he'd _____ himself.
6. It was a great holiday apart from the fact that it rained _____ for most of the first week.
7. What does your brother do _____?
8. My parents emigrated to Australia because they thought there would be more _____ out there.
9. I want _____ that new restaurant that Peter has been going on about. Can we go there this weekend?
10. I wanted to do intermediate _____ Spanish, but they've put me in the advanced class and it's really difficult. I think I need to get some_____ instead.
11. There's no way I can afford a mortgage in my current _____ so I'll just have to carry on renting.
12. The Royal Opera House is partly _____ by the Government, but it also gets donations from corporate and individual sponsors.
13. I've _____ got to get a new phone. This one's rubbish.
14. We _____ most of our time in the garden in the summer.
15. Why don't you get Roberto to have a look at your car? He's a _____ mechanic.
16. He makes enough money _____, but not enough for holidays.
17. She's a qualified accountant but she can't get a job because she doesn't have enough work _____.

18. I was going to go by train, but then someone told me the bus is much
_____.

19. Now that Paul's not working we _____ to go out for dinner every
weekend like we used to.

20. I'm a bit _____ at the moment so I'm going to ask my parents for
a loan.

B Transformations

Change the word in each bracket that appeared in the interview to form
a word that fits the gap, if necessary.

Here's an example to help you:

Example: I can make you a sandwich if you're (hunger) **_hungry_**.

1. He studies international (relationship) _____ at university.

2. You need to keep (constantly) _____ pressure on the wound so
that the bleeding stops.

3. If you've got a degree you could always go into (taught) _____.

4. I don't know if I can afford to go on holiday this year. I need to check
my (financial) _____.

5. Passing your driving test first time is a huge (achieve) _____.
Well done!

6. We've decided that for this job experience should take (precedent)
_____ over qualifications, so we'd like to offer you the position.

7. My aunt's having a brain (scanning) _____ on Friday so I'm
taking her to the hospital.

8. Please fill out the attaching (applying) _____ form and send it
back before the closing date of 15th August.

9. I'm going on a (trained) _____ course next week so I'll have five
days away from the office. I can't wait!

10. Could you try and get the (waiting) _____ attention?

11. Have you got any (lines) _____ paper? I want my writing to look
neat.

12. They say (proud) _____ comes before a fall.

13. The new couple next door aren't as (socialise) _____ as our
previous neighbours, which is a shame.

14. I'm finding this new job very (challenges) _____ because there's
so much to learn.

15. Leeds used to be a very (industry) _____ town, but now most of
the factories have closed down.

C Prepositions and adverbs

Put the correct preposition or adverb into the gaps in these sentences based on the interview.

1. How do you feel _____ going to that new gym and checking it out?
2. Why don't we go and talk to those guys _____ there?
3. I really like Jake, but he's impossible to work _____.
4. I've just applied _____ a fantastic job – head of entertainment on a cruise ship.
5. I would love to get back _____ playing tennis again, but I just don't have enough spare time these days.
6. Try to get it _____ your head – she doesn't love you and she never will!
7. The tickets cost £50, but Thomas fell asleep _____ most of the second act so that was a waste of money.
8. You obviously put a lot of work _____ this essay and it shows.
9. It would be great to catch _____ and hear all your news.
10. I'm sharing a flat _____ three other guys, and it's working _____ really well.
11. I'm not sure if I'll be able to make it tomorrow – it depends _____ how much studying I get done this evening.
12. He came here _____ a long weekend and ended _____ staying here for five years.
13. I'm finding it a bit hard to keep _____ top _____ my work at the moment.
14. I've got tomorrow _____ so we could get together if you're free.
15. The problem _____ living in London is that everywhere's so expensive.

I: OK. How did your mum and dad feel...

R: ...that was great.

I: ...or your family feel about you coming over to live in England?

R: I think er, my, my parents and I hit a lovely point in our relationship where they're just happy that I'm happy and er, I'm so much more interested in this country than I ever was in the States. It was too easy over there **(1) to fall into a menial job** that, you know, would pay the bills **(2) and get you by** and, and **(3) you never really pushed yourself for anything above and beyond.** And I first moved over here in '99 and I was in London for six months before I went to Edinburgh for five and half years. Sorry, Edinburgh, Edinburgh *(laughs)* I have to say that one right – I lived there too long, so I *(laughs)*... Yeah, and in Scotland I just found that I, I was always constantly finding somebody to work with, or somebody that wanted to write something, or somebody that needed an actor **(4) to pull up cards** or help them direct a show, or...

I: Mmm, hmm.

R: ... so I've, I've just found that over here it's um... **(5) It's not just bill-paying**, you know. It's a way to **make a living** and...

I: Mmm.

R: ...and **(6) the opportunities are rife**. No different than New York. I know I could have ended up happily in New York as well, but er, I think **(7) the grass is always greener and** it was nice to er ...

I: Yeah.

R: ...**(8) to check out something different.**

I: And you, you finished your degree, what, what did you do then? Did you start as a music... music teacher?

R: No um, I would have happily taught at a college or university level, but um, as far as my parents' financial situation and mine, coming out of four years' private er, college, there's no way I could have gone to **(9) grad school**...

I: Mmm.

R: ...so I never could have achieved the education that I needed to teach university kids.

I: I see.

R: And I didn't want to teach **(10) high schoolers** music. I've seen too many bad music programmes in my life and...

I: I see.

R: ...it's not something that's funded very well in the States, you know. **(11) Sports kind of takes the precedent**, especially in smaller towns, you know...

I: Mmm. So what are you up to these days?

R: Er, at the moment I am er, job-hunting, as always, as **(12) a freelancer** must do.

I: Mmm.

R: Um, economic climate is not the greatest, so you definitely have to stay out there and fight for it. Um, I spend about three hours a morning **(13) scanning for jobs** and applying for things that I find interesting and...

I: What, what kind of jobs are you applying for? 'Cos you're a trained actor and music teacher, I think.

R: Yeah, um, I've, I've, **(14) I've posted a few places for um, indi... er, individual tuition.** I would like to get back into teaching some lessons and stuff, but you really have to have the right... You have to have the music and the piano ready, you know, and a place where you can teach these people and, and all that kind of stuff.

I: OK.

R: And I'm, **(15) I'm not necessarily stocked up with everything that I would need to start giving brass lessons again**, which I would love to do, you know um... **(16) Voice lessons, acting lessons I can get by on.**

I: Right.

R: So um, as usual most actors pay the er, pay the bills with barwork and er, **(17) waiting some tables.** *(laughs)*

R: I get up in the morning and er, I go for my run and then I come back and shower and er, and search for a job. And I spend a good three hours on that.

At the moment um, my next show... **(18) We start rehearsal on February 23rd...**

I: Mmm, hmm.

R: ...so I've started um, **(19) attacking that script** and trying to get it into my head and, and learn the couple of tunes that I have to sing for that. And er...

I: So it's words and music you're having to learn?

R: Yeah.

I: So you're practising that af... afternoons, I suppose, learning the lines...

R: Yeah, the afternoons I'm learning some lines and, and I pretty habitually sing at least two hours a day, **(20) just to keep my chords up** and...

I: Mmm, hmm.

R: ...that's something I enjoy doing so it's relaxing for me as well.

I: Do you sing at home?

R: Yeah, **(21) belt away** to the... to the disgrace and dismay of the neighbours! *(laughs)*

I: So do you have a bedsit or a studio flat?

R: Er, no, I'm, I'm in a two-bedroom flat.

I: OK.

R: Um...

I: Just, just on your own?

R: No, I have a flatmate - Northern Irish guy - he lives there. And he works during the day so I make sure I sing during the day so he's not there, and not too late at night.

I: Do you have a piano in the flat?

R: I do have a piano, yeah.

I: That's lucky, isn't it?

R: Yeah.

I: Did you have to buy that?

R: Um, it was a gift from a friend of mine that I composed a show with in... up in er, Scotland.

I: That's wonderful!

R: So it's...

I: How nice.

R: ...it's full 88 keys and it's digital, but nonetheless it's...

I: Right.

R: ...touch-sensitive and you get a good sound out of it.

I: OK. So er... yep, right: running, job-hunting in the mornings, learning your lines, whatever, in the afternoon and then?

R: Um, **(22) get some dinner on** *(laughs)*. I love to cook. I love to keep my flat clean. I'm quite a homely person.

I: Right.

R: Love the house and er, put a lot of work into it. We've been there two years, so...

I: Mmm.

R: ...so really quite proud of what it is and like to keep it clean. Um...

I: But you're renting – you, you haven't bought it?

R: No, we're renting. Er, the landlord's great. She takes care of all the problems that we need.

I: OK. Good.

R: It's a, it's a pretty good situation.

I: Mmm. **(23) So you've landed on your feet?**

R: Yeah.

I: Yeah.

R: And then um, a lot of part-time work in the evenings at bars or **(24) I try to socialise and catch up with people** and er... Just constantly on the look-out for new things to do and new **(25) challenges** and...

I: Oh, that's great. But how can you make enough money with barwork? I didn't think that was very well paid. How can you make enough to pay the rent in London?

R: Um, one of the reasons I live south of the river is because it's cheaper. *(laughs)* When we were flat-hunting, you know, we found a place that we knew we could afford.

I: Mmm.

R: And I can get by bill-wise on probably about 3½ -4 shifts a week, you know...

I: OK.

R: ...in a bar, which I'm... which works out well. You just have **(26) to budget** what's important and what's not and, you know, the grocery shopping is very carefully spent **(27) and divvied out** and, you

I: know, we take good care to budget and finance ourselves as best we can so that, you know, you can enjoy having a life without...

I: Mmm.

R: ...**(28) slaving away** at a job 50 hours a week.

I: Right. So how many hours would you say you worked?

R: Um, right now I'm on about – now just up to 30 hours a week.

I: OK, yep. Um, does a lot of the barwork pay minimum wage – which I think is about £5.80?

R: Um, some... You're always paid depending on experience in this industry, which is the great thing. And er, and, and my problem is **(29) if I start to get strapped for cash** and I find a place that I enjoy working I will end up being there 50, 60 hours a week, managing the bar or general managing the restaurant and the bar and the American experience of waiting...

I: Mmm.

R: ...and waiting tables and bartending, and the customer service is, you know, second to none. It's, it's...

I: So because you're good at it...

R: You get trained hard in the States.

I: Oh, I see.

R: And the minute you start working for somebody, because you're good they want you there all the time and...

I: I see.

R: ...and it's really hard to keep that balance of yes, but, I need time to, you know, **(30) audition** and do my shows **(31) and keep on top of my artistic life. (32) It's too easy to get sucked in** and then all of a sudden...

I: Yeah.

R: ...you're working six doubles a week and the, the 24 hours you have off **(33) you're recuperating** because...

I: Mmm, hmm.

R: ...it's, it's... It's dang... It's dangerous, but sometimes you do need to pile away the cash so that you have six months to, to relax and...

I: Concentrate on the art stuff, yeah.

R: ...work on what's important, yeah.

I: Um, what's the latest you finish work when you're working in a bar?

R: Oh, it can be three in the morning – three, four in the morning. Couple of night buses across town! (laughs)

I: So if you finish then do you um, still do your run in the morning?

R: Um, it might become more an afternoon, evening run.

I: But you do run every day?

R: Five, five times a week.

I: Not Saturdays, Sundays?

R: No.

I: Um, have you ever worked anywhere really awful?

R: Oh, yes! (laughs) Haven't we all! Oh, where do I begin? No... (laughs) I suppose for me the worst kind of bar jobs are just... It, **(34) It might sound a bit snobby**, but I, I do like the **(35) gastro bars** and, and the places that do offer a little bit more **(36) upscale** than some place where you just walk in and watch football on TV and, and drink pints out of dirty glasses. **(37) It drives me nuts.** I have a real serious standard to what I offer as far as service and er...

I: Mmm, hmm.

R: ...and I can't stand dirt and **(38) grime** and, and filth, you know. I, I like someplace that, that, it, you know, offers a good product and offers nice service and somewhere that you want to go in, but not because you're going **(39) to get wasted** on a bottle of wine for £5. You're going to have a bottle of wine that's £30 - £40 because it's lovely and you're going to enjoy it with people and...

I: Mmm.

R: ...you know, have that experience **(40) rather than just down it** and, you know...

I: I'm not going to invite you to my local pub, then! (laughs)

R: (laughs) I'm not saying I don't drink in places like that, but I'm just saying I wouldn't want to work there! (laughs)

I: Oh, what time do you try to get to bed by?

R: Um, on... *(coughs)* The problem with working late nights um, is usually when you do get home it takes a couple of hours **(41) to wind down** before you can sleep. So I would say on non-work nights I definitely am in bed by midnight.

I: Mmm.

R: That's me. **(42) I try to shut down at that point.** It doesn't always work, but I try.

I: Mmm.

R: But, you know, sometimes when you're pushing yourself and I always... I try to get up at half-seven every morning as well.

I: Do you? Even though you don't need to?

R: Regardless of whether I gotten up at six or not. *[sic – gotten home]*

I: Yep. You don't need to. You could get up any time you want, really, in the mornings.

R: Yeah. At the moment **(43) my schedule's pretty open** and I, I, I could waste it just sleeping late but er, life, life's too short to lay in bed and do nothing and I have, I have enough things that I want to be doing so...

I: So you're quite di... disciplined like that?

R: Yeah. I, I don't sleep very much. *(laughs)*

I: How, how many hours would you say you slept per night?

R: If I was going to say average it out over a normal seven-day week I probably sleep...... four to six hours a night.

I: **(44) Crikey!**

R: On an average, yeah.

I: And then do you catch up like on a Sunday, or...?

R: Um, there... Don't get me wrong. There are days where I will hibernate and 14 hours later my eyes will open up and life will be great again... *(laughs)*

I: You are reasonably normal.

R: *(laughs)* No, there are always **(45) hibernations** – hibernation moments – especially in the winter.

I: Mmm.

R: And I think everybody feels that in this country – that the sun comes out in the summer and you want to be out in it and during the winter you just want your bed.

I: And everybody's smiling, yeah.

1   **to fall into a menial job** – to end up doing a boring, unskilled job without making any effort

2   **and get you by** – and which would pay you just enough money to live on

3   **you never really pushed yourself for anything above and beyond** – you never really forced yourself to do anything more challenging

4   **to pull up cards** – a theatre expression meaning to get parts, i.e. acting roles without having to audition

5   **It's not just bill-paying, you know. It's a way to make a living** – It's not just a question of making enough money to pay the bills. It's a way to earn good money.

6   **the opportunities are rife** – there are a huge amount of opportunities

7   **the grass is always greener** – things always look better somewhere else

8   **to check out something different** – to go to a place to see what it's like

9   **grad school** – (AmE) a college for post-graduates, i.e. students who already have a degree who want to study further

10 **high schoolers** – (AmE) children attending high school in the USA (broadly equivalent to a combined secondary school and sixth form college in the UK)

11 **Sports kind of takes the precedent** – Sport is viewed as being more important than, in this case, music.

12 **a freelancer** – a person who is self-employed, but who works for other organisations on a contractual basis

13 **scanning for jobs** – trying to find a job by looking through newspapers, magazines, website advertisements, etc.

14 **I've posted a few places for um, indi... er, individual tuition** – (AmE) I've put advertisements up in a few places offering one-to-one teaching.

15 **I'm not necessarily stocked up with everything that I would need to start giving brass lessons again** – I don't really have the right equipment or things I need to teach people to play brass instruments such as the trumpet, trombone, etc.

16 **Voice lessons, acting lessons I can get by on.** – I can give these lessons without needing special equipment.

17 **waiting some tables** – (AmE) – being a waiter

18 **We start rehearsal on February 23rd** – We start run-throughs of the show on February 23rd, a period of preparation before the first official opening performance.

19 **attacking that script** – working hard to learn the lines of a play, etc.

20 **just to keep my chords up** – just to keep my vocal chords in good shape

21 **belt away** – sing really loud

22 **get some dinner on** – start cooking dinner

23 **So you've landed on your feet?** – So you have ended up in a good situation?

24 **I try to socialise and catch up with people** – I try to meet friends and see people I haven't met for a while

25 **challenges** –things which require hard work to be done successfully, but which make you feel good if you succeed

26 **to budget** – to plan carefully how you spend your money

27 **and divvied out** – and shared out

28 **slaving away** – working extremely hard at something

29 **if I start to get strapped for cash** – if I begin to be short of money

30 **(to) audition** – When an actor wants a part he or she has to attend an audition and perform something, generally in front of the show's director and other people.

31 **and keep on top of my artistic life** – and make sure that my artistic life doesn't suffer due to my other work

32 **It's too easy to get sucked in** – It's too easy to get involved in something without choosing to be...

33 **you're recuperating** – you're recovering, i.e. you're getting your health and strength back

34 **It might sound a bit snobby** – It might sound that I think I am better than ordinary people

35 **gastro bars** – bars which offer high quality food

36 **upscale** – (AmE) upmarket (BrE)

37 **It drives me nuts** – (AmE) It makes me really angry.

38 **grime** – a layer of dirt or dust on something

39 **to get wasted** – to get very drunk

40 **rather than just down it** – rather than just drink it very quickly

41 **to wind down** – to relax gradually

42 **I try to shut down at that point** – I try to switch off at that point.

43 **my schedule's pretty open** – (AmE) I haven't got a lot of things on at the moment, i.e. I have a lot of free time

44 **Crikey!** – an old-fashioned expression of surprise

45 **hibernations** – Some animals hibernate during the winter, i.e. they enter a period of deep sleep. Here the meaning is long periods of sleep.

UNIT 9 Eileen

We heard Eileen talking about her family in Unit 4. Eileen is the mother of two children in their early 20s, Hannah and Andrew. She works in the Town Planning department of a London borough and lives with her husband Andy in north–east London. She has a strong east London accent.

A Schema building – predicting which words will come up

Which 10 of these 20 words do you expect to hear during the interview?

> flexitime, butterfly, tray, shower, dust, station, gravy, fence, forms, cloudy, lunch, museum, dog, socks, statistics, pattern, cook, boring, crunchy, stressful

B Discussion

Discuss these questions in pairs or small groups and share your answers with the class:

1. Eileen and her daughter get up around the same time on weekday mornings. What do you think the atmosphere is like in the kitchen?
2. Eileen's husband Andy is her line manager. What are the potential problems?
3. What does a London accent sound like?

C Normalisation – freestyle listening comprehension

This exercise is designed to help you get used to Eileen's voice.

Eileen talks about her job and the start of a working day. How much do you find out from this short excerpt?

A True/False

Eileen talks about getting to work and what she does when she arrives. Answer true or false. Be prepared to give reasons for your answers.

1. _____ Eileen usually doesn't eat anything before she leaves for work.
2. _____ She gives her daughter a cuddle before she leaves.
3. _____ It takes Eileen 20 minutes to walk to her local Tube station.
4. _____ Eileen's workplace is very close to the Tube station she travels to.
5. _____ Eileen doesn't like the drinks machine in the kitchen at work.
6. _____ She usually has toast for breakfast.
7. _____ Eileen's computer is clearly very hi-tech.
8. _____ Eileen and her colleagues process planning application forms.
9. _____ Eileen clearly finds her job very interesting.
10. _____ Eileen finds it difficult that her husband is her line manager.

B Gap-Fill

Eileen talks about her work colleagues.

Before you listen, try to predict which words, or which types of words (nouns, adjectives, prepositions, parts of verbs, etc.) will fill the gaps. Listen and check your answers.

1. Four of the people in Eileen's team do the _____, i.e. they enter information on the computer.
2. Eileen and her colleagues get _____ _____ _____.
3. One of Eileen's colleagues comes from _____.
4. The colleague from New Zealand has only worked in the planning department for a _____ _____ _____.
5. He shares a house with _____ _____.

C Questions

Eileen talks some more about her work and then her lunch break. Listen and answer the questions.

1. Which word does Eileen use to describe her work?
2. What does the team deal with, in addition to processing planning applications?
3. Where in Holloway Road does Eileen normally have lunch?

4. Who does she usually have lunch with?
5. Who started working at the Council first – Andy or Jane and Pat?
6. Do Andy and Eileen have any contact with Jane and Pat outside work?
7. What does Eileen say they talk about at lunch? (tick the correct options)

a) what they've read in the newspaper
b) their families
c) the weather
d) the food they're eating
e) annoying things at work
f) the weather
g) the pressure they're under at work

D Gap-Fill

Eileen talks about the rest of her working day. As with Exercise B, try to predict your answers before you listen.

1. Eileen says the work in the afternoon is the _____ as the morning – not very _____.
2. If they've had a really _____ day, someone will go to the _____ and they have _____ or something to cheer themselves up.
3. The Council doesn't like people eating at their _____ because of the computers.

E Questions

Eileen talks about getting home from work. Listen and answer the questions.

1. Who prepares the evening meal during the week?
2. Who is Max?
3. What does Andrew have to do while his parents are at work?

F Gap-Fill

Eileen talks about her husband's work.

As with Exercises B and D, try to predict your answers before you listen.

1. Andy usually leaves work at _____.
2. At the moment someone is _____ the work that Eileen and her colleagues do.
3. They want to find out how _____ it _____ to do each task.
4. Part of Andy's job is to go through all these figures and produce _____.
5. Andy starts work _____ than Eileen.

G True/False

Eileen talks about her children. Answer true or false. Be prepared to give reasons for your answers.

1. _____ Andy and Eileen usually have dinner with their children.
2. _____ Andrew has generally gone out by the time his parents come home.
3. _____ Hannah comes home from work before going to see her boyfriend.
4. _____ Hannah makes a point of seeing her parents at least once over the weekend.

G Gap-Fill

Eileen talks about evenings at home. As with Exercises B, D and F, try to predict your answers before you listen.

1. Eileen says 'We do _____ _____ sometimes.'
2. Andy is _____ by maps.
3. Eileen's _____ lives in Norfolk.
4. Eileen is finding television quite _____ at the moment.
5. In the evening Eileen reads or does the _____ or tidies _____.
6. She usually has the television on in the _____.
7. Eileen says she and Andy very _____ see their _____ these days.
8. She explains that both children have got their own _____ now.
9. Because work is quite _____ at the moment, Eileen says it's quite nice for her to just sit down and _____ in the evenings.
10. Eileen doesn't have a _____ _____ when she comes home, but she has occasionally _____ _____ on the sofa.

A Four features of an east London accent

Remember, a good language learner will realise that when a speaker produces one non-standard pronunciation feature, the speaker is likely to produce this feature in all other words in English containing that sound.

1. A typical feature of an east London accent is for the speaker not to pronounce the initial letter *h-* at the start of words such as *'ouse, 'ad, 'appy*, etc.

    Listen to these examples:

    > *I usually 'ave a shower.*
    > *and then 'e takes the dog out for a walk*
    > *and 'e's only been there a couple of weeks*
    > *sorts out 'is breakfast*

    How would a person with an east London accent say the following sentences?

    1. We're **hoping** to buy a new **house** next year.
    2. I **hope he** comes **home** soon.
    3. **How** was your **holiday**?

2. A second feature of an east London accent is a tendency to drop the final letter **-g** at the end of words. Listen to these examples:

    > *A typical day is the alarm **goin'** off at 7...*
    > *I don't talk much in the **mornin'.** I'm not a very happy person in the **mornin'.***
    > *So while the computer is **warmin'** up and **gettin'** ready...*
    > *and he walks him in the **mornin'***

    How would a person with an east London accent say the following sentences?

    1. Are you **coming** out tonight?
    2. Can we stop **walking** for a bit? I'm **getting** tired.
    3. We're **growing** our own tomatoes this year.

3. A tendency to use a vocalised /l/ when the /l/ sound is not at the start of a word.

    Instead of the normal /l/ sound in words such as *cradle* or *battle*, speakers with this accent tend to say *–ul*, *–uwl* or even *–uw* at the ends of words ending in the letters *–le*. Listen to these examples:

    > and a really old **kettle**
    > and he shares a, a house with eight **people**

    How would a person with an east London accent say the following sentences?

    1. Where's the baby's **rattle**?
    2. Oh no! Now I've dropped the **needle**.
    3. Would you like an **apple**?

4. Another feature of an east London accent (and many other British accents) is the *glottal stop*. A glottal stop happens when the speaker tightens his or her throat and very briefly stops the air from getting through. This results in the /t/ sound at the end of words such as *got* or *lot*, or the /t/ sound in words such as *bottle* or *kettle* not being fully pronounced. This can make it difficult for students to recognise words containing this feature. Listen to these examples:

    > ...and me continually knocking **it** off till **about** 8!
    > As long as you **get** in by 10 o'clock, you just do your seven hours from there.
    > So I usually **get** up **about** 8.
    > and then he takes the dog **out** for a walk
    > coffee, **chocolate**
    > I actually work in a planning **department** and we process um, applications forms...
    > And there's four of us **that** do the **input**...
    > he has to do a **lot** of figures
    > **Saturday** or Sunday

    How would a person with an east London accent say the following sentences?

    1. We've **got** a new **cat**.
    2. Would you like another **bottle** of **water**?
    3. Just give me a **little bit**, please.

A Gap-Fill

Fill in the blanks in these new sentences with words you heard during Eileen's interview. The words are listed in the box to help you.

alarm	busy	cakes	(to) chill	desk
disgusting	dozed off	flexitime	(a) lie down	(to) process
kettle	rarely	(to) remind	(a) ride	shower
socially	(to) sort out	(to) tidy	(to) stagger	stressful

1. I'm going to set the _____ for 6 as I've got to be in work for 7.
2. I need to bring some _____ in tomorrow because it's Sophie's birthday.
3. Our company has just announced it's going to introduce _____, so I'll be able to socialise more during the week in future.
4. We _____ cook meals from scratch these days because we're both so busy at work. We just buy ready-meals or get takeaways instead.
5. Our _____ is broken so we can only have baths at the moment.
6. I wanted to get my mother a helicopter _____ for her birthday, but they were charging 35 euros for a six-minute trip which I thought was a bit steep.
7. I'm just going to go for a _____ _____. I'm exhausted.
8. Could you try not to _____? I don't want the neighbours to see you drunk again.
9. There's a _____ smell coming from next door. Do you think we should phone the police?
10. I can't believe it takes them 10 weeks to _____ a passport application.
11. Are you very _____ at the moment? I could do with a chat.
12. I never meet my manager _____. I prefer to keep work separate from pleasure.
13. Your _____ is a real mess! I don't know how you can work like that.
14. Could you _____ me to call Claire tonight? I don't want to forget.
15. This freezer's in a terrible state. I need to _____ _____ what we've got in there.
16. Can you _____ up your bedroom, please? It's a disgrace.
17. I've had a really _____ day, so I'm just going to sit in the garden and _____ for a while.
18. Last night I went to put the _____ on and by the time I came back he'd _____ _____. I really think he's working too hard.

B Transformations

Change the word in each bracket that appeared in the interview to form a word that fits the gap, if necessary.

Here's an example to help you:

> *Example: I can make you a sandwich if you're (hunger)* ___hungry___.

1. Mike's the (lucky) _____ person I've ever met. He always lands on his feet.
2. They said on the weather forecast to expect (shower) _____ today, so don't forget your umbrella.
3. You're (stagger) _____ a bit. Do you want me to carry it for a while?
4. I've just (application) _____ for a new job with Network Rail.
5. We're thinking of (extensions) _____ our kitchen into the garden a little way, but it's going to cost a fortune.
6. There was a real air of (exciting) _____ before the match began.
7. Would I like to come white water rafting? No, thanks. That sounds a bit too (adventures) _____ to me.
8. Her new boyfriend's not very (friends) _____, is he?
9. Stop being so (annoyed) _____!
10. There seems to be a (tend) _____ now for people go on city breaks rather than longer holidays in the sun.
11. I forgot to pay the gas bill last month and they've already sent me two (reminder) _____.
12. They didn't tell us our work was being (monitor) _____, which was a bit unfair really.
13. This book is (fascinated)_____! You must read it.
14. My old teacher used to say 'If you're (boring) _____ you're boring', which was really annoying.
15. Try to be patient with her. She's really (stressful) _____ at the moment.

I: Can you tell me about a typical day, please?

E: A typical day... A typical day is the alarm going off at 7 **(1) and me continually knocking it off till about 8!** *(laughs)* Um, we're quite lucky. I work at _____ Council and we have what they call 'flexitime', so you can work 35 hours a week. So if... as long as you get in by 10 o'clock you just do your seven hours from there. So I usually get up about 8. I usually have a shower. Um, I don't talk much in the morning – I'm not a very happy person in the morning. Er, my daughter also gets up for work and, *(laughs)* and we don't talk to her either. So I usually have a shower first and then she has a shower. Um, my husband gets up, has a quick shower and then he takes the dog out for a walk. **(2) He escapes.** Um, I usually just have a cup of tea – I, I don't do... Um, I think my daughter and I **(3) grunt** at each other as we say goodbye. Um, I go to the station – it's, it's a 20-minute **(4) ride.** It's only a 20-minute ride on the Victoria line. Er, get off there and it's two minutes' walk from the station so **(5) I usually just stagger up there.** Um, we have a small kitchen there – it's got like a microwave. It's got this horrible coffee **(6) contraption** – you know, one of those machines that do coffee, chocolate – disgusting contraption – and a really old kettle. Um, so I usually have a cup of tea and I usually make those **(7) Ready–Brek** breakfasts there.

I: They're like warm break... porridge oats, or something?

E: Yeah, and you put them in the microwave.

I: Mmm, hmm.

E: I usually have that then, when I get into work because I'm awake. *(laughs)* So that's the first thing. So while the computer is warming up and getting ready I usually have a bowl of porridge and my cup of tea. **(8) That just gets me into line.** I actually work in **(9) a planning department** and we process um, application forms, so if people do extensions or **(10) dormers** or whatever and they, they send in application forms we process them. It's a really exciting job. *(laughs)* Er, there's um, six of us in the team. My husband is actually **(11) my line manager.**

I: Oh.

E: Um *(laughs)* It works out quite well, you know, with not too much of a problem. And there's four of us that do **(12) the input** and we get on very well. We have um, an African lady. We have a lady who actually lives in Islington. And we have **(13) a young lad** that's just started um, and I don't know much about him, but he's from New Zealand and he's only been there a couple of weeks. And he's just started. But he has porridge in the morning as well. And he shares a, a house with eight people, so I think he has quite a few adventures to come. Um, so basically that's what we do – we just work on the computer and um, it's quite busy – sort of input thing. And we, we deal with a lot of phone calls as well. We have a lot of people phone up, you know: 'Can I park my car in front of the window?' and 'Where's my application?' That, that sort of thing. We have lunch um, actually at a Greek cafe at the end, in Holloway Road. Um, they do sandwiches or they do... you can... national food as well. Sometimes we have a nice Greek salad or whatever.

I: You say 'we', so do you go for lunch with your husband?

E: Yeah, I go with my husband and actually two of the typists. It's um...

I: Oh.

E: My husband's worked at planning for about 30 years now and, and Jane and Pat have also... He's known them actually since they started, so they're quite good friends. So we tend to, you know... We're, we're friends socially as well. We see each other socially. So we tend to go to lunch. Sometimes um, we just talk about, you know, our families. Or sometimes we might – I don't know – there might be something at work **(14) that might**

annoy us or how much work we have. **(15) We have a little moan about that.** Um, the afternoon's basically the same as the morning, really. It's not very exciting. We don't have tea breaks as such. We just make our tea and our coffee as we will. If we have a really busy day we tend to go into the supermarket just up the road and get some cakes or something, just to make us feel a bit better. Um, they actually don't like you eating at your desk because of the computer, so we, we tend to turn round and eat at the non-desk and then turn round and go to the computer. *(laughs)*

I: Do you travel in with your husband in the morning?

E: No, we never travel in together.

I: Do you come home together?

E: No.

I: *(laughs)*

E: *(laughs)* Never, ever because the reason we don't come home is 'cos I cook the dinner usually.

I: Right.

E: Um, so I usually... I usually get in before him. Because he takes the dog out, as I say. He usually takes the dog out – **(16) the Labrador** – and he walks him in the morning. Um, takes him back, sorts out his breakfast and whatever. Um, Andrew, my son Andrew's just passed for university, so he's actually at home now. Um, but he usually stays in bed till about 12 or 1 o'clock. So he'll put Max in the back of the house and then go upstairs, wake Andrew up and remind him he's got to take the dog out and then, *(laughs)*, and then he comes into work. Andrew... Andy usually works till about half-past six 'cos he actually is a line manager and um, he has to do a lot of figures. We have to, we have to... They're monitoring our work at the moment to see how long it takes us to do each job um, to see the volume of work that we're dealing with, and Andy has to sort all these figures out, so he's quite busy doing statistics at the moment and...

I: And does he normally start later than you?

E: Yeah, he usually gets in about half-past... well, 10, usually.

I: Right.

E: He usually gets in about 10 o'clock.

I: So you come home and you cook the dinner, and then Andy comes home a bit later and...

E: Yeah.

E: ...takes the dog for a walk. And then... Do, do the four of you have dinner together? You and your children?

E: Very, very rarely. Um, usually when I come home from work Andrew is usually out. He's usually out with one of his friends or whatever. Um, my daughter's um, has a boyfriend and she goes straight up to his house. We don't usually see Hannah till about 12, 1 o'clock... If she comes home. Sometimes she don't come home at all. Er, we may see her over the weekend – Saturday or Sunday.

I: Um, what do you do in the evening af... after dinner, you and your husband?

E: Not very exciting. Um, most evenings... we do go out sometimes, but most evenings I usually just sit down, really. We just er... *(laughs)* Andy reads. He's quite um... Andy reads a lot. Andy actually does read a lot. He's fascinated with maps. He likes maps. And he likes um, to read about different towns in for example, if... when... Because we were going down my sister's to Norfolk um, we were going to go to Hunstanton, so he will, he will read that up. He'll go on the web and actually read up on it and where we can go and what we can see. Um, the television is actually a bit boring at the moment, so...

I: And what do you do? You said you just sit down, but do you read as well?

E: Yeah, I read. Or I might do some washing or tidy up, but.... It's... There's not, there's not really much on the telly. Sometimes I do. **(17) I usually just put it on just for background, really.**

I: Um, what time do you go to bed?

E: About 11, half-eleven.

I: So that's actually before your daughter's come home quite often.

E: Yeah, we very rarely see the kids. *(laughs)* Which is

quite nice. Well... But we very rarely see... because they, you know, they're at an age now, they've sort of got their own life, really. It's, it's, it's quite stressful at work, so it's quite nice just to sit down and **(18) chill**, really.

I: What, what's the latest you leave work?

E: The latest? Ten o'clock.

I: Oh, sorry, leave work – when you finish in the afternoon.

E: Um, half-five. I, don't... I can't do any longer than that. It's... *(laughs)*

I: Do you have a... ever have **(19) a lie down** when you come home?

E: **(20) I have dozed off** on the sofa.

I: Right.

E: I have done that, yeah. *(laughs)*

1 **and me continually knocking it off till about 8!** – and me pressing the 'snooze' button again and again
2 **He escapes** – He gets away from it all. (i.e. the rather tense atmosphere in the kitchen between Eileen and her daughter)
3 **(to) grunt** – to make a short, low sound instead of speaking
4 **(a) ride** – a journey in a car, bus, Tube train etc.
5 **I usually just stagger up there** – To stagger means to walk with a lack of balance, for example if you are drunk or you are carrying something very heavy. Here Eileen means she's not walking 100% because it's still quite early in the morning.
6 **(a) contraption** –a machine or device that looks very old-fashioned or is awkward to use
7 **Ready-Brek** – a brand of ready-made porridge – a thick, soft food made from oats boiled in water or milk which is eaten hot for breakfast
8 **That just gets me into line** – *(unusual usage)* That gets me up and running for the day.
9 **a planning department** – a department of local government which deals with planning applications. If you want to put up a new building or make substantial alterations to an existing building you have to apply to this department for planning permission.
10 **dormers** – A lot of people are now turning the attic or the loft of their house (i.e. the empty space under the roof) into a spare room or rooms and these have dormer windows, i.e. sloping windows in the roof. So Eileen is using dormers to mean loft extensions.
11 **my line manager** – the person who manages me directly
12 **the input** – the information or date which is entered onto the computer
13 **a young lad** – a boy or young man
14 **that might annoy us** – that might make us cross or angry
15 **We have a little moan about that** – We complain a bit about that.
16 **the Labrador** – a big yellow, brown or black dog with short hair (often used as guide dogs for the blind)
17 **I usually just put it on for background, really** – I usually just put it on to break the silence.
18 **(to) chill** – to relax
19 **a lie down** –a short period of rest or sleep, usually in bed
20 **I have dozed off** – I have occasionally found myself falling asleep... Generally *to doze* means to fall asleep for a short period in the daytime, often while sitting up.

UNIT 10 Peadar

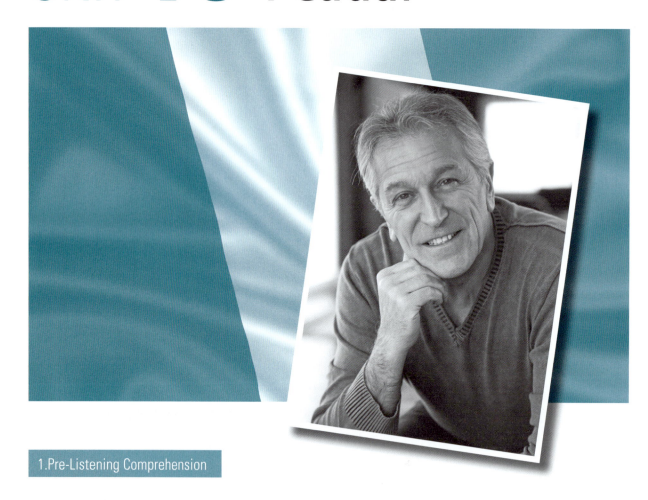

The name Peadar is the Irish or Gaelic form of Peter. Peadar comes from County Cork in the Irish Republic but moved to England at the age of 17 to see life outside Ireland. He works on building sites in the London area where he specialises in digging tunnels. Peadar has a strong Irish accent despite having lived in London for forty years. Another challenge for the students is that people from County Cork are renowned for speaking extremely fast.

A Discussion

Discuss these questions in pairs or small groups and share your answers with the class:

1. What do you think of when you hear the word 'Ireland'?
2. What does an Irish accent sound like?
3. What are the advantages and disadvantages of working on a building site?
4. Peadar gets up very early in the morning and does hard, physical work all day. What do you think he does in the evenings?

B Normalisation –
Questions

This exercise is designed to help you get used to Peadar's voice.

Peadar talks about the start of his working day. Listen and answer the questions.

1. What time does Peadar get up on a work day?
2. What does he have instead of breakfast?
3. How does he get to work?
4. What does he have before he starts work?
5. How long does he work before his first break?

2. Listening Comprehension

A True/False

Peadar talks about his day at work. Answer true or false. Be prepared to give reasons for your answers.

1. _____ Peadar never buys food for lunch.
2. _____ He always has a cheese sandwich for his morning break.
3. _____ His working day is from 8am to about 4pm.
4. _____ He generally has less than an hour for lunch.
5. _____ He has to make his own way home from work.

B Gap–Fill

Peadar talks about his journey home.

Before you listen, try to predict which words, or which types of words (nouns, adjectives, prepositions, parts of verbs, etc.) will fill the gaps. Listen and check your answers.

1. Peadar never knows exactly when he'll get _____ – it all _____ on which part of London he's working in.
2. It can take him up to _____ _____ to get home from Putney, depending on the _____.
3. Peadar mentions two tunnels – the Rotherhithe Tunnel and the _____ Tunnel.
4. He usually has his _____ about 30 minutes after getting home.

C True/False

Peadar talks about what he does in the evenings. Answer true or false. Be prepared to give reasons for your answers.

1. _____ Peadar can't stand watching television.
2. _____ It takes him 10 minutes to drive to his local pub.
3. _____ Peadar goes out for a drink every night.
4. _____ He only drinks Guinness in the pub.
5. _____ When he goes home, Peadar usually has a small whisky.
6. _____ Peadar's wife is generally in bed when he gets home.
7. _____ Peadar has less than six hours' sleep a night.
8. _____ He has had the same routine for 14 years.

Hertfordshire Libraries
Hatfield Library
Kiosk 2

Borrowed Items 24/02/2015 11:21:12
XXXXX1640

Item Title	Due Date
The best friend wish	05/03/2015
Real lives, real listening.	17/03/2015
Collins practice tests for	17/03/2015
English grammar in use	17/03/2015

Indicates items borrowed today
Please remember to unlock
our DVDs and CDs

Enquiries and Renewals phone number
0300 123 4049
go to : www.hertsdirect.org

A **Features of English spoken by an (older) Irishman**

Nowadays it seems that young people from the Irish Republic, i.e. people in their 30s and below, have acquired a more mid-Atlantic accent than their parents and grandparents. It is interesting that Peadar has retained his strong Irish accent some 40 years after moving to the UK.

Ask your students to consider why Peadar has not lost his accent.

1   **Saying *has* instead of *have***

Note how Peadar uses has instead of have in the following extracts:

> *I get up at 5.30 in the morning and I **has** a, a cup of tea and a fag.*
> ***Has** our sandwiches at 10.*
> *and then... then I **has** my dinner*
> *I **has** a shower, watch television*

2   **Pronouncing the initial *th-* sound in words such *think* (/θ/) as the /t/ sound in words such as *tame***

Note how Peadar pronounces **thirty** in the following extract:

> *I get up at five-**thirty** in the morning...*

Peadar would pronounce **through** as **true** and **thought** as **taught.**

Remember, a good language learner will realise that when a speaker produces one non-standard pronunciation feature, the speaker is likely to produce this feature in all other words in English containing that sound.

How might Peadar and other people of his age from his part of Ireland pronounce the following words?

Thursday three thumb thorn throat throw

A Transformations

Change the word in each bracket that appeared in the interview to form a word that fits the gap, if necessary.

Here's an example to help you:

> *Example: I can make you a sandwich if you're (hunger)* **hungry**.

1. I hate (get) _____ up in the mornings when it's dark.
2. Is it OK if we (picked) _____ you up at 6.30 tomorrow?
3. What a beautiful rose bush! Do you know what (varies) _____ it is?
4. Can you give me a (roughly) _____ idea of when you'll be arriving?
5. (depends) _____ on the weather we'll either have a barbecue or a casserole indoors.
6. The kids were playing with the hosepipe in the garden yesterday and they took great pleasure in (shower) _____ me with water when I came home.
7. You'd get a lot more done if you didn't spend so much time (chat) to your friends on your mobile all the time.

B Prepositions and adverbs

Insert the correct preposition or adverb into the gaps.

1. What time will you be _____ tonight?
2. I was just coming home _____ work when I saw Paul, so we went _____ a drink.
3. I'm just going to phone Kate. I need to have a chat _____ her about next Sunday.
4. What would you like _____ your sandwiches – cheese or ham?
5. I'm starving! I haven't had anything to eat _____ ages.
6. Anders was just telling me _____ his holiday. It sounds fantastic.
7. I normally go _____ work _____ bus, but the traffic's been so bad lately I've been walking _____ work instead.
8. Patrick only gets half an hour _____ lunch.
9. Shall we have beef or lamb _____ dinner tomorrow? It's _____ to you.
10. I was really scared the first time we went _____ the Channel Tunnel, but now I've got used _____ it.

I: Peadar, can you tell me about a typical day? What time you get up and everything?

P: I get up at five-thirty in the morning...

I: Uh, huh.

P: ... and I has a, a cup of tea and **(1) a fag.**

I: Mmm, hmm.

P: And I'm picked up at half-past six.

I: By car?

P: By **(2) van**, working van.

I: Right.

P: Firm's van. And we go to work and we have a cup of tea and we start work at eight o'clock. Has our sandwiches at ten.

I: Mmm, hmm. You take in your own sandwiches?

P: Yeah.

I: What kind of sandwiches do you have?

P: Well, it varies - cheese, ham - varies. And um, have the sandwich at 10 o'clock and work away till dinner time and... finish around four o'clock, like.

I: What time's dinner time?

P: Well, it... one o'clock, **(3) roughly**, you know.

I: And do you get an hour for lunch?

P: Oh, it is up to ourselves, really, like, you know. We'll take half hour, 40 minutes. It all depends and er, that's it and come home and...

I: So you finish at four?

P: Four o'clock, yeah.

I: And you get **(4) a lift** home in the van?

P: Yeah, the same firm's van again.

I: So what time are you back home?

P: It all depends. We could be working in **(5) Putney** – could be an hour and a half, two hours. It all depends what part of London we're in and traffic, like.

I: What's the latest you get home?

P: It could be six, it could be half past six. Traffic, you know. It could get... You could come through

(6) Rotherhithe Tunnel and you can have a breakdown anywhere. **(7) Blackwall Tunnel** and...

I: Do you have dinner as soon as you get in?

P: Well, not straight away, but **(8) the missus** know *[sic – knows]* what time I'll be in roughly and it'll be about a half an hour before I'm in, and then I has my dinner.

I: What do you do after dinner?

P: I has a shower, watch television, and **(9) then I go up for my few pints**.

I: In your local pub?

P: In my local pub.

I: How far is it from where you live?

P: About 10 minutes' walk.

I: OK. Right. You do that every day?

P: Every day.

I: And you're an Irishman, so what do you drink in your pub?

P: I drink **(10) Guinness**, the best of it.

I: *(Laughs)* OK. And you get home. What do you do when you get home?

P: I has two *(laughs)*. I have... watch the television, have a cup of tea and I go to bed.

I: Is your wife home when you come home?

P: Yeah.

I: Yeah. So you have a chat with her as well.

P: Yeah.

I: And you go to bed what, what's, what time do you go to bed?

P: Roughly around 12.

I: OK. That's brilliant.

P: And the same thing next day and the same for the last 40 years! *(laughs)*

I: *(laughs)* Thanks a lot!

1   **a fag** – a slang word for a cigarette
2   **(a) van** – a medium-sized road vehicle used for carrying goods which has no windows at the side or the back
3   **roughly** – approximately
4   **a lift**– a free journey in somebody else's vehicle, as in *'Would you like a lift as it's raining?'*
5   Put**ney** – a district in south-west London
6   **(the) Rotherhithe Tunnel** – a road tunnel beneath the River Thames in east London connecting the London Borough of Tower Hamlets north of the river with the London Borough of Southwark
7   **(the) Blackwall Tunnel** – another road tunnel beneath the River Thames in east London connecting the London Borough of Tower Hamlets north of the river with the London Borough of Greenwich
8   **the mis**s**us** – a slang word for *my wife*
9   **then I go up for my few pints** – then I go out for a few pints (Beer and lager in the UK is sold in a half-pint or a pint measure. A pint is equivalent to just under half a litre.)
10 Guin**ness** – a popular Irish dark beer known as 'stout' which has a creamy head

A Place I Know Well

UNIT **11** Trudie

Trudie is a very successful businesswoman who works in the City — the financial centre of London. In this interview she talks about her home and the area in London where she lives. Trudie has an RP accent and speaks quite quickly at times.

A Schema building – predicting which words will come up

Which 10 of these 20 words do you expect to hear during the interview?

brick-built, builders, a burglar alarm, a church, converted, a cul-de-sac, dentures, a diet, feathers, files, greenery, a hallway, ink, nylon, a patio, perfume, poverty, semi-detached, a strike, toothache

B Normalisation – anticipating the next word

 to

This exercise is designed to help you get used to Trudie's voice.

Listen to Track 276. There is a word missing from the end of each excerpt. When you hear the beep sound, try to guess the missing word and write it down. Then listen to Track 277 to check your answers. How well did you guess?

1. _____
2. _____
3. _____
4. _____
5. _____
6. _____
7. _____
8. _____

C Discussion

You now know a little bit about Trudie from the Introduction and from hearing her speak. No doubt you have subconsciously formed your own conclusions about her. Discuss these questions in pairs or small groups and share your answers with the class:

1. What do you expect Trudie's home to be like?
2. What do you expect the road where Trudie lives to be like?
3. What do you expect the area where Trudie lives to be like?

A True/False

(278)

Trudie talks about her home. Answer true or false. Be prepared to give reasons for your answers.

1. _____ Trudie's house was built in the first half of the 20th century.
2. _____ Trudie likes the pebble-dash effect on the front of her house.
3. _____ Trudie has clearly made a lot of changes to her house.
4. _____ When Trudie bought the house it had four bedrooms.
5. _____ The reception room is divided by French doors.
6. _____ Downstairs there is a huge kitchen.

B Gap-Fill

(279)

Trudie continues to talk about her home and the road where she lives.

Before you listen, try to predict which words, or which types of words (nouns, adjectives, prepositions, parts of verbs, etc.) will fit in the gaps. Then listen and check your answers.

1. Trudie has _____ the garage into a _____ room.
2. There is a _____ downstairs.
3. Trudie says the _____ is a reasonable size.
4. The _____ is about 50 foot long.
5. Access to the garage is from the _____ round the _____ of Trudie's house.
6. Trudie doesn't know how _____ the _____ is at the end of her _____.
7. The _____ at the _____ of the house is quite small.
8. Trudie's road is quite quiet because it's a _____.

C True/False

(280)

Trudie talks about her neighbours. Answer true or false. Be prepared to give reasons for your answers.

1. _____ Trudie thinks her neighbours are wonderful.
2. _____ The woman across the street complained about the noise Trudie's builders made.
3. _____ Trudie felt the builders could have worked harder.
4. _____ Trudie's street is a popular location for families with children.
5. _____ Trudie gets on very well with the mixed-nationality couple who live opposite.

6. _____ The couple across the road clearly trust Trudie.
7. _____ Trudie's next-door-neighbour had nothing to do with her after she complained about the building work.

D Gap-Fill

Trudie talks about East Finchley. As with Exercise A, try to predict which words, or which types of words, will fit in the gaps. Then listen and check your answers.

1. East Finchley is one of the many _____ of London.
2. There is a _____ of shops in the _____ Street and also a _____.
3. Trudie says East Finchley is a _____ community.
4. Some people have _____ there _____ their lives there while others have recently moved in.
5. A lot of the houses in East Finchley are being _____ _____.
6. East Finchley isn't a very _____ area, but it does have a lot of family houses which are quite _____.
7. It doesn't _____ long to get to the _____ from East Finchley.
8. You can travel to the _____ of London in around 40 minutes.
9. There is a _____ station in East Finchley.
10. East Finchley is quite _____ up.
11. Trudie says Muswell Hill is a good place to go for _____.
12. The _____ from Muswell Hill on a clear day is _____ fantastic, according to Trudie.

E Questions

Trudie talks about the parks in East Finchley. Listen and answer the questions.

1. Where do the antique fairs take place in Alexander Park?
2. What is the name of the woods near Trudie's home?
3. What is the main aim of the East Finchley Festival?
4. What can you buy to eat at the Festival?
5. How long does it take Trudie to get to Hampstead Heath by car?
6. What is special about the concerts at Kenwood House?
7. What lies between the audience and the orchestra at these concerts?
8. What usually happens at the end of each concert?
9. Do you get a refund if the weather's too bad for the concert to take place?

A Negative statements with a positive meaning

It is very common in British English to use negative statements instead of positive statements, as in these examples, with their actual meanings:

> **I don't feel very well.** = I feel really ill.

> **I haven't got much money on me.** = I have almost no money on me.

> **I'm not very hungry.** = I'm quite full up from when I last ate.

Look at Trudie's use of negative statements taken from the interview:

> *It's not particularly attractive...*
> *I don't have really much garden to the front of the house...*
> *there aren't really many cars coming down the road*
> *she didn't really like the noise*
> *There's aren't actually many children in my street.*
> *It wouldn't take you very long to get to the countryside.*

Now try to make up your own examples of negative statements with positive meanings.

B Qualifying statements

It is also very common in British English to qualify statements rather than to make direct statements. This is probably one of the reasons British people have a reputation for being reserved.

Trudie uses the word *quite* throughout her interview. (NB This is not the quite = exactly/precisely meaning, but a way of qualifying the following word to make it less strong.)

> *quite nice, quite noisy, quite nice, quite close, quite big and spacious*

She also makes a number of qualified statements:

> *I do actually know quite a few of my neighbours.*
> *East Finchley is probably what you would perhaps call the suburbs of London.*
> *it's probably not necessarily the most fashionable area in London*

C Intensifying statements

At other times in the interview Trudie speaks very enthusiastically about certain things. Look at these examples:

> *he's absolutely lovely*
> *you really, really are high up here*
> *an absolutely fantastic view of London*
> *you can see for absolutely miles*
> *And that's huge. I mean that is absolutely massive.*
> *fantastic music*

Now try to make up your own examples of intensifying statements.

D The passive

There are a number of examples of the passive in the interview:

> *It was actually built in 1923.* **(simple past passive)**

> *The garage has been converted into a breakfast room.* **(present perfect simple passive)**

> *The houses are gradually being done up.* **(present continuous passive)**

> *East Finchley Festival is held in the summer.* **(present simple passive)**

Now try to make your own examples featuring these passive tenses.

E To have something done

We use this construction when someone does something for us. Common examples are:

'Have you had your hair cut?'

(Not 'Did you cut your hair?' This is a common mistake made by non-native English speakers. It implies that the person you are talking to cut their own hair. Definitely not a compliment!)

'We're having our living room decorated next week.'

'Paul had his wisdom teeth taken out last week so he won't be eating peanuts for a while.'

Now look at these examples from Trudie's interview:

I was having some building work done...

But the thing is, when you have building work done it is quite noisy.

Now try to make up some sentences using this construction.

F Word stress

Every word of more than two syllables in English has one prominent stress – the primary stress. There may also be a secondary stress. Mark the prominent stress in these words taken from Trudie's interview:

1.	absolutely	8.	fashionable
2.	attractive	9.	fantastic
3.	classical	10.	festival
4.	community	11.	necessarily
5.	converted	12.	orchestra
6.	countryside	13.	particularly
7.	exhibition	14.	performances

London

A Dictation

 to

At times in her interview Trudie speaks very quickly and consequently some words are not pronounced clearly.

Work with a partner. First listen to the excerpts from Trudie's interview and write down how many words there are in each item. Then listen and write down the words you hear. After that check your answers with another pair.

1. (___ words) _____
2. (___ words) _____
3. (___ words) _____
4. (___ words) _____
5. (___ words) _____

B Elision

In fast spoken English a process called 'elision' often occurs, most frequently with words ending in –d and –t. This results in these sounds not being pronounced when the next word begins with a consonant. This can make it difficult for you to recognise individual words in a stream of speech – even those words which you use regularly when speaking.

Listen to these excerpts from the interview and use a tick (✓) or a cross (✗) to mark whether the final –d or –t of words are pronounced or not pronounced. The relevant letters have been put in capitals for ease of reference.

1. it's a brick-builT house ( )
2. On the fronT it has something calleD pebble-dash… ( ) ( )
3. and thaT is sort of jusT like stone ( ) ( )
4. It's a semi-detacheD house. ( )
5. which has been converteD into a breakfasT room ( ) ( )
6. It has a very large bedroom at the fronT of the house… ( )
7. which useD to be two bedrooms ( )
8. And then nexT door to that we have a kitchen… ( )
9. AnD then at the back I have a garden… ( )
10. there's a roaD that leads rounD the back of my house ( ) ( )

C Glottal stop

289

Another feature of natural spoken English is the *glottal stop*. A glottal stop happens when the speaker tightens his or her throat and very briefly stops the air from getting through. This results in the /t/ sound at the end of words such as *got* or *lot*, or the /t/ sound in words such as *bottle* or *kettle* not being fully pronounced. This can make it difficult for you to recognise words containing this feature.

Try to fill in the gaps before you listen to the excerpts, and discuss your predictions with your teacher. Then listen to check your answers.

1. I do have something _____ used to be a garage attached to my house, _____ I've now converted that into a breakfast room.
2. _____ has three bedrooms.
3. It's _____ one bathroom upstairs.
4. _____ I've knocked it into one huge one
5. And then next door to _____ we have a kitchen...
6. I'm not sure when it was _____, _____ pretty, pretty old.

Can you produce a glottal stop?

D Weak forms, i.e. unstressed grammatical (or function) words

290

The words between the stressed content words are known as grammatical (or function) words. These are the words which bind the speaker's content words together and they are a major contributing factor to the rhythm of English speech. These grammatical/function words tend to be unstressed, which makes them difficult to distinguish. Listen to these excerpts and fill in the missing grammatical/function words.

NB Because this is a listening training exercise don't try to predict the answers before you listen!

1. Um, _____ you describe _____ house _____ _____?
2. _____ the end of _____ street _____ _____ very nice church.
3. I _____ _____ _____ building work done...
4. I wish they did stay until 5 o'clock, _____ _____ _____ _____.
5. _____ _____ other side _____ _____ _____ very nice young family...

6. _____ it _____ take _____ very long _____ get _____ _____ countryside...

7. You _____ see _____ Docklands, _____ _____ see sort _____ all _____.

8. _____ got a little bit _____ green where people _____ kick _____ _____ football

9. you _____ go _____ have _____ cup _____ tea...

10. _____ _____ you call it!

11. ..._____ it _____ be a really nice evening, if _____ fine weather. _____ _____ _____ always fine weather.

A Gap-Fill

Fill in the blanks in these new sentences with words you heard during Trudie's interview. The words are listed in the box to help you.

attractive	keys	knocked	married	neighbours
noisy	park	patio	stone	switch

1. Sorry, can we just stop a minute? I've got a _____ in my shoe.
2. I know he's not very _____, but he's got a lovely personality.
3. We rang the doorbell and _____ on the door, but there was no answer.
4. We usually have dinner on the _____ in the summer, unless it's raining.
5. Where we live in London you need a permit to _____ on the street.
6. When we go on holiday we get our _____ to water the garden and then we do theirs when they're away.
7. I don't think they're _____ — neither of them wears a ring.
8. I've lost my _____ and our neighbour who has a spare set is away, so I'll have to call a locksmith out.
9. How do you _____ it off? Is it this button here?
10. The kids were so _____ the teacher had to shout to make herself heard.

B Transformations

Change the word in each bracket that appeared in the interview to form a word that fits the gap, if necessary.

Here's an example to help you:

*Example: I can make you a sandwich if you're (hunger) **hungry**.*

1. I had to give the police a (describe) _____ of the man I saw because they think he was the getaway driver.
2. We're having some (built) _____ work done, so it's a bit difficult to have anyone to stay at the moment.
3. Most of my friends think Robbie Williams is gorgeous, but I can't see the (attractive) _____ myself.
4. I wish I had a (converted) _____ to drive in the summer, so I could put the top down and get a suntan.
5. Every time we turn our central heating on the pipes start (knocked) _____. I think we've got an airlock somewhere.

6. The beach is no longer (access) _____ by car, so we'll have to go on foot.
7. I was rather (alarm) _____ when I (switch) _____ the lights on and nothing happened, but then I realised there was a power cut.
8. Are flared trousers in or out of (fashionable) _____ at the moment?
9. The one disadvantage with our cottage is that we don't have enough (spacious) _____.
10. I love this time of year when all the (leafy) _____ turn red and yellow.
11. My spatial (aware) _____ is really poor, which is why I'm no good at (park) _____.
12. I'm a bit short of (fund) _____ at the moment. Can you lend me £20?
13. Are you the (owns) _____ of this car?
14. Everybody's very (neighbours) _____ in this street. We're always popping in and out of each other's houses.

C The Passive

Put the verbs in brackets into the correct passive tense.

1. I think he (to operate on) _____ tomorrow morning.
2. The door (to shut) _____ at midnight, so if you come back late you'll have to ring the bell and the night porter will let you in.
3. My car (to repair) _____ so I couldn't fetch her from the station, unfortunately.
4. Have you heard about Peter? He (to fire) _____!
5. Our local swimming pool (to suppose) _____ (to heat) _____, but it gets perishing cold in winter.
6. Penicillin (to invent) _____ by Sir Alexander Fleming.
7. Last year all our courgettes (to eat) _____ by snails so we're not growing them this year.
8. I don't think this bed (to change) _____! I'm going to call reception and complain.
9. I'm sure I (to knock out) _____ in the first round, but I'll give it my best shot.
10. Breakfast (to serve) _____ between 7 and 10am.
11. So while our very important visitors (to show) _____ around the facilities we were frantically trying to get hold of the catering company to find out what had happened to the lunch that, according to our records, (to order) _____ five weeks ago.

I: Um, can you describe your house to me? Because I've never seen it.

T: OK. I live in a 1920s house. It was actually built in 1923. And it's a brick-built house. On the front it has something called **(1) pebble-dash** and that is sort of just like stone. It's quite grey. It's not particularly attractive, actually, on the front. Um... And the windows are small, paned windows – about four-by-four little panes of glass and eight panes of glass per window. It's a semi-detached house. I do have something that used to be a garage attached to my house, **(2) but I've now converted that into a breakfast room**. It has three bedrooms. It has a very large bedroom at the front of the house which used to be two bedrooms, and **(3) I knocked it into one**. It's got one bathroom upstairs. And then downstairs it has one very large **(4) reception room**, which used to again be two reception rooms, but I've knocked it into one huge one which goes from the front of the house to the back of the house. And the back half of the reception room has er, large **(5) French doors** leading on to a **(6) patio**. And then next door to that we have a kitchen, which is a reasonable sized-kitchen, which has a door leading again out to the back of the house. And then **(7) adjoining that** is the garage which has been converted into a breakfast room. We also have **(8) a downstairs cloakroom** and a reasonable size hallway. And then at the back I have a garden which is probably, what? About 50 foot long and within that garden there is also a garage where I can park my car. You get access to the garage because there's a road that leads round the back of my house and the other houses along the street. At the end of my street there's a very nice church – quite old. I'm not sure when it was built, but pretty, pretty old. And that's quite nice because, you know, there's lots of greenery and everything. And um, I don't have really much garden to the front of the house, but that doesn't really matter because there aren't really many cars coming down this road 'cos this road's a cul... **(9) cul-de-sac** so you only really come down the road if you live here, and you can't get access to anywhere else.

I: Have you got nice neighbours?

T: I have quite nice neighbours, yes. Um, **(10) the lady who's adjoined to me** complains to me sometimes. Er, I was having some building work done, but she didn't really like the noise. But the thing is, when you have building work done it is quite noisy.

I: Mmm.

T: But it only happened from 9 o'clock to 5 o'clock. It didn't happen beyond 5 o'clock 'cos then the builders always went home – actually probably about 4 o'clock. I wish they did stay to 5 o'clock, but they never did. To the other side I've got a very nice young family with um, it's just a couple with a little girl who's, what? Three years old. There aren't actually many children in my street. Um, she... There's her, and then there are a couple of children at the house at the end of the street. And then across the road I have a very nice neighbour who's Greek. And he's absolutely lovely. He's married to a very nice Turkish lady. And um, they are really, really nice. So I look after his keys when he's away, so if his burglar alarm goes off I can switch it off for him, or call the police. Um, I do actually know quite a few of my neighbours. I even know other people down the road and, you know, **(11) we do have the odd gathering**. My next-door neighbour, it's [sic – it was] her 70th birthday what, probably two months ago and she had a big party in a... not in her house, but in a, **(12) a venue** nearby, and all the neighbours in the street went, which was really, really nice. And people who'd left the street actually came back and visited, so that was great.

I: And quite unusual for London.

T: Very unusual. But I've actually been very lucky um, with my neighbours, so um, I'm... sort of quite happy. But maybe that's 'cos I'm a really friendly person.

I: Mmm. Right. You live in East Finchley. I've never been there. Can you describe the area?

T: Yeah. Um, East Finchley is probably what you would perhaps call the suburbs of London. It's um, very green, leafly [sic – leafy]. It's a village, or town within itself, you know, it has a row of shops. Um, it has its own community. So you have a High Street and you have, you know, your churches, you have your supermarket. You have your own schools and all the services. There are... It's basically a mixed community in that there are people who've lived here all their life, but then obviously you've got the people who are new and incoming. **(13) The houses are sort of gradually being done up, probably over time**. It's, it's probably not necessarily the most fashionable area in London er, however, it does have nice family houses, **(14) quite spacious houses**, and er, you know, it's green and leafy and it wouldn't take you very long to get to the countryside, you know, into north London, you know, or (unclear) and **(15) Hertfordshire**. So I think that's probably why people live here. And it's only, what, 40 minutes, 30 minutes, 40 minutes from the centre of London. You know, it has **(16) a Tube line**, which is nice. It's very high up as well. You know you really, really are high up here. If you go to the next sort of shopping area along - **(17) Muswell Hill** - you can have an absolutely fantastic view of London. You can see **(18) the Docklands**, you can see sort of all around. You know on a clear day you can see for absolutely miles. So...

I: Have you got any nice parks here?

T: We have um, Alexander Park er, which is quite near, nearby er, which is quite big and spacious. And it has a sort of exhibition hall and everything. That's quite useful 'cos they have lots of **(19) antique fairs** and things like that there. And it does have

sort of nice greenery. In East Finchley itself we have one... I'd... We only actually have one little park that I'm aware of which is Cherry Tree, Cherry Tree Woods, which is quite nice. So you've got the woods and you've got a little bit of green where people can kick about a football. And there's a little cafe there – you can go and have a cup of tea if you've [sic - you're] walking your dogs. And every year they have the er, East Finchley Festival there, which is held in the summer, which is just basically **(20) a fund-raising event**, but, you know, they have a few local bands playing and they have um, people giving little sort of um... What do you call it? Um, oh, what do you call it? Performances. [laughs] That's what you call it! You know, the local children give a dance performance, or whatever. And then people have **(21) stalls** where they, you know, sell home-made cakes or have **(22) a tombola** and just er, **(23) raise proceeds for a local cause**, which is very good.

I: Hmm. Do you always go to that festival?

T: Um, if I'm around I do go, yes.

I: OK. And I think um, Hampstead Heath is quite close, isn't it?

T: It is. That's about, what? A 10-minute walk away, maybe a 15-minute walk away. Five-minute drive. And that's huge. I mean that is absolutely massive. And they have um, **(24) Kenwood House** there, which is an old house which... I think that's **(25) English Heritage**, I think, owns that. And that's very nice to look around and in the summer they have open-air concerts there. They have classical concerts. They have a lake and then they have **(26) an orchestra bowl** beyond the lake. And that's really lovely 'cos you can take a picnic there in the evening and listen to some fantastic music. And it ranges from jazz, classic or just, say, theme tunes from films and things. And they normally end the performance with some fireworks and it can be a really nice evening. If it's fine weather. But it's not always fine weather.

I: What happens if it rains?

T: If it rains you don't go and you lose your money for your ticket.

I: So it's a bit of a risk.

T: It is a bit of a risk.

1   **pebble-dash** – a covering of pebbles (small round stones) in cement
2   **but I've now converted that [the garage] into a breakfast room** – but I have now changed that into a breakfast room
3   **I knocked it into one**. – She (or more probably the builders) knocked down the wall between the two original bedrooms and made it into one large bedroom.
4   **(a) reception room** – (formal) a room in a house where people can sit together (informal) a living room
5   **French doors** – a pair of doors with panes of glass which usually open from the back or side of the house into the garden
6   **(a) patio** – an area outside a house with a solid floor, but no roof, where you can sit outside in good weather
7   **adjoining that** – (in this case) next to the kitchen
8   **a downstairs cloakroom** – a polite word for a toilet
9   **(a) cul-de-sac** – a road with only one entrance and exit
10 **the lady who's adjoined to me** – the lady who lives next door to me
11 **we do have the odd gathering** – we all meet up socially sometimes and do something together
12 **a venue** – a place where a public event happens
13 **The houses are sort of gradually being done up, probably over time**. – The houses are slowly being renovated, i.e. modernised.
14 **quite spacious houses** – quite large houses
15 **Hertfordshire** – a county to the north of London
16 **a Tube line** – an underground train service into London
17 **Muswell Hill** –a suburb in north London less than 10 kilometres from central London
18 **the Docklands** – The development which has grown over the past 30 years on the site of the old London docks. The areas includes Canary Wharf and other skyscrapers and the O2 Arena.
19 **antique fairs** – public events where people buy and sell antiques
20 **a fund-raising event** – an event intended to raise money for charity
21 **stalls** – a large table displaying goods for sale at a fair, market, etc.
22 **a tombola** – a game in which people buy tickets with numbers on in the hope that their ticket will have the same number as a prize
23 **(to) raise proceeds for a local cause** – to raise money for a good cause in the local area, e.g. a nearby children's hospital
24 **Kenwood House** – a beautiful 18th century house situated on Hampstead Heath, a large ancient natural park in north London with spectacular views over the city
25 **English Heritage** – a Government-funded organisation whose mission is to protect England's historical buildings and archaeological sites
26 **an orchestra bowl** - a large round theatre without a roof which is used for outdoor concerts, e.g. the Hollywood Bowl

UNIT 12 Laura and Francis

Laura is a project manager from Vancouver married to Francis, a professional architectural photographer from the village of Millers Falls in Massachusetts. They live just outside Seattle in Washington State in the north-west of the USA. In this interview they talk about Seattle and their recent visit to London.

A **Schema building –**
True/False

How much do you know about Seattle? Mark the following statements True or False.

1. Seattle is the biggest city in the state of Washington.
2. Seattle is less than 50 kilometres from the US-Canadian border.
3. Seattle is the home of the Starbucks coffee chain.

4. Seattle was the location of a famous film called 'Scared Witless in Seattle' starring Tom Hanks and Meg Ryan.
5. Seattle is famous for its Spice Needle.
6. Seattle is a major seaport.

B Normalisation – anticipating the next word

This exercise is designed to help you get used to Laura and Francis's voices.

Listen to Track 292. There is a word missing from the end of each excerpt. When you hear the beep sound, try to guess the missing word and write it down. Then listen to Track 293 to check your answers. How well did you guess?

1. _____
2. _____
3. _____
4. _____
5. _____

Seattle

A Multiple Choice

Laura and Francis talk about Seattle's location. Choose the best answer, a), b) or c).

1. Seattle is protected from the open ocean by

   a) a big island.
   b) a pier.
   c) a peninsula of land.

2. The San Juan Islands can be reached by

   a) boat.
   b) a bridge.
   c) plane.

3. The San Juan Islands are a great place to go to

   a) get good views of Seattle.
   b) go swimming and walking.
   c) observe various wildlife.

B Gap-Fill

Francis talks about the mountain ranges near Seattle.

Before you listen, try to predict which words, or which types of words (nouns, adjectives, prepositions, parts of verbs, etc.) will fill the gaps. Listen and check your answers.

1. The mountains near Seattle are tens of _____ of _____ high.
2. One range is called the Olympic Range and the other, to the _____ of the city, is called the _____ Range.
3. Francis says _____ ocean air gets blown _____ from the _____. It gets _____ against the mountain. The air rises and this forces the _____ out of the air which turns to rain.
4. This is why there is _____ on one _____ of the peninsula.

C Questions

Laura and Francis talk about the region around Seattle. Listen and answer the questions.

1. Which two words do you hear Francis say after the interviewer says: 'OK. What about the other side?'
2. What can you drive to in less than two hours , according to Francis?
3. What are scarce there because it's so dry?
4. What type of man-made land do you find in this area?
5. In which part of the state do you find lots of orchards?

D True/False

Laura and Francis talk about the town where they live. Answer true or false. Be prepared to give reasons for your answers.

1. _____ Burien is a suburb of Seattle.
2. _____ Burien is only a short drive from the centre of Seattle.
3. _____ Laura finds the idea of taking a bus into Seattle amusing.
4. _____ Francis thinks the bus system in Seattle is very efficient.

E Gap-Fill

Francis talks about the history of Seattle. As with Exercise B, try to predict your answers before you listen.

1. The oldest part of Seattle is Pioneer _____, but not much else is _____.
2. Seattle owes its early growth to the logging of timber and _____.
3. The oldest part of Seattle is around _____ years old.
4. Washington State, because of its location, was one of the last states to be _____.
5. In the state of Virginia there are places that are _____ as old as the oldest parts of Seattle.
6. However, Francis says these places are _____ by European _____.

F Questions

Laura and Francis talk about the famous Space Needle in Seattle. Listen and answer the questions.

1. Why does everyone know the Space Needle, according to Laura?
2. How high is the Space Needle in metres?
3. How can you go up the Space Needle?
4. What two things are there at the top of the Space Needle?

G True/False

Laura and Francis talk some more about the Space Needle, as well as Pike Market and the region around Seattle. Answer true or false. Be prepared to give reasons for your answers.

1. _____ Laura says the restaurant is expensive.
2. _____ Laura and Francis often go to the restaurant.
3. _____ It seems the area around the Space Needle is not a good place to leave your car.
4. _____ Francis says Pike Market is famous for selling French food.
5. _____ Laura says it's 'morphed into' more than just a food market.
6. _____ Seattle is just a couple of hours away from mountains, rainforest and desert.

H Gap-Fill

Laura and Francis talk some more about Seattle and the 'Seattle Ducks'. As with Exercises B and E, try to predict your answers before you listen.

1. Laura says Seattle is _____ around two lakes: Lake _____ and Lake Washington.
2. She says there is a lot of _____-_____ property in Seattle.
3. Francis says all the lakes are _____ by _____ and _____ to the ocean.
4. Laura mentions the 'Seattle Ducks' which are World War II amphibious assault _____ which have been _____ for tourism purposes.
5. The Seattle Ducks are both vehicles and _____ which can go on _____ of the water.
6. The Seattle Ducks were _____ carriers in World War II and can take up to _____ passengers.
7. The slogan is '_____ the Duck'.
8. The Seattle Ducks are _____ white.
9. To attract tourists people use _____ to make a quacking noise as people drive by.

I True/False

Francis talks about his current visit to London. Answer true or false. Be prepared to give reasons for your answers.

1. _____ Francis finds London very cold compared to Seattle.
2. _____ He was taught a lot about London when he was young.
3. _____ He has been enjoying looking at all the modern buildings.
4. _____ Francis is disappointed that some of the buildings are covered in scaffolding.
5. _____ He says 'things are being neglected'.
6. _____ He was surprised by the amount of litter in the street.
7. _____ He says the traffic in London is nearly as bad as in Paris.

A Two features of a North American accent

Laura has a Canadian accent and Francis has a North American accent. It is interesting to hear these accents and compare them with a neutral British English accent.

Remember, a good language learner will realise that when a speaker produces one non-standard pronunciation feature, the speaker is likely to produce this feature in all other words in English containing that sound.

1. **A different /t/ sound in the middle of words**

   Listen to how first Laura or Francis, and then the interviewer, pronounce the following /t/ sounds.

   > **Laura/Interviewer:** *it is ocean **water***
   > **Laura/Interviewer:** *there's lots of **little** islands along the way across from the **Seattle** pier*
   > **Francis/Interviewer:** *So we have these two bands of **mountains**...*
   > **Laura/Interviewer:** *It has its own **little** town centre...*
   > **Laura/Interviewer:** *That part's about a hundred and **twenty**-five years old?*
   > **Francis/Interviewer:** *They hold **forty** people.*

   a) What happens to the /t/ sound when Laura and Francis say the following words: **water, Seattle, mountains** and **forty**?

   b) What happens to the /t/ sound when Laura says the word **little**?

   c) What happens to the /t/ sound when Laura says the word **twenty**?

   How might Laura and Francis pronounce the following words?

   daughter, battle, thirty, fountain, seventy

2. **The /æ/ sound**

   Now listen to how first Laura or Francis, and then the interviewer, pronounce the letter **a** in the following extracts. Can you hear the difference?

Francis/Interviewer:	*A big peninsula of **land** protects Puget Sound from the open ocean.*
Francis/Interviewer:	*So we have these two **bands** of mountains...*
Laura/Interviewer:	*it's still very **handy***
Laura/Interviewer:	*that's the **landmark***

How might Laura and Francis pronounce the following words?

sand, jammed, crammed, candy, panda, can, understand

B There's + plural

Although we should use *there're + plural*, it is quite common in spoken US and British English to hear *there's + plural*. This is probably because it is far easier to say 'there's' than 'there're' in a stream of speech. Look at these examples from the interview:

> ***There's** lot of little islands along the way across from the Seattle pier.*
> *Yeah, but **there's** also islands. **There's** Vachon and Bainbridge.*
> ***there's** lots of wildlife*
> ***There's** islands, too.*
> ***there's** mountains*
> *And then **there's** these things called the Ducks....*

C Tense usage

The interview features a number of different tenses in context. Look at these examples:

Present perfect simple

(NB Note how the *have* which forms part of the present perfect simple is normally shortened to *'ve* in a stream of speech.)

> ***We've never been** to Seattle.*
> ***I've heard** so many people say it's a wonderful place to go...*
> *But **it's morphed** into more than just a food market.*
> *World War Two amphibious assault vehicles that **they've converted** to tourism.*
> ***You've just** come over to London.*
> *Um, and... a lot of traffic, despite the... what **I've read** about efforts to reduce it.*

Past perfect simple and past continuous

*I could also keep checking on my car – make sure that nobody **had stolen** it while we **were eating**.*

Simple past and past perfect

*So it was very fun [sic – So it was fun] to see all the places that we'd... that **I'd read** about as being historically significant as a child.*

Past continuous

*But, but were they as good as you **were expecting**?*
*Lots and lots and lots of cars – far more than Paris. **I was expecting** it to be almost the opposite, honestly.*

Now make your own examples of sentences featuring the tenses listed above.

D Uses of get

To have the opportunity to do something:

*So you get to see... Over a leisurely meal **you're getting** to see the entire city.*
*I mean I **got** to see it and everything was in lovely shape...*

To have something (nearby):

*So **you've got** all that – **you've got** the, sort of, ocean quite close and **you've got** this island and peninsula and that's very green.*

***Has it got** an old quarter or...*

*So **you've got** the Space Needle.*

*Pike Place Market is famous... **it's got** everything. **It's got** arts and crafts and food and...*

To become, as part of a process:

*The moist ocean air **gets blown** eastward from the ocean. **It gets pushed** against the mountains.*

*If it's a densely populated area the speed limit **gets reduced**.*

Now make your own examples of sentences featuring the verb **to get**.

E The passive

There are a number of examples of the passive in the interview:

*Washington State... was one of the last areas **to be settled**.*

*Seattle **is built** around two lakes – Lake Union and Lake Washington.*

*Everything **is connected**. All the lakes **are connected** by canals, too.*

*I mean I got to see it and everything was in lovely shape, or **were being fixed**. [sic – was being fixed]*

*things **were being** properly **cared for***

*things **aren't being neglected***

Now make your own examples featuring these passive tenses.

F Word stress in compound nouns

When compound nouns are formed from two separate words, the second word is more likely to be stressed that the first one. Look at these examples from the interview:

*ocean **water***
*town **centre***

However, the interview contains a far greater number of compound nouns made up of two joined or hyphenated words. With these compound nouns the first word is more likely to be stressed than the second one. Look at these examples from the interview:

***salt**water, **wild**life, **rain**forest, **grass**land, **farm**land, **high**way, **free**way, **land**mark, **sun**set*

4. Further Listening Practice

A Dictation

 to

At times during the interview Laura and Francis speak very quickly and consequently some words are not pronounced clearly.

Work with a partner. First listen to the excerpts from the interview and write down how many words there are in each item. Then listen and write down the words you hear. After that check your answers with another pair.

1. (____ words) _____
2. (____ words) _____
3. (____ words) _____
4. (____ words) _____
5. (____ words) _____
6. (____ words) _____
7. (____ words) _____

B Elision

In fast spoken English a process called 'elision' often occurs, most frequently with words ending in –d and –t. This results in these sounds not being pronounced when the next word begins with a consonant. This can make it difficult for you to recognise individual words in a stream of speech – even those words which you use regularly when speaking.

Listen to these excerpts from the interview and use a tick (✓) or a cross (✗) to mark whether the final –d or –t of words are pronounced or not pronounced. The relevant letters have been put in capitals for ease of reference.

1. it's calleD PugeT Sound ( )( )
2. I'm particularly interesteD 'cos it was your firsT time in London. ( )( )
3. A big peninsula of lanD protects Puget Sound from the open ocean. ( )
4. it was nice to see that um, things aren'T being neglected ( )
5. I was expecting it to be almosT the opposite, honestly. ( )
6. you've jusT come over to London ( )
7. anD it's very old and I likeD that. ( ) ( )
8. assaulT vehicles thaT they've converteD to tourism ( )( )( )
9. it's a greaT green rainforest ( )

C Linking

Linking occurs when the end of one word runs_into the start_of the next word. It is very common in informal spoken English, but less so in more formal English, such as speeches or lectures.

Linking makes it difficult for you to distinguish the individual words in a stream of speech.

The most common linking occurs between the letter –s at the end of a word when the next word begins with a vowel, as in these examples from the interview.

tens_of thousands_of feet
two bands_of mountains

However, linking also occurs with other sounds, for example when one word ends in the same letter as at the start of the next word, as in these examples from the interview:

So can you do boat_trips from there?

Linking also occurs when the final letter –s merges with the start of the next word, as in this example:

it's_not the ocean

Mark where you expect linking to occur in these excerpts from the interview. Then listen and check your answers.

1. but there's also islands
2. are not too far away
3. lots and lots and lots of irrigated farmland
4. And it's called the city of Burien, where we live.
5. And so it's still very handy.
6. Has it got an old quarter?
7. and then there's also a revolving restaurant
8. It's right down near the waterfront and it's got everything. It's got arts and crafts and food and...
9. everything was in lovely shape...

D People talking over each other

In real life, as opposed to coursebooks, it is very common for two or more people to talk over each other at the same time. Fill in the missing words in these excerpts from the interview where the participants are talking at the same time.

Please note this is a very difficult task that many native speakers would find tricky!

L: Laura   F: Francis   I: Interviewer

Excerpt 1

L: There's islands, too.
I: OK.
L: Mmm, hmm.
I: Right.
F: There are, indeed. Lovely islands, and the San Juan Islands, which are very famous, is er...
L: _____.
F: Not too far away _____.
L: You can take _____.

Excerpt 2

I: Why are they famous?
F: They're, they're magnificently beautiful. _____ _____...
L: And you can do whale-watching...
F: ... _____.
I: Whale-watching?

Excerpt 3

I: What about the other side?
F: Equally wet.
I: Equally wet.
L: Well, the city side is...
F: The city side...
L: ... it rains a lot.
F: _____.
L: And if you go two hours east of the city then you're in the desert. Then you cross over...
F: _____.
L: High desert. yeah.

Excerpt 4

F: And they're very... they're bright white and they have people with little whistles...

I: Mmm.

F: ...that make duck sounds...

L: Yeah, quack, quack.

F: ..._____.

I: Lovely!

E Revision gap–fill activity

These sentences are all taken from the interview. Try to fill in the missing words then listen and check your answers.

1. A big peninsula of land _____ Puget Sound from the open _____.

2. It's _____ _____ for trees, but not too dry _____ _____, so it's big rolling gentle _____ with grasses.

3. There are buses. They're just um... not as _____ as you're _____ to here.

4. Washington State being on the far _____-_____ portion of the _____ was one of, was one of the last _____ to, to _____ settled.

5. Everybody knows the Space Needle, because that's the _____...

6. And you can go up in an _____ and then when you _____ to the _____ there's a, an observation _____ and there's also a revolving _____ that you can _____ at.

7. And it was good 'cos then I could also keep _____ on my car – make _____ that nobody had _____ it _____ we were eating.

A Gap-Fill

Fill in the blanks in these new sentences with words you heard during the interview. The words are listed in the box to help you.

blown	crop	handy	invited	landscape	original	portion
pricey	quarter	ride	romantic	salt	shape	sheer

1. Pierre called to say that you're _____ to his party as well.
2. Our garden was in terrible _____ when we moved in, so we decided to get a _____ gardener in to re-design it.
3. Would you like a glass of water? I think I put too much _____ in the soup.
4. We had to drive very carefully because on one side of the road there was a _____ drop to the bottom of the mountain.
5. Their yacht was _____ off course in the storm, but luckily they had GPS.
6. We had a good _____ of runner beans this year. What were yours like?
7. My brother and I are the same size, which is very _____ because we can borrow each other's clothes.
8. It should only have been a short car _____, but the traffic was terrible so it took nearly an hour.
9. It's a really old house and it's still got some of the _____ features.
10. Could I just have a small _____ of chips, please? I'm not very hungry.
11. The hotel was quite _____, but we didn't mind because it was right in the middle of the old _____.
12. We often have dinner by candlelight because it's _____.

B Transformations

Change the word in each bracket that appeared in the interview to form a word that fits the gap, if necessary.

Here's an example to help you:

*Example: I can make you a sandwich if you're (hunger) **hungry**.*

1. I've put your (invited) _____ in the post.
2. Have you (water) _____ the plants today? They look a bit dry.
3. This is a nice spot for a picnic because it's (protects) _____ by the wind.
4. Did you know you've got a (spotted) _____ of gravy on your shirt?
5. That patch of (dry) _____ on my leg turned out to be eczema.

6. Economic (grow) _____ has picked up since last year.
7. My parents say we can't have a holiday this year because they're going to spend loads of money on (modern) _____ the kitchen. But I'd rather have a holiday than a new kitchen, wouldn't you?
8. All the land around here (original) _____ belonged to a farm.
9. My general (know) _____ is quite good, but don't ask me anything about modern music!
10. I think this country needs a (revolver) _____!
11. What with it being 30 degrees every day, (combination) _____ with 90% humidity, I have to say I spent most of my time in the room because of the air-conditioning.
12. I was (amazing) _____ when he told me how old he was.
13. The number of seats is (limit) _____ so make sure you book early.
14. We watched a (fascination) _____ programme on television last night about the planets.
15. The weather wasn't as good as we (expecting) _____, but we still had a great holiday.
16. I'm sorry for (neglected) _____ you on your first day, but we're really busy at the moment. How have you been (settled) _____ in?
17. The critics (rubbish) _____ Mamma Mia when it first came out but I loved it.
18. The motorway gets so (congestion) _____ on weekdays that it's generally quicker to go by train.

C Prepositions and adverbs

Put the correct preposition or adverb into the gaps in these sentences based on the interview.

1. He's _____ very good shape _____ his age.
2. Switzerland and Belgium are both famous _____ their chocolate.
3. Megan and I had a lovely chat _____ a cup of coffee last week.
4. I'll just check _____ the kids and make sure they're not fighting.
5. I usually go to work _____ car, but this week I'm going to cycle instead.
6. What's 10 centimetres _____ inches?
7. We've been invited _____ a party next Saturday but we can't make it because we're _____ holiday from the Thursday.
8. What's the garden _____ in your new place?
9. My grandmother used to tell us wonderful stories _____ the old days.
10. There are far more cars _____ the road than there used to be.
11. It's too late _____ a cooked meal. Shall I just make a sandwich instead?
12. Is there any cake _____?

I: OK. Er, you very kindly invited us to come and see you in Seattle. We've never been to Seattle. I don't know what the landscape's like. I don't know if it's on the sea, or on a lake or anything. So can you tell me about Seattle, please?

L: It's on the sea.

I: Mhm, hm.

L: Er, it's not the ocean, it's called **(1) Puget Sound**, so it is ocean water - it's salt water, but er, there's lots of little islands along the way across from the Seattle pier.

F: **(2) Peninsula**, actually.

L: It's a...

F: A big peninsula of land protects Puget Sound from the open ocean.

L: Yeah, but there's also islands. There's Vachon and Bainbridge.

F: Yes.

L: There's islands, too.

I: OK.

L: Mhm, hm.

I: Right.

F: There are, indeed. Lovely islands, and the San Juan Islands, which are very famous, is er...

L: Are not too far away.

F: Not too far away in the northern part of the Sound.

L: You can take ferries.

I: Why are they famous?

F: They're magnificently beautiful. **(3) Sheer cliffs** that ...

L: And you can do whale-watching...

F: ...run right into the water.

I: Whale-watching?

F: Very... very, very clear cold water, so there's lots of s... wildlife, sea life – **(4) seals** and whales and orca which are, which are killer whales.

I: OK.

F: Black and white spotted ones.

I: So can you do boat trips from there?

L: Yes.

F: Mhm, hm.

L: Yes.

I: OK. So... So you've got all that – you've got the, sort of, ocean quite close, and you've got this island and peninsula and that's very green. Not rainforest, though.

F: Yes, rainforest.

I: Is it rainforest?

F: Because there's mountains um, moun... er, very, very tall – tens of thousands of feet, so - I'm not sure what that is in metres - on each side of this of er, er, there's **(5) the Olympic range** on the Olympic Peninsula...

I: Mhm, hm.

F: ...and the Cascade range to the east of the city. So we have these two bands of mountains, so the warm ocean... moist ocean air gets blown west... eastward from the ocean. It gets pushed against the mountain. It rises and the, that forces the rain out of, forces it to rain a lot, forces the moisture out of the air and it's a great green rainforest...

I: Mmm.

F: ...on that side of the peninsula.

I: OK. What about the other side?

F: Equally wet.

I: Equally wet.

L: Well, the city side is...

F: The city side...

L: ...it rains a lot.

F: It rains a lot, but it's not rainforest.

L: And if you go two hours east of the city then you're in the desert. Then you cross over...

F: It's high desert, they call it.

L: High desert, yeah. I think it's very dry.

I: What, what does that mean, high desert?

F: Like, um, Russian steppe land.

I: Nope!

F: Er, grassland.

I: OK. Grassland.

F: Not many trees.

I: Right.

F: It's too dry for trees, but not too dry for grassland, so it's **(6) big rolling gentle hills** with grasses. And it's um, lot of irrigated farm... lots and lots and lots of **(7) irrigated farmland**.

I: OK.

F: And in the southern part of the state um, there are irrigated, irrigated areas that um, they grow apples. Washington is very famous for its apple crop.

I: So this is Washington State, not Washington DC?

F: Washington State, as opposed to Washington DC.

I: Yes.

F: Washington State is about the size of Great Britain.

I: Goodness me! *(laughs)* Um, so do you live in the centre of Seattle, or out on the outskirts?

L: We live about a mile out, out of the city of Seattle. And it's called the city of Burien where we live. And it was part of Seattle until about 12 years ago.

I: Mhm, hmm.

L: Yes. And so it's still very **(8) handy**. Er, it has its own little town centre with lots of little shops and boutiques and all the grocery stores and things that you need there. But then it also is a really quick ride down the, down the highway to end up back at Seattle, downtown Seattle.

I: So you'd go in by car? You wouldn't take a bus?

L: Yeah! *(laughter)* No, we'd go in by car.

F: There are buses. They're just um... not as convenient as you're used to here.

I: Right, OK. Hmm. So Seattle itself is quite a modern city, isn't it, from what I know. Has it got **(9) an old quarter** or...

F: Hmm, yes, it does.

L: It does.

F: It's called **(10) Pioneer Square**. It's what's left of the original... It used to be **(11) a logging town**, a timber town.

I: Oh, right. Yeah.

F: And fishing.

L: So it's maybe about how old? That part's about 125 years old?

F: Yes. And that's very old for Seattle. *(laughter)* We were... the... Seattle... Washington State being on the far north-west portion of the continent was one of, was one of the last areas to, to be settled.

I: I see. That makes sense 'cos Virginia you'd have...

F: Virginia you'd have stuff that was more than twice that old...

I: Yeah.

F: ...which is still young by European standards. But for us...

L: It's ancient.

F: It's ancient, yes.

I: OK. So what can you see in Seattle? Why, why... I mean, I've heard so many people say it's a wonderful place to go, but...

L: Yeah. Space Needle. Everybody knows the Space Needle, because that's the landmark and it's... I think it's about er...

F: 1960.

L: ..six hundred and something feet high.

F: Six hundred and eighty feet.

L: So like two hundred and something metres high.

I: And can you go up that?

L: Yeah, you can go up in **(12) an elevator** and then when you get to the top there's a, **(13) an observation deck** and then there's also a revolving restaurant that you can eat at that's quite lovely.

F: It...

L: Pricey, but lovely.

F: ...it revolves once an hour.

I: Oh, nice.

F: So it's very... So you get to see... Over a leisurely meal you're getting to see the entire city.

I: Have you ever done that? Had a meal up there?

L: Yeah, we did for our anniversary one year.

F: Yes, we did. It was very...

I: Oh, that's nice.

F: It was very lovely.

L: Yeah.

I: Good. Romantic.

L: Yeah.

F: It's beautiful. You go up at sunset and you can see both mountain ranges.

I: Oh, right.

L: Yeah. And it was good 'cos then I could also keep checking on my car — make sure that nobody had stolen it while we were eating.

F: Because we could see it.

L: Yeah. *(laughs)*

I: OK. So you've got the Space Needle. What, what else can you see?

L: Pike Place Market is famous. It's the um, it's right down near the waterfront and it's got everything. It's got arts and crafts and food and...

F: It's famous for its fish, fresh fish.

L: Yeah, famous for the fish market, yeah, yeah, yeah.

F: Fish and vegetables, but yes. Lots of...

L: But **(14) it's morphed into more than just a food market**.

I: Right. OK. What else?

F: The mountains and the rainforest. It's all in easy... Or the desert area. It's all within... By car it's two hours, or so. Or maybe a com, combination drive and the ferry. And the ferries...

L: Oh, and you can ride...

F: ...are all car ferries. Very easy. They're very, very large. They're six hundred feet...

I: OK.

F: ...ferries.

L: And you can ride the Duck, because Seattle...

F: Oh, yeah.

L: ...is built around two lakes — Lake Union and Lake Washington. So even though the Sound is... So there's... You can be... You can live right on Puget Sound and you can also live around a lake, which is very lovely. There's lots of lake-front property.

F: There's the canal....

L: And there's the...

F: ...they're all connected to... Everything is connected.

L: Yeah.

F: All the lakes are connected by canals, too – canals and locks to the ocean.

L: Yeah. Yeah.

I: Oh, that's fantastic.

F: So you can sail big ships up there.

L: And then there's these things called the Ducks where you, they drive through the city, and then they get to the lake and they go 'Phiii' and then they're in the lake. And then they... *(laughs)*

F: They're, they're **(15) amphibious**.

L: Yeah.

F: World War Two amphibious assault vehicles that they've converted to tourism.

I: Do they go under the water?

L: No.

I: But they go into the water?

F: They go right on top. They turn into... they're boats...

L: They're *[unclear]* that turn into boats!

I: Oh, that's amazing!

F: But they're very, very large.

L: They're fun.

F: They were personnel carriers in World War Two.

I: Oh, yeah?

F: They hold 40 people.

I: Right.

L: And you see them driving around the city and they're massive, yeah. 'Ride the Duck'! *(laughs)*

F: And they're very... they're bright white and they have people with little whistles...

I: Mmm.

F: ...that make duck sounds...

L: Yeah, quack, quack.

F: ...and they blow them at you as you drive by.

I: Lovely! Um, you've just come over to London. I'm particularly interested because it was your first time in London. Can you tell me your impressions of this city of ours?

F: Um, it is old!

I: Mmm.

F: And it's very old. I liked that. Um, and we hear lots of... being colonial... at one point **(16) a colonial**...

I: Mmm.

F: ...um, **property of yours**, um, it's... We learn quite a lot about um, England, particularly London, in um, as children in school.

I: Yeah.

F: At least I did.

I: Right.

F: And so there's a certain fascination with it and so it was very fun to see all the places that we'd... that I'd read about as being historically significant as a child.

I: Right.

F: Trafalgar Square and to see the... you know, **(17) Lord Nelson perched up on his...**

I: That's it. But, but were they are good as you were expecting?

F: Honestly?

I: Yeah, honestly.

F: Yes and no.

I: OK.

F: Yeah, yes bec... I mean I got to see it and **(18) everything is in lovely shape...**

I: Mhm.

F: ...or being fixed. And er...

I: When you say 'being fixed', you mean...

F: Being repaired. **(19) There's scaffolding up.** That things were being properly cared for. And it was nice, nice to see that um, **(20) things aren't being neglected and...**

I: OK.

F: Um, a lot of rubbish about, I noticed.

I: Mmm.

F: Um, and... a lot of traffic, despite the... what I've read about efforts to reduce it. Lots and lots and lots of cars – far more than Paris. I was expecting it to be almost the opposite, honestly.

I: Really. Yeah, when **(21) the congestion charge** came in initially there was a huge um, decrease in traffic, but very quickly...

L: Hmm.

I: ...it got up to the normal standards. OK. Mmm, hmm. Anything else? *(laughs)*

L and F: Come visit us!

I: Yes, I think we will. Thank you very much.

L: OK.

1 **Puget Sound** – a sound is a passage of sea which connects two larger areas of sea, or an area of sea which is surrounded by land

2 **Peninsula** – a long piece of land which sticks out from a larger piece of land into the sea or into a lake

3 **Sheer cliffs** – **(plural)** high areas of rock by the coast with extremely steep sides

4 **seals** – **(plural)** a seal is a large fish-eating mammal which lives partly in the sea and partly on ice or land

5 **the Olympic Range** – a range is a group of hills or mountains

6 **big rolling gentle hills** – gently rising and falling hills

7 **irrigated farmland** – farmland which is supplied by water to make crops grow

8 **handy** – (in this sense) convenient

9 **an old quarter** – a part of the town which is older than the rest of the town

10 **Pioneer Square** – A pioneer is a person who was one of the first people to do something – a pioneering scientist. Pioneer Square is the area in Seattle where the first settlers established the town in the mid-19th century.

11 **a logging town** – in the early days Seattle was an important source of timber, i.e. wood used for building. Logging is the activity of cutting down trees for wood.

12 **an elevator (AmE)** – a lift (BrE), i.e. a small room that carries people or goods up and down a building

13 **an observation deck (AmE)** – an observation deck or an observation platform (BrE) is part of a building designed to offer people a good view

14 **it's morphed into more than just a food market** – it has changed into more than just a food market

15 **amphibious** – An amphibious vehicle operates on both land and water.

16 **a colonial property of yours** – Here Francis refers to the fact that the USA used to be a colony controlled politically by Britain.

17 **Lord Nelson perched up on his (column)** – Here Francis refers to the statue of Lord Nelson which stands on a tall column in Trafalgar Square. The verb *to perch* is normally used in reference to birds resting in a high position or near the edge of something or a person perched on the edge of a seat, etc.

18 **everything is in lovely shape** – everything is in very good condition

19 **There's scaffolding up.** – Scaffolding is structure of metal poles and wooden boards which is put against a building for workers to stand on.

20 **things aren't being neglected** – things are being looked after with care and attention

21 **the congestion charge** – The congestion charge was introduced in central London in 2003 with the aim of reducing the amount of traffic. Drivers currently have to pay a fee to enter the congestion zone between the hours of 7am and 6pm, Monday to Friday.

UNIT 13 A group of friends

This is an interview with a group of friends, Val, Peter and Jill, who all live in Walthamstow in north-east London. The interview took place in a pub. The three talk about their local area – things to see and do and local history. Val is a true Cockney, as she was born within the sound of the bells of Bow Church, and has a Cockney accent. Peter has lived in London all his life and has a strong London accent. Jill is originally from North Wales and has retained her Welsh accent.

It is very noticeable in this interview that turn-taking is occurring, with each person tending to speak in a short bursts consisting of a short sentence, or just a few words. The speakers obviously know each other well because they tend to talk over each other and to correct each other.

NB For the first one minute, 47 seconds the machine washing the glasses in the pub is making a noise in the background which makes this section particularly challenging.

A Schema building – predicting which words will come up

Which 10 of these 20 words do you expect to hear during the interview?

museum, custard, fluff, original, fur, rebuilt, lick, cart, tights, bandage, haunted, market, curdle, farmland, sharpen, transport, fledgling, village, yolk, multi-ethnic

B Normalisation 1: Anticipating the next word

323 and 324

This exercise is designed to help you get used to Peter, Val and Jill's voices.

Listen to Track 323. There is a word missing from the end of each excerpt. When you hear the beep, try to guess the missing word and write it down. Then listen to Track 324 to check your answers. How well did you guess?

1. _____
2. _____
3. _____
4. _____
5. _____
6. _____

C Normalisation 2: Questions

325

In this first part of the interview Val and Peter talk about various places they like in Walthamstow while Jill listens in. Listen and answer the questions.

1. What two things does the first speaker, Val, like about Walthamstow, besides the William Morris House and the Vestry Museum?
2. What does Peter like, in addition to Lloyds Park?
3. What are often held at the William Morris House?
4. What does the Vestry Museum have a continuous exhibition of?
5. Why does the Vestry Museum contain an original jail?
6. Who thinks Val may have got her facts wrong, Jill or Peter?
7. Where are the almshouses in relation to the Vestry Museum?

A Questions

Here the friends talk some more about the history of Walthamstow. Listen and answer the questions.

1. Which other building is nearby?
2. Which two words does Peter use instead of 'renovated'?
3. What mistake does Val make when she talks about the car?
4. What was the car based on?
5. In which century was the car built?
6. Who is really scared of ghosts – Jill or Val?

B Gap-Fill

Peter tells Jill how two roads in Walthamstow got their names.

Before you listen, try to predict which words, or which types of words (nouns, adjectives, prepositions, parts of verbs, etc.) will fill the gaps. Listen and check your answers.

1. The other side of Willow Walk used to be marshland which was _____ so that _____ could be built.
2. The area from Willow Walk to Hoe Street used to be _____.
3. Jill finds it _____ to imagine that the local area used to be so rural because it's so _____-_____ now.
4. Hoe Street got its name because the farm _____ used to walk home that way with their hoes and _____.

C Questions

Now Val joins in. Listen and answer the questions.

1. What caused the Walthamstow area to expand towards the end of the 19th century?
2. What exactly does Val have a photo of?
3. What do you think 'a bustle' was?
4. What is the correct term for a line of houses?

D Gap–Fill

The three friends talk about why Walthamstow is a good place to live.

As with Exercise B, try to predict your answers before you listen.

1. Peter says Walthamstow is convenient 'For me _____, from my _____ of _____, for transport.'
2. Peter says 'From here you _____ _____ anywhere _____.'
3. Walthamstow is just _____ _____' drive from the _____ motorway and seven miles from the _____, the orbital motorway _____ London.
4. Jill says you _____ _____ into _____ London in 20 minutes from Walthamstow.
5. She says there is an _____ train line to _____ Street, as well as the Victoria line.
6. Val says there are _____ into central London as well.
7. It takes Val 45 minutes to get to _____, door-to-door.
8. Val is very interested in _____.
9. Epping Forest, one of the _____ forests in England, is only 10 minutes away.

E Questions

Jill talks about her impressions of Walthamstow. Listen and answer the questions.

1. When did Jill move to Walthamstow?
2. Why did she find it 'a culture shock'?
3. What does she like about Walthamstow?
4. What haven't changed in Walthamstow since Peter was born there?

F Gap–Fill

The three friends talk about things to do in Walthamstow.

As with Exercises B and D, try to predict your answers before you listen.

1. Val says there is a _____ of different _____ in Walthamstow, including _____ and _____.
2. There are a _____ of Italian restaurants in the old _____, as well as a _____-style restaurant.
3. Jill says the fact that there are so many different restaurants _____ the make-up of the local _____.
4. She mentions _____ restaurants and Caribbean restaurants.

5. Peter says it doesn't _____ what time of _____ or _____ it is in Walthamstow, you can always buy _____, as well as milk and _____.

G Questions

The three friends talk about some important buildings in Walthamstow. Listen and answer the questions.

1. Which two buildings does Peter mention, in addition to the Assembly Hall?
2. Who both went to see the same Russian ballet performed in the Assembly Hall?
3. What is the Assembly Hall famous for?
4. Which advertisement did Walthamstow Town Hall appear in?

A Four features of an east London accent

Remember, a good language learner will realise that when a speaker produces one non-standard pronunciation feature, the speaker is likely to produce this feature in all other words in English containing that sound.

1. **Dropping the initial letter *h–***

   A typical feature of an east London accent is for the speaker not to pronounce the initial letter *h–* at the start of words such as *'ouse, 'ad, 'appy*, etc.

   Listen to these examples from the interview:

   > Peter: *Vestry **'ouse** Museum was the original police station.*

   > Peter: *It's changed a lot. Buildings **'aven't.***

   > Peter: *I've lived **'ere** all my life.*

   How would a person with an east London accent say the following sentences?

   > **1.** We're hoping to buy a new house.
   > **2.** I hope he comes home soon.
   > **3.** How was your holiday?

2. **Dropping the final *–d* of *and***

   Another typical feature of an east London accent is for the speaker not to pronounce the final *–d* of the word ***and***.

   Listen to these examples from the interview:

   > **Val:** ***An'** then it was a poor house.*

   > **Peter:** *Was it a poor house first, an' then the museum, **an'** then a police station.*

Val: *No, I think it was the, the police station first **an'** then a poor house.*

Val: ***An'** I work at Tottenham Court Road...*

Jill: *it's colourful **an'** it has a nice buzz about it*

3. The glottal stop

Another feature of the London accent (and many other British accents) is the *glottal stop.* A glottal stop happens when the speaker tightens his or her throat and very briefly stops the air from getting through. This results in the /t/ sound at the end of words such as *got* or *lot*, or the /t/ sound in words such as *bottle* or *kettle* not being fully pronounced. This can make it difficult for you to recognise words containing this feature.

Listen to these examples from the interview:

Peter: *Or was **it** the other way round? Was **it** a poor house first...*

Peter: *... which has just been **rebuilt***

Peter: ***It** was the first car **that** was ever **built** as a, as a **motor** vehicle.*

Peter: *Willow Walk, which is down the **market**.*

Val: *'Cos I've **got** a picture of my house in 1904.*

Peter: *From here you can **get** anywhere quickly.*

Jill: *Yeah, and you can **get** into central London in 20 minutes.*

Val: *You've **got** the buses as well.*

Val: *Different variety of restaurant.*
Interviewer: *Like **what**?*
Val: *Chinese, Indian...*

Val: *And the um, the town hall next door to the Assembly Hall, **that** was featured in a McDonald's **advert**.*

How would a person with an east London accent say the following sentences?

1. We've got a new cat.
2. Could you put the kettle on, please?
3. Cup of coffee?

4. **Using the letter *f* instead of the /θ/ sound**

Another typical feature of an east London accent is to use the letter *f* instead of the /θ/ sound found in ***think, thimble, thin***, etc.

Peter: *It was made in Walfamstow.*

Peter: *Which is a major norfartery.*

Just for fun ask your students how a person with a strong London accent would say the following sentences:

1. I think she's a bit thick! *
2. I thought I saw you at the theatre last night.
3. I worked in Germany for three months.

* ***thick*** is a British English slang word for 'stupid'

Now can your students combine these different features of an east London accent?

1. I haven't decided yet – I'm thinking about it.
2. I'll see him later.
3. My daughter's just had a little girl.
4. He just goes on and on and on.
5. I'm gutted Kate's got married to Harry. *

* The meaning of ***to be gutted*** is 'extremely upset'. It's a typical east London slang expression.

B Pausing mechanisms

1. 'um' and 'er'

We often use *um*, or *er*, in informal spoken English. These sounds indicate to the listener(s) that we are thinking and so no one should interrupt us. Look at these examples from the interview:

*It was the first ever **um**, motorised car...*

*What do I like? Um, I like the leisure centres, **er**, the library.*

*It's got **er**, the old jail in there.*

What equivalent sounds do you make in your own language?

Remember that when you hear *er* it sounds the same as the indefinite article *a,* so don't automatically assume that a noun is going to follow. Look at this example from the interview where it's impossible to hear if Peter is saying *a* or *er*:

Peter: *...and the college, of course, which is **a/er**, quite a... attractive set of buildings.*

2. Repeating the question

At the start of the interview the interviewer has obviously asked the three friends this question: 'What do you like about Walthamstow?'

Val replies: *What do I like?*

By repeating the question she is giving herself time to think, whilst at the same time indicating that she is about to say something so no one should interrupt her.

This is a useful technique to acquire and works with any question.

C Ways of expressing surprise

Because Jill hasn't lived in Walthamstow for as long as Val and Peter, she is often surprised by the things they tell her.

1. With questions: Part A

We often use a question formula to express surprise and to seek confirmation from the speaker that we have understood correctly. Our voice tends to rise and then fall on the final word. Listen to these examples from the interview:

Val:	*It's got er, the old jail in there. That was... Before that it was er...*
Jill replies:	*The old jail?*
Val:	*Jail.*
Peter:	*And of course it is haunted.*
Val:	*What, the museum?*
Peter:	*Yeah*

2. With exclamations

We can make exclamations in various ways. We normally use falling intonation with exclamations. Listen to Jill's intonation in the following excerpts:

1   When Jill finds out the car was made in the 18th century she says:

   My goodness!

2   When Jill finds out Willow Walk got its name because it was lined with willow trees, she replies:

   My God!

(NB This exclamation can cause offence to religious people, so be careful how you use it.)

3   When Jill finds out the Assembly Hall was featured in a McDonald's advertisement she says:

   Oh, please!

D The passive

There are a number of examples of the passive in the interview:

Present simple passive:

> And of course **it is haunted.**
> **It is listed** as a haunted building.

Simple past passive:

> It was the first car **that was ever built...**
> So **it was made** round here?
> It was made in Walthamstow.
> **it was based** on a cart
> **house was built** in 1896

Present perfect simple passive:

> Peter talks about the Tudor house which **'has just been rebuilt'.**

Now make your own examples featuring these passive tenses.

E must have + past participle for logical assumptions

Peter tells Jill: *I was born here. I've lived here all my life.*

Jill replies: *So you must have seen quite a lot of changes.*

We use the must have + past participle structure when we are making logical assumptions based on the speaker's statement. Look at these other examples:

Andy:	Last week I had lunch with an old girlfriend from when I was at school.
Patrick:	That must have been interesting.
Chelsea:	Do you like this scarf? I knitted it myself.
Rosalind:	That must have taken you ages!
Kate:	I went to see Take That at the O2 last night.
Sam:	That must have been amazing!

NB Tell your students that the word *have* in this construction is often pronounced more like *of* in a stream of speech.

Now make your own examples using *must have + past participle.*

A Dictation

 to

At times during the interview the three friends speak very quickly and consequently some words are not pronounced clearly.

Work with a partner. First listen to the excerpts from the interview and write down how many words there are in each item. Then listen and write down the words you hear. After that check your answers with another pair.

1. (___ words) _____
2. (___ words) _____
3. (___ words) _____
4. (___ words) _____
5. (___ words) _____
6. (___ words) _____

B Weak forms, i.e. unstressed grammatical (or function) words

The words between the stressed content words are known as grammatical (or function) words. These are the words which bind the speaker's content words together and they are a major contributing factor to the rhythm of English speech. These grammatical/function words tend to be unstressed, which makes them difficult to distinguish. Listen to these excerpts and fill in the missing grammatical/function words.

NB Because this is a listening training exercise don't try to predict the answers before you listen!

1. And _____ course _____ is haunted.
2. Because _____ the cells.
3. And it _____ called Willow Walk because it was a road lined _____ willow trees. Because the other side _____ _____ was the marsh.
4. And _____ Willow Walk up here, up _____ this end _____ the market, _____ Hoe Street, was farmland.
5. it was basically nothing more _____ a pathway
6. the farm workers used to come _____ _____ the end _____ _____ day _____ _____ wheelbarrows _____ _____ hoes
7. So _____ _____ only with the introduction of _____, of _____ trains, actually, _____ it took off.
8. _____ right.
9. _____ really convenient _____ me personally, _____ my point _____ view, it's, it's really convenient _____ transport.

10. _____ five minutes _____ _____ motorway...
11. The M11, _____ _____ _____ major north artery.
12. So _____ _____ _____ _____ take you, say,
_____ get to Oxford Circus?
13. _____ I work _____ Tottenham Court Road...
14. it reflects _____ community

C Linking

(NB A full explanation of linking occurs in Exercise B in Section 4 of Unit 2.)

Mark where you expect linking to occur in these excerpts from the interview. Then listen and check your answers.

1. It was a police station.
2. Was it a poor house first...
3. So it was made round here?
4. Was it?
5. It's steeped in history.
6. Willow Walk, for example's where the waters, the Marshes stopped.
7. Willow Walk, which is down the market.
8. the other side of that was the marsh
9. It was all marshland.
10. that's the way the farmers used to come back
11. with their wheelbarrows and their hoes
12. It was all farmland up here.
13. From my point of view
14. The M11, which is a major north artery.
15. Oxford Circus, it takes me 25 minutes.
16. It's good for eating.

D People talking over each other

In real life, as opposed to coursebooks, it is very common for two or more people to talk over each other at the same time. Fill in the missing words in these excerpts from the interview where the participants are talking at the same time.

Please note this is a very difficult task that many native speakers would find difficult!

P= Peter   V= Val   J= Jill

1. P: Lloyds Park
   V: Lloyds Park is good.

J: Yes, _____ _____ _____.

P: Lloyds Park's nice.

2. V: ...police station.

P: It was the original police station.

J: What, Vestry House? Was it?

P: Vestry House Museum was...

J: Oh, _____.

P: ...the original police station.

3. P: It was the first car that was ever built as a, as a motor vehicle. Not electric.

V: Wasn't it?

P: No.

J: So _____...

P: No, it was petrol.

J: ... is that _____?

V: It was made in Walthamstow. It was made in Walthamstow?

P: Yeah, it was made in Walthamstow and it was...

J: Oh, well, _____!

P: ...it, it, it was... it the first ever um, motorised car...

4. P: ...our house was built in 1896, and

_____.

J: They kind of did them in, in rows, didn't they? Yes, that's right.

5. I: Of course one of the things Waltham's got, Walthamstow's got is the, the Assembly Hall – the town hall...

V: Oh, yeah!

J: I'd _____.

P: ...and the college, of course, which is a, quite a... attractive...

J: Yes.

P: ...set of buildings.

V: 'Cos I saw the Russian Ballet there as well, I think um...

J: I did.

V: That was good.

J: _____ _____.

V: And Elkie Brooks was there.

J: That was wonderful.

P: _____.

J: It's famous for its acoustics. It's got brilliant acoustics, apparently.

V: Yeah, it really is good.

A Gap-Fill

Fill in the blanks in these new sentences with words you heard during the interview. The words are listed in the box to help you.

advert	based	change	couple	drained
haunted	imagine	lined	matter	original
rows	shock	variety	exhibitions	right

1. Have you been to any good art _____ lately?
2. This is an _____ recipe handed down to me by my grandmother.
3. It's a novel _____ on the life of a student in the 1980s.
4. It's such an old house I'm sure it's _____.
5. When we looked inside the nest we could see it was _____ with moss.
6. There was an old swimming pool in the garden when we moved here but we _____ it and filled it with soil to make a vegetable patch.
7. I can't _____ my grandmother ever being a schoolgirl.
8. I don't think it's _____ that children have to stay on at school until they're 16 nowadays.
9. We planted the peas in _____ about 12 inches apart.
10. To get to work I have to _____ trains twice.
11. When I moved to New York from Milan I found it quite a culture _____.
12. The hotel laid on a huge _____ of activities for the children during the day.
13. Caroline and Robert are a very nice _____.
14. No _____ what time I come home my partner always waits up for me.
15. Have you seen the new _____ for Pilkington Pies? It's hilarious.

B Transformations

Change the word in each bracket that appeared in the interview to form a word that fits the gap, if necessary.

Here's an example to help you:

> Example: I can make you a sandwich if you're (hunger) **hungry**.

1. Would all (visiting) _____ please report to reception.
2. It says the last time this painting was (exhibitions) _____ was in 1827.

3. My mother was very (art) _____ when she was younger, but then she stopped painting when she got married.
4. This room was (original) _____ the garage.
5. The Government wants to put up income tax, but the (opposite) _____ say they'll cut it if they get into power.
6. Who starred in the original (produced) _____ of My Fair Lady?
7. English Heritage is responsible for preserving sites of (history) _____ interest.
8. The jacket's is made of silk, but the (lined) _____ is polyester.
9. Sorry about the awful smell! I think our (drained) _____ need checking.
10. What do you think is the (basically) _____ of a good relationship?
11. I prefer doing (culture) _____ things on holiday rather than lying on a beach all day.
12. I have to say we were both a bit (shock) _____ when we met our son-in-law for the first time.
13. What's your estimated time of (arrived) _____?
14. The menu is quite (variety) _____ here so I'm sure you'll find something you like.
15. Isn't that beautiful – the (reflects) _____ of the willow trees in the water?
16. Everyone else in my family loves skiing, but I can't see the (attractive) _____ myself. I hate being cold and wet.

C Must have + past participle for logical assumptions

Match the utterances to the responses below.

1. I grew up on a farm. _____
2. We were a bit noisy, so we got thrown out of the restaurant. _____
3. When I was 21 my parents sat me down and told me I was adopted. _____
4. Have you seen Tom's new car? It's a brand new Mercedes. _____
5. I got hit by a golf ball the last time I went for a walk. _____
6. I got stuck in a lift at work last week. _____

    A. That must have hurt!
    B. That must have been a bit embarrassing!
    C. That must have been a bit scary.
    D. That must have been wonderful!
    E. That must have cost a fortune!
    F. That must have been a shock.

V: What do I like? Um, I like the leisure centres er, the library. I also like er, visiting **(1) William Morris House** and also the Vestry Museum.

P: Lloyds Park.

V: Lloyds Park is good.

J: Yes, that's really nice.

P: Lloyds Park's nice. **(2) The Marshes.**

V: William Morris is quite good, actually, because of the exhibitions they have in there – different art exhibitions. And the Vestry Museum has a continuous exhibition of life in Walthamstow as it was in the past. It's got er, the old jail in there. That was... Before that, it was er...

J: The old jail?

V: Jail, the old jail.

P: It was a police station.

V: Police station.

P: It was the original police station.

J: What, Vestry House?

P: Vestry House Museum was...

J: Oh, I didn't realise.

P: ...the original police station.

V: And then it was **(3) a poor house.**

P: Yeah. Or was it the other way round? Was it a poor house first, and then the museum, and then a police station? I think it was...

V: No, I think it was the, the police station first and then a poor house.

P: Yeah. And you've got the almhouses just... **(4) the almshouses**...

V: Just opposite.

P: ...just opposite.

J: Yes.

V: Then you've got **(5) the old Tudor house**...

P: That's right. The Tudor...

V: ...which is original.

P: ...which has just been rebuilt, completely re-established.

V: And also in there is the first electric car.

P: Well...

J: Is it?

P: ...it's the first car ever produced. It was the first car that was ever built as a, as a motor vehicle. Not electric.

V: Wasn't it?

P: No.

J: So it was made round here?

P: It was petrol.

V: It was made in Walthamstow. It was made in Walthamstow?

P: It was made in Walthamstow and it was...

J: Oh, well, get down!

P: It was, it was the first ever um, motorised car and it was based on **(6) a cart.**

J: Was it?

P: Horse's cart, yeah, yeah. And it's still there. It's, it's 17 something or other.

J: My goodness!

P: Yeah, it's really interesting.

V: That's fantastic.

J: It is! I didn't realise that.

P: And of course **(7) it is haunted.**

J: Oh, don't!

V: What, the museum?

P: Yeah, yeah.

J: By?

P: It is listed as a haunted building.

J: Is it?

V: Because of the jail, or?

P: Yeah, because of the cells...

V: Hmm.

P: ...cell.

V: One cell, yeah, 'cos it's...

P: But it is listed as a haunted building.

P: The h..., the history's good. It's got... **(8) it's steeped in history.** Willow Walk, for example's where the waters, the Marshes, stopped.

J: Willow Walk?

P: Willow Walk, which is down the market. And it was called Willow Walk because it was a road lined with **(9) willow trees**.

J: My God!

P: Because the other side of that was the marsh. It was all marshland.

J: So **(10) they drained all that** and kind of built houses.

P: All drained that, refilled back to, to build on, basically.

J: OK.

P: And from Willow Walk up here, up to this end of the market, to Hoe Street, was farmland.

J: OK.

P: Of... Hoe Street...

J: It's so hard to imagine because it's very built-up now.

P: Hoe, Hoe Street... It was called Hoe Street because that's the way the farmers used to come back – it was basically nothing more than a pathway.

J: OK.

P: And it was the way the farm, and the farm workers used to come back at the end of the day with their **(11) wheelbarrows** and their **(12) hoes**.

J: Oh, right, yes.

J: So it was only with the introduction of the, of the trains, actually, that **(13) it...**

P: Yeah, yeah.

J: **...took off.**

V: In the late 1800s.

P: Yeah, that's right. That's right.

J: OK.

P: Because er...

V: Because my road was farmland as well.

P: It was all farmland up here.

V: I...

P: It was all farm.

V: 'Cos I've got a picture of my house in 1904.

J: Mmm.

P: Yeah.

V: A woman with **(14) a bustle** behind walking past my actual house! And you just...

P: Our, ours...

J: Oh, that's amazing!

P: ...was built, our house was built in 1896, and probably yours was the same.

J: They kind of did them in, in rows, didn't they?

V: Yes, that's right.

P: Yeah.

I: Why's Walthamstow a good place to live?

P: It's really convenient for me personally, from my point of view, it's, it's really convenient for transport.

V: Yeah.

J: Yes.

V: That's, that's **(15) a selling point**.

I: In what way?

P: From here you can get anywhere quickly.

I: All right.

P: You can... You're five minutes from the motorway...

I: Which motorway?

P: Well, the, **(16) the M11...**

I: Mhm, hmm.

P: ...which is **(17) a major north artery**. It's about seven miles from the M25 which is the orbital motorway round London.

J: Yeah, you can get into central London in 20 minutes.

P: You can... yeah.

I: Which line is it?

J: Well, you've got an overland line to Liverpool Street or you have the, **(18) the Tube**.

V: And if they break down...

J: The Victoria line.

V: You've got the buses as well, haven't you, if they break down?

J: Yes, also.

I: So how long would it take you, say, to get to Oxford Circus?

V: Er, Oxford Circus, it takes me 25 minutes.

I: Mhm, hmm.

V: And I work at Tottenham Court Road and then cha... change trains, so I allow 45 minutes door-to-door, but you can do it in 30...
(Noise of people in the pub)

V: And for me, of course, another incentive is birdwatching because you've got **(19) Walthamstow Reservoirs.**

P: And in Walthamstow you're 10 minutes away from one of the biggest forests in, in, in England.

J: Yes.

V: **(20) Epping Forest**, yeah.

J: That's right.

J: I, I've lived here since '93, I think, and er, **(21) it was quite a culture shock**, I think, when I arrived 'cos **(22) it's very multi-ethnic**. And it's colourful and **(23) it has a nice buzz about it**. I quite like living in Walthamstow.

P: I was born here. I've lived here all my life.

J: So you must have seen quite a lot of changes.

P: It's changed a lot. Buildings haven't, but...

I: What kind of things can you do in the evenings here?

P: Eat, drink.

I: Right.

V: It's good for eating. It's very good.

I: In what sense?

V: Different variety of restaurants.

I: Like what?

V: Chinese, Indian. You've got... In the village you've got – in the old village – you've got Italian – a couple of Italians. Er, um, there's a Mediterranean-type restaurant there.

J: There's lots, I mean **(24) it reflects the community**. There's Turkish...

P: Oh, there's every type of...

J: Absolutely.

P: ... eating, eating house.

J: And West, West... Caribbean.

P: And of course one of the things about Walthamstow is no matter what time, what time of day or night it is, you can always get food. You can always buy food.

J: Yes.

V: Yes, that's true.

P: Milk, tea - there's always somewhere open.

P: Of course one of the things Waltham's got, Walthamstow's got is the, the Assembly Hall – the town hall...

V: Oh, yeah!

J: I forgot about that.

P: ...and the college, of course, which is a, quite a... attractive...

J: Yes.

P: ...set of buildings.

V: 'Cos I saw the Russian Ballet there as well, I think um...

J: I did!

V: That was good.

J: I went to that!

V: And Elkie Brooks was there.

J: That was wonderful.

P: They have lots of stage shows there.

J: It's famous for its **(25) acoustics**. It's got brilliant acoustics, apparently.

V: And the er, the town hall next door to the...

J: Mmm.

V: ...Assembly Halls, that was featured in a McDonald's advert.

J: Oh, please!

V: The fountain, 'cos it's so old-fashioned. And they did **(26) the backdrop**.

I: Oh, right.

J: Really?

V: Yeah. They used Walthamstow Town Hall as the backdrop.

1   **William Morris House** – William Morris (1834–1896) was born in Walthamstow. He was a famous textile designer, artist, craftsman, writer and socialist and you can visit his family home set in Lloyd Park in Walthamstow which houses a permanent exhibition of his work.

2   **The Marshes** - Marshes are areas of land near a river which are always wet. The Marshes in Walthamstow have been partly drained.

3   **a poor house** – a building used, in the past, to house and feed extremely poor people with no means of supporting themselves which was paid for by the local community

4   **the almshouses** – houses built in a community in the past by charitable trusts to provide affordable housing, often for men, or the widows of men, who had worked in a particular trade

5   **the old Tudor house** – A period of history dating from 1485 to 1603 when England was ruled by kings and queens from the Tudor dynasty, the most famous being Henry VIII and his daughter Elizabeth I. Tudor buildings were often half-timbered, i.e. the wooden framework was exposed, and can still be seen in many towns and villages today.

6   **a cart** – a vehicle with four wheels often pulled by a horse

7   **it is haunted** – there is a ghost in the building

8   **it's steeped in history** – the area is full of history

9   **willow trees** – trees that grow near water with long, thin branches which hang down

10 **they drained all that** – they removed the water from the ground

11 **wheelbarrows** – a wheelbarrow is an open container used to move things which has a wheel at the front and two handles at the back

12 **hoes** – a hoe is a garden or farm tool with a long handle and sharp blade used to remove weeds

13 **it took off** – it expanded

14 **a bustle** – In the second half of the 19th century it was fashionable for women in England to wear dresses or skirts with a bustle - a metal framework worn under the material at the back just below the waist which changed the woman's shape and stopped her skirt or dress dragging on the ground.

15 **a selling point** – (in this case) something that makes Walthamstow an desirable place to live (**a selling point** is usually the characteristic of something that will persuade someone to buy it)

16 **the M11** – the motorway which links London with Cambridge

17 **a major north artery** – (in this case) an important road heading north (an artery is a major blood vessel that carries blood from the heart to other parts of the body)

18 **the Tube** – London's underground train system

19 **Walthamstow Reservoirs** – large artificial lakes which supply water to parts of London once it has been treated

20 **Epping Forest** – an area of ancient woodland and the largest public open space in the London area

21 **it was quite a culture shock** – it was very different from anything she'd experienced before because

22 **it's very multi-ethnic** – there are people from lots of different countries (i.e. races) living there

23 **it has a nice buzz about it** – it has a nice atmosphere; it's lively; it's full of energy
24 **it reflects the community** – the variety of restaurants mirrors the ethnic diversity of the area
25 **acoustics** – the quality of its sound
26 **the backdrop** – the view behind something

UNIT **14** Dorah and Letta

1.Pre-Listening Comprehension

Dorah and Letta are sisters who grew up under apartheid in South Africa. Here they talk about the township they grew up in and how it has changed in recent years. Dorah and Letta now both live in England where they work as nurses. They speak excellent English, but they have retained their South African accent.

A Normalisation – Questions

This exercise is designed to help you get used to Dorah and Letta's voices.

Dorah and Letta talk about their township. Listen and answer the questions.

1. What is the name of the township Dorah and Letta come from?
2. Why do you think Dorah and Letta both laugh when the interviewer asks if their township is near Cape Town?
3. How far is Dorah and Letta's township from Johannesburg by car?

A Gap-Fill

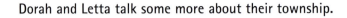

Dorah and Letta talk some more about their township.

Before you listen, try to predict which words, or which types of words (nouns, adjectives, prepositions, parts of verbs, etc.) will fill the gaps. Listen and check your answers.

1. Dorah doesn't know how many people _____ in the township because it has _____ so much in recent years.
2. Dorah says the main reason for this is because the _____ is building new _____ everywhere.
3. Letta talks about '_____ houses' – new houses which people are buying in the township.
4. Dorah equates 'RDP houses' with _____ houses in the UK.

B True/False

Dorah and Letta talk some more about their township. Answer true or false. Be prepared to give reasons for your answers.

1. _____ As you enter the township you see lots of jacaranda trees.
2. _____ Jacaranda trees are well-known for their distinctive leaves.
3. _____ Jacaranda trees lose all their leaves in the summer.
4. _____ The 'mortgage houses' are situated on the hill near the entrance to the township.
5. _____ One of the sisters is clearly very proud of her township.
6. _____ One of the sisters says the people who live in the township are 'lovely'.
7. _____ The black people who live in Dorah and Letta's township are mainly of the same race, or tribe.
8. _____ Atteridgeville doesn't have any 'no-go areas', according to Dorah and Letta.
9. _____ Letta says it can be a bit dangerous in the township at night.

C Gap-Fill

Dorah and Letta talk about the different tribes and different languages they are familiar with. As with Exercise A, try to predict your answers before you listen.

1. People from the Xhosa tribe, such as Nelson Mandela, have the sound of a _____ in their language.
2. Dorah says many people in Gauteng can _____ three or four _____.
3. This means everyone can _____ with each other.

D Questions

Letta and Dorah talk about a new development in their township. Listen and answer the question.

Why have people in Atteridgeville stopped going to Pretoria to do their shopping?

E Gap-Fill

Dorah and Letta talk about the changes in their township since apartheid. As with Exercises A and C, try to predict your answers before you listen.

1. The interviewer asks Dorah and Letta what _____ they have seen in their township over the years.
2. Dorah says there used to be no houses on the _____.
3. A lot of _____ people have moved to Atteridgeville since Apartheid ended.
4. Dorah says during apartheid any white person who moved to a township would have ended up in _____.
5. She says now you can _____ anywhere you _____.
6. Looking back, Dorah wonders what the _____ was of all the bad things that happened in her country.

A Four features of Dorah and Letta's South African accent

Remember, a good language learner will realise that when a speaker produces one non-standard pronunciation feature, the speaker is likely to produce this feature in all other words in English containing that sound.

1. The long *i* sound found in the word *sheep* tends to be much shorter.

    Listen to these excerpts from the interview:

    > It's **clean.**
    > there are **these** jacaranda **trees**
    > And plus **these** er, mortgage houses...
    > the first thing that you see is **these** beautiful houses

    How might a South African say these words?

    fleas, peas, keys, please, tease

2. The letter *a* found in *hat* and **cat** is pronounced the same as the letter *e* in *bed*.

    Listen to these excerpts from the interview:

    > **At** the entrance...
    > different **nationalities**
    > **black** South Africans
    > There were white people who wanted to be with **black** people.

    How might a South African say these words?

    map, tap, lack, sat, flap

3. There is a tendency to roll the letter *r*:

    Listen to these excerpts from the interview:

    > *Jacaranda trees*
    > they're just ala... along that **area.**
    > They are more accessible to **everybody**...
    > different **groups** of...

How might a South African say these words?

freeze, fridge, transport, trade, cried

4. The v sound found in English words such as *of* and *have* is pronounced more as the letters *ff* in the word *off*:

    there's er, a lot of um, of new people that have moved in

    How might a South African say these words?

    cave, love, sieve, over, cover

South Africa

A Gap-Fill

Fill in the blanks in these new sentences with words you heard during the interview. The words are listed in the box to help you.

close	expanding	friendlier	get	miss
mortgage	moved	safe	special	view

1. We live quite _____ to the station, but we can pick you up in the car if your hip's still playing up.
2. Sorry the house is in a bit of a mess – we only _____ in last week.
3. Our company is _____ so we're having to take on more staff.
4. I want to buy my own place, but first I need to see if I can get a _____.
5. You're a really _____ person and I'm glad you're my friend.
6. We wanted a room with a _____ of the sea, but they were all booked so we ended up looking out at the car park.
7. Please come home soon – I _____ you.
8. I think people are _____ in London than in Paris.
9. I wish you kids would try to _____ along better – you're always fighting!
10. Is it _____ to walk around here at night?

B Transformations

Change the word in each bracket that appeared in the interview to form a word that fits the gap, if necessary.

Here's an example to help you:

*Example: I can make you a sandwich if you're (hunger) **hungry**.*

1. According to the latest figures, economic (grown) _____ fell to 0.6% in the year to June.
2. The 19th century saw a huge (expanding) _____ of the rail network in England.
3. Have you heard the latest about Josh and Kiki? There's been a new (developing) _____.
4. My friend is a lawyer (special) _____ in divorce cases so I could give you her work number if you like.
5. I wish I could help you, but my (known) _____ of employment law is pretty basic.

6. What do you do for a (lively) _____?
7. One of the reasons we decided to move to Canada is because people are more (tolerance) _____ here towards gay people.
8. My grandfather (fighting) _____ in the First World War.
9. What is the (minimal) _____ wage in the USA?
10. The thing I remember best about our holidays in Wales when we were kids is all the (flocking) _____ of sheep everywhere.
11. Sorry to disturb you, but I need to (accessible) _____ my computer.
12. If you think that dog's ugly you should see his (own) _____!

I: So your **(1) township** – what's the name of it?

D: Atteridgeville.

I: I'm sorry?

D: Atteridge…

L: Atteridgeville.

D: Atteridgeville.

I: Atteridgeville.

D: Mmm.

I: Can either of you spell that? *(laughs)*

L: A-double t-e-r-i-d-g-e-v-i-double l-e.

D and L: Atteridgeville.

I: I see. All right. And is it close to Cape Town?

D and L: No! *(laughing)*

I: No. Is it close to Johannesburg?

D: No, it's in a, it's er, it's in the um… It's just 40 minutes from…

L: Johannesburg.

D: …from, from, from Jo'burg. It's in **(2) Pretoria**. It's one of the townships of Pretoria. It's in Pretoria West.

I: How many people live there?

D: In Atteridgeville? Well, I don't know. I… Phew! I don't know. Um, now it's, it's… It has grown so much and there's a lot, there's er, a lot of um, of new people that have moved in.

I: Right.

D: So it is expanding.

I: I see.

D: It's just expanding and expanding. You know the government is building new houses everywhere…

L: Yeah.

D: …everywhere. So it um, it's a beautiful township…

L: Yeah.

D: … – one of the best in South Africa.

L: And there are a lot of er, **(3) mortgage houses** around…

D: Mmm.

L: It's more developing.

I: Right.

L: Yeah.

I: So people are buying places out there.

D and L: Yes.

D: Buying. And even the - we call them **(4) the RDP** - like um…

L: Government.

D: The council houses here.

L: Council houses, yeah.

I: OK. So, so is it a, a nice place to live?

D: Yeah.

L: It's is, yeah. It is.

I: Wha… You said it's one of the best townships.

D: Oh, yes.

I: What makes it, what makes it special?

D: Um…

L: At the entrance when you go to Atteridgeville there are these jaca… Pretoria is being known by, by these….

L and D: (5) Jacaranda trees. There's…

I: Right. They're the ones with the blue flowers?

D and L: Yes!

L: The petals especially, yeah.

D: And they're huge.

L: Yes. So um, the entrance… When you get into Atteridgeville from the entrance, there are these jacaranda trees, especially during the summer.

D: Mmm! It's lovely.

L: Oh, it's beautiful!

L: It's beautiful.

D: *(laughs)*

L: And plus these er, mortgage houses, they're just ala… along that area…

D: Yeah, and it's in a, in a kind of a hill.

L: Hilly, yeah.

D: So you have these beautiful…

L: Yes!

D: …houses…

I: Mmm.

D: …as you…

L: It's a nice view to look at.

D: ...yeah, get into Atteridgeville so you... the first thing that you see is these beautiful houses.

I: I see.

D: Big houses...

L: And the jacaranda trees.

D: And the yeah, and the jacaranda. And you drive in – you know, just get in and...

I: Yeah.

D: It's a beautiful...

L: It's a beautiful view.

D: Yeah.

I: You, you both seem to miss it.

L: Yes! A lot, a lot.

D: It's um... It's a, it's a, it's a beautiful township. It's the best! The best! It's clean.

I: OK, yeah.

D: Um, er, the people um, are friendlier.

I: Mmm, hmm.

D: Um, they...

L: **(6) They're bubbly.**

D: *(laughs)*

I: Bubbly?

L: Yes.

I: You mean lively and...

D and L: Yes.

I: Happy?

D: There's, there's um...

L: Happy, yeah.

D: And we, we... I think it's, it's one of the... one of the townships where **(7) there's a lot of tolerance.**

I: Mmm.

D: Because we do have er, different nationalities, different groups of, of, of, of, of black South Africans. Then we just get along.

I: Right. So there's never any trouble – never fighting or...

L: Even it is like at a minimal rate.

I: Oh, I see.

L: If you understand what I mean.

I: A little bit, but...

L: Yeah, yeah. It's not...... There... I know there are places where you find that people like the no... I

would say the no-go areas.

I: Mmm, hmm.

L: But Pretoria Atteridgeville is...

D: We don't have.

L: You can go anywhere. You are free to go anywhere, anytime. You'll always be safe.

I: Oh, right. That's brilliant, isn't it?

D and L: Yeah.

I: So you don't feel it's dangerous at all.

L: No, not at all.

I: OK.

I: Um, can, can I ask what tribe you were because we thought you were Huts...Huts... Soto.

D: Soto. We are Sotos.

I: Are they the ones that do the clicking nose when you talk?

D: No.

L: No, it's Xhosas. Xhosas are clicky.

I: Oh, right.

L: That's Mandela's language. They click when they talk.

I: I see.

L: Mmm.

I: But you can both do that.

D and L: Yes, yes.

I: I've heard you do it. Yeah. But just for a laugh.

L: *(laughs)*

D: No! Um, one of the, one of the, the, the good things of being in a township, especially in um, Gauteng area – we're called Gauteng area which involves Pretoria, Johannesburg and um...

L: Rastelberg.

D: Er, no, not Rastelberg. Johannesburg and Pretoria, they're called Gauteng. So because that's where it's happening, so you find that you've got er, different people. So you find that even if you are, you are a Xhosa you can speak Soto.

L: Mmm.

D: If you are a Soto you can speak Xhosa or Zulu or... So you can speak more than three, four languages.

L: Languages, yeah.

I: You can all communicate with each other.

D and L: Yes.

I: So in your township you would find those...

D: Yeah.

L: Yes.

I: ...different groups of people.

D and L: Yes.

I: And it's... You, you never come across someone you can't talk to them.

D: No.

L: No.

I: You can manage?

D and L: Yeah.

I: That's brilliant, isn't it?

L: Yeah.

D: We can, we can.

I: OK. Where's um, the nearest city? Is it Pretoria?

L: Yes, yes.

I: To your township?

L: So you would go there for big shopping, or...

L: Yeah.

D: No.

L: No, at the moment... No, they've er, built...

D: They've built **(8) malls.**

L: ...built malls.

D: In the townships.

L: In the township, so people are no longer flocking more to town because their shopping which they used to do in the town centre...

I: Mmm.

L: ...they can do it in the...

D: ...in the township.

L: ...in the township now.

I: Oh, that's, that's much better.

L: Yeah.

D: They've building malls and, and, and er...

L: Mmm.

D: ...shopping centres and...

L: Yeah.

D: ...so there's no need to go...

L: Yeah.

D: ...to town.

L: They are more accessible to everybody, even if one doesn't have money for... to take him or her to town, you can...

D: You can walk.

L: Yeah.

D: You can walk to the mall.

L: Yeah.

I: That's a big difference...

L: It is, yeah.

I: ...from when you were growing up.

L: It is, yeah.

I: What changes have you seen in, in that township since you were children there?

L: Oh.

I: I mean when you were growing up was it only...

L: When we were growing up this hilly part of Atteridgeville – **(9) it was just a plain hill**.

I: Where all the rich houses are?

D: Yeah.

L: Now there are these mortgages houses...

I: Mmm, hmm.

L: And er, this mall is around there.

D: Mmm.

L: And what else, Dorah?

D: Um...

L: Um...

I: Were there any white people living there?

D: Yeah, yeah. There are.

L: At the moment yes. A lot of them, yeah.

I: But there weren't before.

D and L: No, no.

L: There weren't before. Now there are a lot of them.

I: Uh, huh.

L: Mmm.

I: OK. Is that all right?

L: Yeah, it's fine. It's fine.

I: Are they the ones, though, who own all those nice houses?

D: No...

L: No.

D: ...it's not only them.

I: Oh, that's good.

D: Um... Remember that it, it was not everybody who, who was um... There were white people who wanted to be with black people.

I: Mmm.

D: But because of **(10) the system and everything**, you know, they...

L: they couldn't.

D: They, they, you, you couldn't.

L: No.

D: You know, otherwise you were going to jail. You know.

I: So they couldn't move...

D: Yeah.

I: ...to your township then.

D and L: Yeah.

I: You had to be...

L: We, we couldn't move to their town... to their places by them and now...

D: And they couldn't come to our places, because there were laws, you know? There were laws that were governing you, telling you can't go this, you can't...

L: **(11) Boundaries**, yeah.

D: Boundaries, yeah. So now you just live anywhere you want.

L: Anywhere you want.

I: Yeah. Brilliant.

L: Mmm, hmm. And you're, you're happy about that.

L: Yes, yes.

D: Yeah. It's um...

I: Much better than when you were growing up.

L: Yeah, it's nice. It's very nice.

D: And it's... you.... er, you just ask yourself – what was all about, you know?

I: Mmm.

D: It's um...

I: It's changed so much.

D: There's no point, yeah. There's no point. There was no point anyway from the beginning, you know?

I and L: *(laugh)*

I: Thank you very much. That was absolutely fantastic. Thank you, you two.

D and L: Thank you.

1 **township** – a town in South Africa where only non-whites were allowed to live under apartheid (Apartheid, a period of legal racial segregation, lasted from 1948 until 1994.)

2 **Pretoria** – a city in north-eastern South Africa which is one of three capital cities of South Africa, the others being Cape Town (the legislative capital) and Bloemfontein (the judicial capital)

3 **mortgage houses** – these are newly built houses in the township that people have taken out loans (i.e. mortgages) to buy

4 **the RDP** – cheap houses built as part of the Reconstruction and Development Programme (RDP) launched by the ANC (African National Congress) government of Nelson Mandela in 1994

5 **Jacaranda trees** – tall trees that during the late spring in South Africa (i.e. between October and November) are covered with purple-blue flowers (Pretoria is known as The Jacaranda City.)

6 **They're bubbly.** – Usually this word is used to describe the personality of someone who is very lively. Here Letta uses it to refer to the people who live in the township, the meaning being that they are lively and full of energy and enthusiasm.

7 **there's a lot of tolerance** – people there are willing to accept behaviour and beliefs which are different from theirs, even if they don't approve of them

8 **malls** – large (usually enclosed) shopping areas with lots of shops and a large car park outside the mall itself

9 **it was just a plain hill** – there were no buildings on it

10 **the system** – the system of apartheid, a period of legal racial segregation, that lasted from 1948 until 1994

11 **Boundaries** – Here Letta means restrictions.

UNIT **15** Muriel

Muriel lives just outside Cannes with her husband and young son. She speaks good English, but has a strong French accent. In this interview she talks about the place she lives now – Mougins – and the place she lived before which was in the mountains near the Swiss border.

A **Schema building – predicting which words will come up**

Which 10 of these 20 words do you expect to hear during the interview?

famous, wallpaper, ink, sea, crumbs, stones, crust, tray, sand, shampoo, mountains, intellectual, hot, housework, storms, saucer, snow, coast, frame, space

B Discussion

Discuss these questions in pairs or small groups and share your answers with the class:

1. Can you identify this sound, recorded in Muriel's garden? What does this sound remind you of?
2. How much do you know about Cannes and the South of France?
3. If you had a choice, would you prefer to live by the sea or in the mountains and why?
4. What does a French accent sound like?

C Normalisation – Questions

This exercise is designed to help you get used to Muriel's voice.

Muriel talks about Mougins and Cannes.

1. Which place(s) in the USA do people sometimes compare Cannes with?
2. How far from the sea is Muriel's home?
3. What can you see in the distance?

Cannes

A True/False

Muriel talks some more about Mougins, Cannes and the surrounding region. Answer true or false. Be prepared to give reasons for your answers.

1. _____ Muriel lives half-way between the sea and the mountains.
2. _____ Muriel would prefer it to be a bit cooler in Mougins during the summer.
3. _____ It seems it's best to avoid Cannes in January and February.
4. _____ The interviewer clearly loves going on holiday to hot places.
5. _____ Sometimes there are water shortages in Cannes because it gets so hot in summer.

B Sentence completion

Muriel talks about where she lived before she moved to Mougins.

Before you listen, try to predict which words, or which types of words (nouns, adjectives, prepositions, parts of verbs, etc.) will fill the gaps. Listen and check your answers.

1. Muriel has only been living in Mougins for _____ _____.
2. Fillinges is surrounded by _____.
3. Fillinges is only 15 kilometres from the _____ _____.
4. Big towns make Muriel feel _____.

C True/False

Muriel talks about the differences between Fillinges and Mougins.

Answer true or false. Be prepared to give reasons for your answers.

1. _____ Muriel's home in Fillinges was an hour's drive from the mountains.
2. _____ Muriel enjoyed going on long walks in the mountains.
3. _____ Muriel used to park the car somewhere nice and then go walking in the mountains.
4. _____ Muriel seems to have enjoyed the winters in Fillinges more than the summers.
5. _____ Muriel says even in summer you have to wear warm clothes in the mountains around Fillinges.
6. _____ Muriel's philosophy in life is to live for the moment and be spontaneous.
7. _____ There was no swimming pool in Fillinges.
8. _____ It takes Muriel the same time to go to the sea now as it used to take her to get to the nearest ski slope in Fillinges.
9. _____ Muriel grew up in the centre of Nîmes.

A Three features of a French accent

Remember, a good language learner will realise that when a speaker produces one non-standard pronunciation feature, the speaker is likely to produce this feature in all other words in English containing that sound.

1. The letter *h* is not pronounced in French and therefore French speakers tend not to pronounce it in English either. Muriel speaks very good English, but sometimes she misses out the letter *h*, as in these examples:

    > Beverly *'ills*
    > and er, we *'ave* nice weather until December
    > **Per'aps** four times in a year.
    > So I can *'ave* a, a walk for one hour...
    > you *'ave* to um...
    > But we *'ave* skiing just near the house.

2. Replacing the /ð/ sound with the /s/ or /z/ sounds.

    Listen to these excerpts from the interview:

    > **Th**e nice wea**th**er?
    > It was **th**e opposite of here.
    > Like here **th**e sea, in fact.
    > **Th**e sea's **th**e same situation...

3. Not distinguishing between a long i sound and a short i sound. (ship – short i; sheep – long i)

    Listen to these excerpts from the interview:

    > And *it's* er, very often raining. (long i)
    > Er, *it's* um... not exactly north. (long i)
    > Ah, for me it's a *little* bit difficult (long i) because I *feel* oppressed. (short i)

B The influence of the mother tongue (L1)

Muriel also has a tendency to use French grammar, although it must be noted that this rarely causes communication to break down. Can your students make these excerpts sound more English, i.e. make them more accurate?

perhaps four times in a year – perhaps four times a year

There are in summer a lot of storms. - There are a lot of storms in summer.

Have you always lived here in Mougins?
No, it was only since two years. – No, only for two years.

For me it's a little bit difficult... – It's a little bit difficult for me...

And what for me was very important... – And what was very important for me...

you can have to put on an anorak – you sometimes have to put on an anorak...

I can go on feet to the swimming pool. – I can walk to the swimming pool./I can go to the swimming pool on foot.

I am born in Nîmes. – I was born in Nîmes.

A Gap-Fill

Fill in the blanks in these new sentences with words you heard during the interview. The words are listed in the box to help you.

border	break	coast	famous	feet	funny
joins	just	landscape	like	main	middle
opposite	oppressed	positive	problem	sand	situation
space	temperature				

1. I won't be a minute. I'm _____ switching off the computer.
2. The city of Bath is _____ for its Georgian architecture.
3. I heard a really _____ joke yesterday. Do you want to hear it?
4. We tried to sunbathe, but we had to give up because it was so windy the _____ kept getting in our eyes.
5. My brother is a _____ gardener.
6. What was the weather _____ while we were away?
7. What's Paul's _____ now? Is he still married?
8. We've got a bit of a _____. Our computers are down so I can't get those figures to you.
9. The hip is where the thigh bone _____ the pelvis.
10. St Andrews is a beautiful city on the east _____ of Scotland.
11. Unfortunately we live next to a _____ road, so there are always cars going past, no matter what time of day or night.
12. I've got two older brothers and two younger sisters, so I come in the _____.
13. You don't even need to show your passport when you cross the _____ between France and Switzerland.
14. The Welsh were _____ by the English for centuries.
15. The only problem with this cottage is there's not enough storage _____.
16. I think we're all getting a bit tired. Shall we have a _____ for 10 minutes and then reconvene at 11?
17. You feel really hot. I think you might have a _____.
18. The neighbours who live _____ are really nice. We see them quite a lot.
19. It's really important to give _____ feedback as well, otherwise people tend to get discouraged.
20. When I stand for too long my _____ swell up so much I can hardly get my shoes on.

B Transformations

Change the word in each bracket that appeared in the interview to form a word that fits the gap, if necessary.

Here's an example to help you:

Example: I can make you a sandwich if you're (hunger) **hungry**.

1. What's the cost of (live) _____ like in Norway now? Is it still really expensive?
2. Can you tell me where the (near) _____ bank is, please?
3. Does Bournemouth have a (sand) _____ beach?
4. Before I start the car, is everyone sitting (comfortable) _____?
5. I usually have (dry) _____ apricots on my cornflakes.
6. The cottage is (situation) _____ on a little hill just outside the village.
7. I'm thinking of (joins) _____ Weightwatchers. I really need to lose a few pounds.
8. We took the (coast) _____ road which took much longer than the motorway, but the views were spectacular.
9. What's the (mean) _____ of the French word 'commune' in English?
10. The weather at the moment is so (oppressed) _____ – really hot and humid. We need a storm to clear the air.
11. I think the Government should provide more affordable (house) _____ for key workers - nurses and teachers and people like that.
12. If you don't ask (nice) _____ you won't get any more cake.
13. It was so (fog) _____ that it was too dangerous to drive so we just walked around the town until it cleared.
14. I think the (happy) _____ time of my life was when I was a student.
15. My next essay is on the (important) _____ of the wool trade in the 18th century, so I'm really looking forward to that!

I: So er, you live in **(1) Mougins**, I think?

M: Yes.

I: Which is just near **(2) Cannes**?

M: Yes.

I: Can you tell me about the place where you live?

M: Um, it's er, it's like a little town.

I: Mmm, hmm.

M: But it's very green and it's a famous place because it's er... Somebody tell me, huh, it's like Bever... **(3) Beverly Hills**.

I: Oh, really?

M: Yes in er, **(4) Hollywood**, or I don't know where.

I: Yeah.

M: So I said, 'Really?' Because when I said I live in Mougins, the people say 'Ah! Like Beverly Hills in...!' So **(5) it's so funny for me** because for me it's er, like another part of the world, huh.

I: Right. Is it near the sea, I suppose?

M: Oh, we are four kilometres from the sea.

I: Hmm.

M: Ten minutes by car.

I: OK *(laughs)*. Hmm. Um, the sea, what – is it um, stones or sand on the beach?

M: We have er, sand...

I: Mhm, mm.

M: And er, it's very beautiful because we have mountains not f... far. So we have a look, er, landscape.

I: Mhm, hm. So it's beautiful?

M: Yes.

I: So you've got mountains and then you've got the sea as well.

M: Yes.

I: How long does it take to go to the mountains by car?

M: Oh, around er... the, the first mountains – small mountains – is around er, 20, 25 kilometres.

I: OK. That's very close.

M: Yes, that's very close.

I: So you have the best of both worlds – the sea and the mountains.

M: Yes.

I: Yeah, OK. What, what's the weather like in Cannes, or Mougins?

M: A little bit warm in er, summer...

I: Mhm, mm.

M: ... and er, we have nice weather until December.

I: Right. When does the nice weather begin?

M: The nice weather?

I: Yes.

M: Oh, in March, April.

I: So it starts to get quite hot?

M: Not hot, just fine.

I: Right. Lots of sun?

M: Yes, lot... always. Always a lot of sun.

I: Does it rain at all in the summer?

M: Oh, perhaps four times in a year.

I: Four times in a year!

M: Yeah. Sometimes it's four times or five times.

I: God!

M: Yeah.

I: It must be very hot.

M: Yes, yes.

I: Uncomfortable. Um, with the mountains what... is the weather also dry in the mountains?

M: Oh no. There are in summer a lot of storms.

I: Mhm, mm.

M: In winter, snow. And er, and it's er, very often raining. So that, that situation give to us a lot of water.

I: OK.

M: So we never have no water.

I: Mhm, mm. Because the water comes down from the mountains.

M: Yes, exactly.

I: Have you always lived here in Mougins?

M: Always? No, it was only since two years and before we were in **(6) Haute-Savoie** in the middle of the mountains.

I: Right, OK.

M: Completely!

I: So is that in north France?

M: Er, it's um... not exactly north.

I: Mhm, hm.

M: But it's er... north-east?

I: OK.

M: Perhaps.

I: Right. And what was the name of the town you lived in?

M: Oh, it was a small village named **(7) Fillinges**.

I: Mhm, hm.

M: And it was just between Genève and Annecy, around.

I: OK. So Genève, you mean Geneva in Switzerland?

M: Geneva, in Switzerland, yeah.

I: OK. So you were very close to the Swiss border?

M: Yes, we were only 15 kilometres.

I: Oh excellent. And... So there it was more green, more mountains, more snow...

M: Oh yes. And more space!

I: More space. You don't like to live in big towns?

M: Ah, for me it's a little bit difficult because I feel **(8) oppressed**.

I: Ah, ha.

M: Because too many people, too many... not enough space.

I: OK. Right. Um, when you lived in Fillinges did you go walking in the mountains?

M: Oh yes! All the time! And what for me was very important – I can go er, from my house and I can walk as I want around the mountain because we were in, in the mountain.

I: Mhm, hm.

M: So I can have a, a walk for one hour, for two hours from my house. And for me it's very important I don't take er, a car or something else. I can just walk.

I: OK.

M: For me it's really – phew! – nice because I can have a break for one... in the day for one hour.

I: OK. The temperature there was much colder, I guess.

M: Ah yes, of course. Yes. It was the opposite of here. A lot of fog, a lot of rain and um, and the winter – phew – was very long.

I: Mmm.

M: And sometimes in er, July you can have to put on **(9) an anorak**.

I: Really?

M: Ah, yes.

I: It's so cold?

M: Yes. Sometimes.

I: OK. Um, so are you happier living here, or back in Fillinges?

M: No, I'm happy, in fact, because when you take a decision, you have to um...

I: Be positive?

M: Exactly! Or you don't live. So I... before coming here I, I thinking about, and then I am here I change my life, that's all. So I, I go to work by bi... bicycle – in Fillinges it was not possible. I can go on feet to the swimming pool. I can't do that in Fillinges because it was 20 kilometres to, to find a swimming pool.

I: Mhm, hm.

M: Er, but we have skiing just near the house. You know it's very different.

I: It is. And the skiing – I mean here in the, in the winter you can go skiing.

M: Yes.

I: But not for so long.

M: We have to, to take all the day when we are, we are skiing because you have to go and to be back. In Fillinges it was near the... it was...er, phew!

I: Near the house.

M: Ten minutes? Yes. Like here the sea, in fact.

I: Yeah.

M: The sea's the same situation than the skiing's in Haut-Savoie.

I: OK. *(laughs)*

M: So we have to take the positive things.

I: Mhm, hm. So where were you born?

M: I am born in **(10) Nimes**.

I: Ah, ha.

M: It was in er, department Le Gard.

I: Right.

M: And er, it was quite a big town, but we were in a small village – **(11) Caissargues** – so it was nice.

I: OK. OK, that's brilliant. Thank you very much.

M: You're welcome.

6. Words and Phrases

1   Mougins – a small town 15 minutes' drive from Cannes

2   **Cannes** – one of the best-known cities on the French Riviera, situated next to the Mediterranean and famous for its Film Festival

3   **Beverly Hills** – a city within Los Angeles which is one of the most affluent cities in the world and home to many Hollywood celebrities

4   Hollywood – a district of Los Angeles famous historically for being the home of American cinema

5   **it's so funny for me** – I find it very strange (*funny* has two meanings 1. humorous – something that makes you laugh and 2. strange, peculiar)

6   **Haute-Savoie** – a department in the Alps in eastern France which shares borders with Switzerland and Italy and is home to Mont Blanc

7   **Fillinges** – a small town in Haute-Savoie equidistant from Annecy in France and Geneva in Switzerland

8   oppressed - feeling anxious and uncomfortable

9   **an anorak (BrE) – a parka (AmE)** – A short, waterproof coat that protects the wearer from the cold, wind and rain

10   Nîmes – a city in southern France dating back to Roman times located in the Gard department

11   **Caissargues** – a small town just outside Nîmes